A New Translation Of The Nichomachean Ethics

Aristotle Aristotle

ADVERTISEMENT.

THE following Translation professes no rivalry with former versions of the same treatise. Its utmost aim is to be a faithful interpreter of its original, which it has constantly followed as closely as the different idioms of the two languages will allow. Let it be recollected, that instances have been where a translator has disguised, or endeavoured to disguise, in pretty no-meaning sentences, his ignorance of his author. In the present attempt no artifice of that kind is employed. Difficulties are fairly met, and in most instances, it is hoped, satisfactorily cleared; and if any ambiguity appears in the English, the same uncertainty will be found in the same passage in the Greek: for it is to be remarked, that the words and phrases of doubtful import in the two languages remarkably correspond.

The Notes are chiefly illustrative; discussion has been generally avoided, as of little use to those for whom this work is principally intended. They are added by the translator of the four last books. The former six are by a different hand. Both are Gentlemen, the sufficiency of whose knowledge has been approved from high authority, and whose names would be no disadvantage to the work were they to be made public.

ARISTOTLE'S ETHICS.

BOOK I.

CHAP. 1.

*That every action has an end.   Ends divided into chief
and subordinate.*

1. EVERY art and every institution, and in like manner
every action, as well as predilection[a], seems to aim at some
good: wherefore men have well defined *the good* [or *summum
bonum*] to be "that which all things desire."

2. But there appears to be a kind of difference in ends ; for
some are operations ; others again beyond these, certain productions : but in things which have certain ends besides the
actions, in these the productions are naturally better than the
energies[b].

3. Now there being many actions, and many arts and
sciences, there arise also many ends ; for of medicine the end
is health ; a ship, of ship-building ; victory, of generalship ;
wealth, of economy.   But as many of such arts as are contained under any one superior, (as for instance, under the
equestrian art is contained the making of bridles, and as
many other arts as belong to the equipment of horses ; this

---

[a] Προαίρεσις, that which is chosen, after mature deliberation, in preference to any thing else : choice, predilection, or principle of action.

[b] Thus the act of riding is an operation, or energy, ἐνέργεια.   Health,
which follows, is a production, ἔργον.   It is evident that health is better
than riding.

art and every warlike action under the art of generalship; and in like manner others under their respective arts;) in all these [series of arts] the ends of all the master arts are more eligible than the ends of those contained under them; because for the sake of the former, the latter also are pursued. It makes, however, no difference whether the operations themselves are the ends of actions, or something else beyond these, as we have seen, in the forementioned sciences[c].

CHAP. II.

That there is a chief end—that it belongs to the science of politics.

1. If, therefore, there is any end of the subjects of actions, which we wish on its own account, and other things on account of this; and if we do not choose every thing for the sake of something else, (for thus the question would proceed to infinity, so that desire would be empty and vain,) it is evident that this must be *the good*, and the best good. Has not then the knowledge of this end a great weight with respect to life? and, like archers, should we not be more likely to obtain that object which is right, if we have a mark? If so, we must attempt to sketch it, at least coarsely; shewing what it is, and to which of the sciences or faculties it belongs: but it would appear to belong to the most important, and most superior.

2. Now of this kind the political science appears to be: for this ordains which of the sciences are necessary in states, and what sort each class of men should learn, and to what extent. Moreover, we see that even the most honourable of the facul-

---

[c] Although it has been said above, that when *the same* art admits both an operation and a production, the production is better than the operation: yet if the end of the master art be an operation, and the end of one of the subordinate arts be a production, the former is still superior; i. e. the operation is an higher end than the production.

ties are subordinate to this, as that of generalship, of economy, of rhetoric.   Since then this science employs the other practical sciences, and moreover lays down laws for what we ought to do, and from what to abstain, the end of this must include those of the others; so that this end must be *the good* of man.   For though the good of an individual and a state be the same, yet to obtain and preserve that of a state appears to be greater and more perfect; for it is a thing to be contented with, to find the good of even a single individual: but to find what is the good of nations and cities, is more noble and divine.   The plan [of our treatise] therefore pursues these objects, being a kind of political treatise.

CHAP. III.

That the accuracy with which any treatise is written, depends on the nature of the subject.   What are the qualifications of a disciple in the school of morality.

1. OUR argument would be sufficiently discussed, if it were explained according to the subject matter.   For accuracy is not to be required equally in all disquisitions, as neither in all productions of mechanic art.   But things noble and just, which the science of politics has to consider, admit so great a difference, and so much uncertainty, as to seem to exist only by compact, but not by nature.   So likewise things good possess a similar want of certainty, because calamities have befallen many out of them.   For some, we know, have perished through wealth, and others through fortitude.   It is then sufficient that, as we are treating of such subjects and drawing our arguments from them, we should point out the truth rudely, and merely in a sketch; and that in treating of and from things contingent, we should also draw similar conclusions.

2. By the same rule also ought we to admit each of the propositions laid down; for it is the sign of an educated man to require accuracy in each class of subjects, just so far as the

nature of the subject admits; for it appears nearly the same to allow a mathematician to reason on probabilities, as to demand demonstrations from an orator.

3. Now every one judges well of those things which he knows; and of these he is a good judge. In particular sciences therefore, he is a good judge who has been instituted in these; but universally, he who has been instructed in every thing. Wherefore the young man is not a proper hearer of politics, for he is inexperienced in the actions of life: but these discussions are from such, and concerning such actions. Moreover, being apt to follow his passions, he will be a disciple in vain and to no purpose, since the end is not knowledge, but practice. But it differs nothing, whether he be a youth in age, or youthful in manners; for the defect arises not from the time, but from his living according to passion, and running after every thing; for to such knowledge becomes useless, as it does to the incontinent; but to those who conform their appetites and actions to reason, the knowledge of these things must produce vast utility. Concerning the hearer, and in what manner he is to admit [the discussion,] and what we propose to treat of, let thus much be prefaced.

CHAP. IV.

The name of the chief end. False opinions of men concerning it. Whether we should argue from effects [particulars] to causes [universals] or contrariwise.

1. BUT to return; since every knowledge and predilection aims at some good, let us shew what it is, which we say that the political science aims at, and what is the highest good of all subjects of action. As to name indeed, it is almost agreed upon by most men; for both the vulgar and learned call it *happiness:* but they conceive that to live well and to act well[d]

---

d Eὖ πράττιιν generally signifies to be fortunate, *bene rem gerere:* but Aristotle seems to use the phrase in its literal sense, and for an obvious reason; as he makes happiness depend upon action, εὖ πράττιιν is at once the cause and effect.

are the same as to be happy. But concerning happiness, what it is, they disagree, and the many do not give the same definition of it as the wise; for some fancy it to be an obvious and well known object, such as pleasure, or wealth, or honour; but different men think differently: and frequently the same person thinks it a different thing; for, when diseased, he believes it to be health; when poor; riches; but, feeling their own ignorance, they admire those who call it something great and above their comprehension. Some again have supposed that, besides these [e] many goods, there is another self-subsisting good, which to all these is the cause of their being goods. Now to examine all the opinions would perhaps be rather unprofitable; but it will suffice us to examine those which are most prominent, or seem to carry some reason with them.

2. Let it not, however, escape our notice, that arguments *from* [f] principles differ from arguments *to* [g] principles; for well did Plato also start this question, and enquire whether the way is *from* principles or *to* principles; as in the course [whether a race is] from the presidents to the goal, or the contrary. For we must begin from those things that are known, and things are known in two ways; for some are known to *us* [h], but others simply in themselves [i]; perhaps therefore we should begin from things known to *us*.

3. Wherefore it is necessary that he should have been well brought up in his moral conduct, who is to listen with advantage to a discussion of things noble and just, and political things in general. For the existence of a thing is the principle; and if that were proved to satisfaction, there would be no necessity for the reason why it is so. Such an one either possesses, or would easily acquire, the principles. But let

---

[e] Plato v. c. 6.

[f] The synthetical method.

[g] The analytical method.

[h] The knowledge of them is acquired by each individual from his own personal experience, as the principles of moral action.

[i] Abstractedly, without any reference to action, as the principles of pure mathematics.

him, who has neither of these advantages, hear the sentiments of Hesiod :——

> Far best is he, whose own instinctive pow'r
> With cautious wisdom weighs each coming hour:
> He too is good, whom borrow'd counsels guide:
> But he who, slave to ignorance and pride,
> Scorns or forgets what wiser tongues have said,
> Alive is useless, and despised when dead [i].

CHAP. V.

The opinions of most men concerning the nature of happiness are considered, and proved erroneous.

1. BUT let us proceed, whence we have digressed; for men seem not unreasonably to form their notion of *the good*, and of happiness, from different lives. The many and most worthless class [suppose] pleasure [to be the good,] wherefore they are satisfied even with a life of enjoyment.

2. For there are three kinds of lives which are most prominent; that just mentioned, and the political, and a third, the contemplative.

3. Now the many appear entirely slavish, deliberately choosing the life of brutes; but they find a plea for it, because many persons, filling places of power, are led by the same passions, as Sardanapalus.

4. But the well-educated and active, [consider] honour [as the great good;] for this is nearly the end of political life; but it appears to be too superficial for the object of our enquiry; for it seems to have its being more in those who honour, than in him who is honoured [k]: but we have a natural conception, that the good is something peculiarly one's own, and difficult to be taken away. Moreover, men seem to pursue honour, that they may believe themselves to be good; at

[i] See the same sentiment in Livy, lib. xxii. c. 29. and Sophocles, Antigone, v. 720. Cicero pro Cluentio. Herodotus, Polymn. 16.

[k] Vide book viii. chap. 8. at the beginning.

least they seek to be honoured by prudent men, and by their acquaintances, and on the score of their virtue: it is plain, therefore, that at least in *their* opinion virtue is superior. But perhaps one would rather suppose *this* [virtue] to be the end of the political life; but this also appears too imperfect; for it seems possible for a man, while in possession of virtue, either to sleep, or be inactive through life; and besides this, to undergo calamities, and be in the highest degree unfortunate: but a man living thus, no one would pronounce happy, unless in defence of a favourite opinion. Enough, therefore, of these things; for we have treated of them at considerable length in our miscellaneous writings.

5. The third life is the contemplative; concerning which we shall institute an enquiry hereafter.

6. But the money-getting life is under a kind of restraint; and it is obvious that riches are not the good which we are tracing; for they are merely useful[1], and for the sake of something else. Wherefore one would rather suppose, that the ends before mentioned [were the goods;] for they are loved on their own account; but not even those appear to be so, although many arguments have been built upon them. Let these things then be dismissed.

[1] The term *useful*, χρήσιμον, is here used to denote something, whose end is not in itself, but it is merely useful towards the obtaining some higher end: ωφέλιμα, is used in the same sense in c. vi. §. 7.

CHAP. VI.

Plato's doctrine of happiness considered.

INTRODUCTION.
UPON PLATO'S DOCTRINE OF IDEAS.

An abstract idea is the notion of some property common to many objects, wholly abstracted from its existence in those objects, and generalized in the mind: so that the mind conceives an idea of this property unconnected with any thing material, and without requiring any operation of sensation to form the idea. Thus my eye tells me that a house is white, snow is white, and paper is white, and by the operation of sense, I have a distinct notion of a white horse, white snow, and white paper: but when I abstract this common notion from the objects themselves, and contemplate whiteness without reference to any object, in which it is inherent, I have a general or abstract idea of whiteness; and this is an operation of pure intellect, without any intervention of sensation.

The same general or abstract idea is acquired of properties, which are not, like whiteness, perceived by the senses. Thus I see different men performing different virtuous actions, and I obtain an abstract idea of virtue: I see different men obtaining happiness by different pursuits, and I obtain an abstract idea of happiness.

But as these abstract ideas could not exist in matter, and every thing must exist somewhere, the ancient Philosophers, and Aristotle amongst them, assigned them a place in the mind of the Deity: they considered these as the archetypes or patterns of every thing in the material world, as truly eternal, and unchangeable, in contradistinction to corporeal forms, which are in a constant vicissitude of generation and corruption.

Thus far Plato and Aristotle agreed. Aristotle however and his School, although they acknowledged these self-existing, eternal, and archetypal forms, yet did not suppose that they had no real existence in those bodies also, which convey the notion of them to the senses, and thence to the mind. Thus they held snow to be really white, although there was only one self-existent whiteness: and though there was only one real form of happiness, (that in the mind of the Deity,) yet they did not deny that those several circumstances, which are commonly said to produce happiness, did really produce what was really and truly happiness.

But Plato went farther, and maintained that those ideas or species of things had a real existence by themselves, not only out of any corporeal form, but out of any mind or intelligence; that they were incorporeal substances, not accidents or qualities of other substances. He considered that these were the only forms, which had any real existence; that shadows or copies might seem to emanate from them, and give names to objects here below; but these objects were nothing more than names. Thus several beings are called by the common name of ἄνθρωπος, man, but they are only called so, because they partake of that one general form, which is the αὐτοάνθρωπος, the very man. So also many things here are called ἄγαθα, goods: but he maintained that none of them were really and intrinsically goods, but only that one αὐτοάγαθον, which was the form and archetype of them all. Consequently the (ἰδέα, εἶδος) abstract idea or form of happiness, was the only happiness which had any real existence.

It is this doctrine of Plato, which Aristotle combats in the following chapter.

1. PERHAPS it is better to investigate the question of universal [good,] and to enquire what is meant by it, although such an enquiry involves difficulties, because men who are our friends introduce the doctrine of *ideas* [or universal *goods.*] But perhaps it may seem to be better, and even necessary, at least for the preservation of truth, that we should overthrow even our own systems, especially as we are philosophers; for both [m] being our friends, it is our sacred duty to prefer the truth.

2. But those who introduced this opinion, did not suppose *ideas* of those things in which they predicated a prior and a posterior; wherefore they did not establish an *idea* of numbers. But the *good* is predicated in substance, in quality, and in relation. But the self-subsistent and the essence are naturally prior to the relative; for this is like a branch, and an accident of being; so that there cannot be any common *idea* in these.

3. Again, since the *good* is predicated in as many ways as being, (for it is predicated in essence, as God and intellect; and in quality, as the virtues; and in quantity, as the mean; and in relation, as utility; and in time, as opportunity; and in place, as a habitation, and so on [in the other predicables [n];]) it is evident, that it cannot be any thing common,

---

[m] Truth, and (Plato) the supporter of this doctrine.

[n] The predicables, or categories, are the various relations in which any being, can stand to another. Aristotle made ten categories, viz. substance, quantity, quality, relation, action, passion, time, place, situation, and habit.

universal, and one : for then it would not have been predicated in all the categories, but in one only.

4. Farther still, since of things under one *idea* there is also one science, there would then be some one science of all goods ; but now there are many sciences even of goods under the same category ; as for instance of opportunity, in war the military art is the science, but in disease, the medical art ; and again of the mean, in food the science is the medical, but in labours the gymnastic.

5. But one might doubt what they mean to say by the *self* of any thing, since in man's-self and man there is one and the same definition of man ; for as far as he is man, they will not differ. If so then, neither will there be difference as far as good is concerned, between good and the self of good ; nor yet will it be more a good from being eternal ; since neither is the white which is of long duration, whiter than that which is for a day.

6. But the Pythagoreans seem to speak more probably concerning it, placing *unity* in the catalogue ° of goods ; whom Speusippus also seems to have followed.

7. However concerning these subjects there must be another disquisition. But in what we have just asserted a doubt suggests itself, because our arguments have not been spoken concerning every good ; but those things, which are pursued and cherished on their own account, are predicated under one species of good ; and things productive of these, or in any way preservative of them, or preventive of the contrary, are said to be goods on account of these, and in another manner. It is evident then, that goods may be predicated in two ways ; and some on their own account, the others on account of the former. Separating therefore goods *per se* from useful [or preparatory] goods, let us consider whether they are predicated under one *idea*. But what kind of goods would one determine to be goods on their own account ? Whether such as are pursued even when insulated, such as wisdom, sight,

° This catalogue may be seen in a note to the Greek text in Wilkinson's edition.

some pleasures, and honours? for these, though we pursue them on account of something else, yet one would class among things good on their own account: or is there nothing good *per se* besides the idea[p]? if there is, then the *idea* is of no use whatever. But if these also are goods on their own account, the definition of good must necessarily shew itself the same in all these; just as the definition of whiteness in snow, and white lead: but of honour, and prudence, and pleasure, there are other and different definitions, in the very particular of their being goods. The good therefore is not any thing common under one idea.

8. But how comes it then [it will be asked] that the same term *good* is predicated [of different things?] for it does not appear to be applied to things accidentally equivocal; is it because all things proceed from one, or tend towards one good? or is it not rather by proportion? For it is as sight in the body, intellect in the soul, and other goods in other substances.

9. But perhaps these things must be dismissed for the present; for it would better become another branch of Philosophy to descant closely upon these subjects, as it would also concerning the *idea*; for even if there were some one good predicated in common, or something separate, independent by itself, it is obvious it would not be practical or to be possessed by man; but for the present this very kind of good is the object of our enquiry. Perhaps, however, it would seem to some one that it were well to know it, as being conducive to those goods, which are to be possessed and acted upon; for having this as a pattern, we shall be more likely to know the goods that are in our reach: and if we know them, we shall obtain them. Certainly this position has some plausibility, but it appears to be at variance with the sciences; for all of them, although aspiring after some good, and seeking that which is deficient, omit the knowledge of this; though, that all artists should be ignorant of an aid of such conse-

[p] This is said ironically: for he means to say that there *is* something good *per se* besides the idea.

quence, and never enquire for it, is not at all reasonable. It is a question likewise how a weaver or carpenter would be benefited towards his own trade by knowing this very good; or how will he who has had an insight into this idea be better suited for a physician, or a general; for neither does the physician appear to regard health in this manner, but the health of a man, and perhaps rather that of a particular individual; for he cures individually. Concerning these things then let so much be said.

CHAP. VII.

The requisites for a summum bonum are explained, and then Aristotle's own definition of it.

1. Now let us again proceed to the good we are in search of, *what it is.* For it seems to be different, in different actions and arts; for it is different in the medical art, in generalship, and so also in the rest. What then is *the good* in each? Is it not that, for the sake of which the other things are done? Now that in the medical art is health; in the art of commanding an army, victory; in architecture, a house; in other arts, other ends. But in every action and predilection it is the end; since for the sake of this all men perform the other things. So that, if there is any end of all the subjects of action, this must be the practical good; but if more ends, these must be it.

2. Our argument at length, often shifting the view, has arrived at this same point[q]. But we must attempt to explain this still farther. Since ends appear many, and of these we choose some for the sake of others, as, for instance, riches, musical instruments, and in fine all things instrumental, it is

---

[q] There are two distinct ways by which happiness is proved to be the *summum bonum*: first, from its being the end of the highest science; secondly, from its being the ultimate end of all human actions.

obvious, that they are not all perfect. But the chief good appears to be something perfect; so that if there is one only perfect end, that must be the very thing, which we are in search of; but if there are many, the most perfect of them. Now we say, that the object pursued for its own sake is more perfect than that pursued for the sake of another; and that which is never chosen on account of another thing, more so than those which are eligible both in themselves, and for sake of that other: in fine, we call that completely perfect, which is always eligible for its own sake, and never on account of any thing else.

3. Of this kind does happiness seem in a peculiar manner to be; for this we always choose on its own account, and never on account of something else. But honour, and pleasure, and intellect, and every virtue we choose in part certainly on their own account, (for were no further advantage to accrue, we should choose each of them,) but we choose them also for the sake of happiness, supposing that we shall attain happiness by their means; but no one chooses happiness for the sake of these, nor in short for the sake of any thing else.

4. But the same result seems also to arise from self-sufficiency [or independence;] for the perfect good appears to be self-sufficient; but we call that self-sufficient, not what is so to a single being leading a solitary life, but also to parents and children, and wives, and, in short, to friends and fellow citizens; since man is naturally a political animal. Some limit, however, must be assigned these; for, if a person extends them to parents and descendants, and to the friends of friends, it will proceed to infinity. But this must be investigated hereafter[r]; and we lay down *the self-sufficient* to be that, which, separated from every thing else, makes life eligi-

---

[r] The stoics defined the *summum bonum* to be αὐτάρκεια ζωῆς. Aristotle was afraid that his own description of the *summum bonum* might seem to lead to the same conclusion: he therefore mentions it here, though he shews the difference more fully hereafter: viz. that his definition of happiness implies αὐτάρκεια, but that αὐτάρκεια does not imply perfect happiness, it being only a part of it.

ble, and in want of nothing. But such a thing as this we suppose happiness to be; and moreover, we suppose it the most eligible of all, even when not added [to any other good;] but when added, more eligible doubtless, in conjunction with the smallest good; for the part added becomes an excess of good; but of goods the greater is always more eligible. Happiness then appears something perfect and self-sufficient, being the end of all things to be done.

5. But perhaps to say that happiness is the best of goods, appears something already allowed; and it is desirable that we should state still more clearly what it is. Perhaps then this may be done, if the peculiar work of man be assumed; for as to the musician, and statuary, and to every artist, and in short to all who have any work or action, the good and excellence of each appears to be in the work; so would it appear to be with man, if there is any peculiar work belonging to him [s]. Are there then certain peculiar works and actions of the carpenter and shoemaker; and is there no peculiar work of man, but is he born to be idle [t]? or as there appears a certain work of the eye, the hand, and the foot, and, in fine, of each of the members, so likewise, would not one assume a certain work of man besides all these?

6. What then can this work be [u]? For *to live* appears to be common to him, even with vegetables; but his *peculiar* work is the question with us; we must therefore abstract the life of nutrition and growth. Then a kind of sensitive life would next follow; but this also appears to be common both to the horse, and the ox, and to every animal. There remains therefore a certain practical life of that, which is in possession of reason; and of this, part is so as being obedient to reason,

[s] The excellence of every artist, considered as an artist, will be known by observing his peculiar work: and as happiness is the excellence of man, considered as man, we shall know what happiness is, by observing what is the peculiar work of man.

[t] Ἀργὸν, i. e. without an ἔργον.

[u] It must be something peculiar to man, and yet common to (or in the reach of) all mankind: the things common to all mankind are ζωὴ θρεπτικὴ, ζωὴ αἰσθητικὴ, and ζωὴ πρακτικὴ. But as it must also be peculiar to man, the two former are excluded.

the other as possessing it, and exercising intellect. But this life also being spoken of in two ways [x], [according to energy and according to habit,] we must take that according to energy; for that appears more properly to be called so. Now if the work of man is an energy of the soul according to reason, or not without reason; and if we say that the work of any man, and of any good man, is the same in genus, as of a harper, and a good harper; (and so, in short, in all cases, superiority in each particular excellence being added to each particular work;) for it is the work of a harper to play, of a good harper to play well: if so, and if we assume the work of man to be a kind of life, and that life an energy of the soul, and actions performed with reason; and the work of a good man to be the same things done well, and excellently; and every thing to be complete according to its proper excellence: if these things are true, man's chief good proves to be *an energy of the soul according to virtue;* but if the virtues are plural, according to the best and most perfect: and besides this, throughout the greater part of life [y]: for as neither one swallow, nor one day, makes a spring; so neither does one day, nor a short time, make a man blessed and happy.

7. Thus then let the good be delineated; for it is necessary, perhaps, first to sketch, then afterwards to complete the figure. But it would seem to be incumbent upon every one to improve and render distinct things, that are correctly sketched, and time would seem to be the discoverer of such things as these, or at least a good assistant; whence also proceed the improvements of arts; for it is the duty of every one to add that which is deficient. But it is necessary to bear in mind what has been mentioned already, and not to demand accuracy equally in all cases, but in each according to its subject matter, and just so far as is appropriate to the plan: for the carpenter and geometrician examine a right angle with different views; the one, as far as it is necessary for his work,

[x] Vide book x. chap. 6. at the beginning.

[y] Βίος τέλειος certainly does not mean a perfect or whole life, as may be seen in c. 10.

the other, what it is, or what qualities it has; for he is a contemplator of the truth. In the same manner then must we act in all other instances, that the ornaments may not become greater than the works themselves. Neither indeed is the cause to be equally required in all things, but it suffices in some cases, as for instance in first principles, that their existence be clearly shewn: but the existence is the first and the principle.

8. Now of principles some are perceived by induction, others by sense, others by a certain habit, and different principles by different modes; but we must endeavour to trace each of them in the manner they are formed by nature; and we must use our utmost skill, that they be well defined, for that has great weight in the discussions which follow. The principle, then, seems to be more than the half of the whole, and many of the subjects of enquiry to become clear by means of this.

CHAP. VIII.

Every thing that is supposed by other writers to be requisite for happiness, is found in Aristotle's definition.

1. But we must consider happiness not only from the conclusion, and the particulars, from which our arguments are drawn, but also from the assertions of others concerning it: for all the real parts of a thing accord with the truth: but the truth is immediately discordant with falsehood [z].

2. Now goods being distributed into three parts, and some called exterior, others said to belong to the soul, and others to the body, we call those belonging to the soul, the superior, and most perfectly good: but we assume, that actions and energies of the soul belong to the soul. So that our definition would be right, according to this opinion at least, which is

---

[z] If Aristotle's definition is true, and the assertions of other philosophers are true, they must necessarily agree.

ancient, and allowed by philosophers: it would also be right, because it has been said, that certain actions and energies are the end; for thus it becomes one of the mental goods, and not one of the exterior [a].

3. Also, that the happy man lives well and acts well is consonant with our definition; for it is there almost called a certain well-living, and well-acting [b].

4. Again, all the qualities required in happiness are shewn to exist in what we have defined; for to some it seems to be virtue, to others prudence, and to others a kind of wisdom: to some again, these, or any of them joined with pleasure, or at least not without pleasure; others again include external prosperity: but of these opinions, many and ancient writers support some; a few, and those men of celebrity, the others; nor is it reasonable to suppose that any of these have totally erred, but that they are right in one particular at least, or in most.

5. With those then, who say it is every virtue, or some virtue, the definition accords; for to this [virtue] belongs the energy according to it. But [c] perhaps it makes no small difference, whether we suppose the chief good to consist in possession, or use; and whether in habit or energy; for it is possible that a habit, when existing, may effect no good: for instance, in one, who is asleep, or in any other way inactive: but for energy to effect no good, is impossible; for it will act from necessity, and it will act well. But as in the Olympic games, not the most beautiful and strongest are crowned, but those who contend, (for some of these are victorious;) thus

---

[a] His argument is this: philosophers have divided *goods* into three kinds, exterior, mental, bodily: of these the mental are most important: I may therefore neglect the rest, and need only prove that my definition contains mental goods: but, as I have made the end to consist in action, external goods cannot be implied: but I have gone farther; I have expressly mentioned actions or energies of *the soul.*

[b] The terms ἀρετὴ, and βίος τέλειος, in the definition imply εὐζωία, and εὐπραξία.

[c] He does not only prove his definition to agree with former opinions, but to go beyond them, as it contains more.

also those, who act rightly, become successful candidates for the noble and good things in life.

6. Moreover, their life is in itself delightful; for to be delighted, is a good of the soul; but that is delightful to every man, of which he is said to be a lover; as a horse to a lover of horses, a spectacle to a lover of spectacles; so also just things to a lover of justice; and, in short, virtuous actions to a lover of virtue. However, those things which are delightful to the multitude, are inconsistent, because they are not such by nature; but to the lover of what is noble, those things are delightful, which are by nature delightful; and such are actions according to virtue; so that they are delightful both to these characters, and in themselves. Their life therefore does not call for pleasure, as a kind of appendage, but has the pleasure in itself; for besides what has been said, he is by no means a good man, who does not rejoice in noble actions; nor would any man call him just, who does not delight in acting justly; nor liberal, who does not exult in liberal acts; and in like manner in the other virtues. If so, actions according to virtue will be delightful in themselves; they will also be good and noble, and each of these in the greatest degree, if the good man judges rightly concerning them; and he does judge so as we have said already. Happiness therefore is the best and most noble, and most delightful; and these qualities are not separated according to the Delian inscription; for all these qualities are attached to the best energies; but we have said that happiness is all these, or that one of them which is the best.

7. At the same time however it seems, as we have said, to stand in need of exterior goods; for it is impossible, or at least not easy to perform praiseworthy actions without exterior means; for many things are performed as it were by instruments, by friends, and wealth, and political power. But men deprived of some things, as of noble birth, fine progeny, or fine form, sully their happiness; for he is not altogether capable of happiness, who is deformed in his body, or of mean birth, or is deserted and childless: and still less so, perhaps, if he have vicious children, or if they were dear and

dutiful, and have died.   As we have said, therefore, it seems to demand such prosperity as this; whence some arrange good fortune in the same class with happiness: but others virtue.

CHAP. IX.

That happiness is acquired by action.

1. HENCE[d] it is also doubted, whether it is acquired by discipline, or habit, or in some other manner by exercise; or whether it comes to us from some divine allotment, or even from chance.

2. If then any other good is the gift of gods to men, it is reasonable to suppose that happiness also is a divine gift, and more so than any thing else, inasmuch as it is the best of human goods.   But this would perhaps be better adapted to another discussion; but, even if it be not a divine gift, but results from virtue, and a kind of discipline or exercise, it appears to be one of the most divine things, for the prize and end of virtue appears to be the best, and something divine, and blessed.

3. But it must also be common to many; for it may be possessed through some discipline and study by all who are not disabled for the reception of virtue.   But if it is better that happiness should be derived in this way, than by fortune, it is reasonable to suppose it is so; since natural productions by nature exist in the best way in which it is possible for them to exist; so also is it with things produced by art, and every other cause, and especially by the best cause. But to commit the greatest and most excellent of things to chance would be very discordant[e].   This question is also cleared up from the definition; for it has been said to be an energy of a certain quality according to virtue; but of other

[d] i. e. from the want of some external goods to make happiness complete.

[e] Lucian. Hermotimus, vol. i. p. 768. ed. Hemst.

goods some necessarily exist with it, others are by nature co-operative and useful in the manner of instruments. But this would accord with what we have said in the beginning; for we have laid down the end of the political science to be the best; but this uses the greatest diligence to render the citizens of a certain character, and good and apt to perform noble actions; therefore that we do not call either an ox, or a horse, or any other brute happy; for it is impossible for any of them to partake of such an energy. And for this reason neither is a child happy; for on account of his age he is not yet capable of acting in this manner; but such as are called so, are pronounced happy through hope; for, as we have said, it requires both perfect virtue, and a perfect life. For there are in life many changes and vicissitudes of all kinds; and it is possible that he, who has the greatest abundance, should in old age fall into the greatest calamities, as is fabled in heroic poems concerning Priam; but him, who meets with such misfortunes and dies miserably, no man will pronounce happy.

CHAP. X.

What effect the vicissitudes of fortune have upon the happy man.

1. Is no man [f] then to be pronounced happy while he lives, but must we according to Solon look to the end? And if this must be admitted, is he then happy when he has died? Or is not this altogether absurd, especially to us who assert that happiness is a kind of energy?

2. But if we do not say that the dead man is happy, and supposing this not to be Solon's meaning, but that one may safely pronounce a man happy at that period, as being beyond the reach of evils and calamities, this also involves a certain question. For there appears to be something both good and

[f] Οὐδ' ἄλλον οὐδένα ἀνθρώπων, no man at all, not only children, but no man at any age.

evil to a dead man, as there may be to one alive, but not conscious[g] of it: as honours and disgraces, and the prosperity and adversity of children and descendants in general. But these things also produce a doubt; for to one who has lived happily till old age, and died accordingly, if it is possible that many changes may happen in his offspring, and that some of them may be good, and obtain a life according to desert, and others the contrary; and it is evident, that even after great intervals of time it is possible for them to affect their parents in various ways. It would then be absurd, if the dead too changed with them, and became one while happy, at another time miserable; it would be also absurd that the affairs of descendants should not be interesting to parents for some time at least.

3. But we must return to the former subject of dispute; for the present question may perhaps be also solved from that[h]. If therefore it is necessary to look to the end, and then to pronounce a man happy, not as being happy, but because he was so before; how is it not absurd, that, when he is happy, his present possession may not be truly predicated concerning him, merely because we are unwilling to pronounce men happy when alive on account of the changes of fortune, and because we have supposed happiness to be something stable, and by no means easily changed; whereas fortune makes many revolutions about the same persons? for it is manifest, that if we follow each change of fortune, we must frequently call the same man happy, and again miserable, exhibiting the happy man as a kind of cameleon,

---

[g] The way in which a dead man may be said to be unhappy by the vicissitudes of his descendants, is illustrated by the case of a living person, who has some calamity befal him, e. g. losing a ship at sea, or a son in a distant country; where he does not know of the misfortune at the time when it happens; but still as it has happened, he must be considered unhappy in consequence.

[h] The two questions are, first, May we not call a man happy whilst he is alive? which leads to the second; Are the dead affected by the vicissitudes of the living? He first answers the former, and by it the latter also.

and seated on an unstable foundation. Or rather is it by no means right to follow the changes of fortune? for the distinction of good or bad does not depend on these, but the life of man, as we have said, requires their presence: but the energies according to virtue are the regulators of happiness, and the contrary energies of the contrary. Moreover, the present subject of dispute bears testimony to the definition. For in no human affairs does stability so exist as in the energies according to virtue; for they seem to be more stable than even the sciences; but of these the most honourable are also the most stable, because happy men chiefly and most stedfastly live in them; which seems like a reason why there is no oblivion concerning them. Consequently that which is enquired after, will be possessed by the happy man, and such will he be through life, for he will be in the practice and theory of the actions of virtue always, or more than any thing else: and will bear his fortune most nobly, and in every way and at all times consistently, as a truly good man, and a square [i] without defect.

4. But the circumstances of fortune being many, and differing in greatness and smallness, it is obvious, that prosperous events, and so also the contrary, when small are of no consequence in life; but many and great events happening prosperously, will render life more happy; for they are naturally adapted to be an ornament, and the use of them is beautiful and good; but happening in the contrary manner, they contract and sully the happiness; for they bring on sorrows, and impede many energies. Nevertheless, even in these circumstances the noble gleams forth when a man bears many and great misfortunes easily, not through insensibility, but being generous and magnanimous. But if energies are the mainsprings of life, as we have said, no happy man can become miserable, for he will never do detestable and vile actions; for we suppose that he, as being

[i] A perfect cube, which, having each of its sides a square, however it be thrown, will rest upon either of its sides perpendicularly. A Greek proverb, v. Rhet. l. iii. c. 11. Plato, Protag. vol. iii. p. 145. ed. Bip.

truly good and wise, bears his fortunes as becomes him, and
from existing circumstances always performs the most noble
deeds; as we suppose that a good general uses the army he
has with him in the most warlike manner; and that the
shoemaker from the skins given him makes the most
beautiful shoe, and in the same manner all other artists.
But if so, the happy man can never become miserable; nor
yet will he be prosperous if he should fall into the calamities of Priam; but he will not therefore be variable and
easily changed, for he will not be removed from happiness
either easily or by common misfortunes, but by great and
many; and out of these he cannot become again happy in a
short time; but if at all, in some long and perfect time,
having in the interval [k] become possessed of great and noble
goods.

5. What then prevents our calling him happy, who energizes according to perfect virtue, and is sufficiently furnished
with external goods, not for a casual time, but through the
greater part of his life? or must we add, who will thus continue to live, and will die accordingly? since the future is
invisible to us, and we have laid down happiness to be an
end, and wholly perfect. But if this be the case, we will
pronounce those among the living blessed, who have and will
have the qualities we have mentioned, but still we must call
them blessed as men. And let so much be explained concerning these things.

CHAP. XI.

*How far the dead are concerned in the fortunes of their
descendants.*

1. THAT the fortunes of descendants and of all friends should
not in any degree affect us, appears a very unfriendly doctrine,
and contrary to the opinions of all men. Now the events
of life being many, and having various distinctions, and
some affecting us more, some less, it appears a long and

[k] Or ἐν αὐτῷ may mean within himself.

endless task to discuss them particularly, and perhaps if the subject were treated generally and in the outline, it would be sufficient.

2. If then of the calamities which befal the man himself, some have a certain weight and consequence in life, while others seem to be lighter; so is it likewise with calamities which befal all his friends: (but it makes a much greater difference whether each of the calamities [of friends] happens to the living or the dead, than whether atrocious and dreadful deeds exist for the first *time* in tragedies, or were actually perpetrated.) [If this be true,] we must conclude the difference to be as stated; or rather perhaps we may conclude the doubt concerning the dead, whether they partake of any good, or of the contrary; for it appears from the above, that if any thing, either good or its contrary, extends to them, it is something weak and small, either in itself or to them; but if not [small,] of such a magnitude and quality as neither to make those happy who are not so, nor to deprive the happy of their haapiness[1]. The prosperity therefore as well as adversity of friends seems partly to affect the dead; but in such a manner and so far, as neither to render those happy who are not happy, nor any thing else of such kind.

CHAP. XII.

That happiness is of the class of things honourable and divine.

1. THESE points then being determined, let us consider happiness, whether it belongs to things praiseworthy, or rather

[1] I consider the whole passage from Εἰ δὴ καθάπερ to ἀφαιρεῖσθαι τὸ μακάριον as one argument: the reasoning of which is this: a man is only affected by great misfortunes; in the same manner the misfortunes of his friends only affect him when they are great: but whether these misfortunes of his friends happen to him when he is alive or dead, makes a great difference: consequently the original question, whether the dead are affected by the misfortunes of the living, may thus be answered: for the case is the same as a man being affected by the misfortunes of his friends while alive, viz. only great misfortunes affect him at all: and when he is dead, those only affect him in a small degree.

to things honourable; for it is evident that at least it is not merely one of the faculties [m], [or powers of action.] Now every thing laudable appears to be praised, in being of a certain quality, and having a certain reference to something [n]; for we praise the just man, the brave, and, in short, the good man, and virtue, on account of works and actions; and the strong, the swift, and every one else, because they are by nature of a certain quality, and have a certain reference to something good and excellent. But this is plain also from the praises given to the gods; for they appear ridiculous when referred to us; but this happens because praises are given by reference [o], as we have said. ' But if praise belongs to such things as these, it is obvious that praise is not given to the best things, but something greater, and more excellent, as also appears to be the case; for we proclaim the gods blessed and happy, and proclaim blessed the most godlike among men; so is it also with goods; for no man praises happiness as he would justice, but pronounces it blessed as being something more divine and excellent. Eudoxus also seems to have well contended for giving the chief rank to pleasure; for its not being praised although it is one of the goods, he thought signified that it was superior to things laudable; but that God and *the good* were of this class, for other things had a reference to these; for praise belongs to

---

[m] Those things which are really and intrinsically goods, and which cannot by any error or persuasion become evils, but must either be goods, or cease to have any existence at all, these the ancient philosophers divided into honourable and praiseworthy. But any thing which depended upon the different characters of men, whether it were a good or an evil, such as money, strength, &c. these they called δυνάμεις, powers or faculties, because though they have the power of being good, they are not necessarily so.

[n] i. e. something *higher* than itself.

[o] *to something higher.* This is not expressed by Aristotle, but is evidently intended: consequently if we praise the gods according to human ideas of merit, we refer them to a standard lower than themselves, which is ridiculous. Nevertheless we certainly *do* praise men, not only for having made advances towards a higher standard, but for having surpassed those below them. This latter kind of praise is not noticed by Aristotle.

virtue, because men are adapted by it to noble actions; but encomiums belong to particular actions, both bodily and mental. But perhaps it would better become those who labour at panegyrics, to discuss these matters closely; but to us it is plain, from what has been said, that happiness belongs to things honourable and perfect. It seems also to be so, because it is a principle; for we all perform all other actions for the sake of this; but we admit the principle and cause of good to be something honourable and divine.

CHAP. XIII.

Of virtue, and the soul, so far as it is connected with virtue.

1. SINCE then happiness is a certain energy of the soul according to perfect virtue, we must consider virtue; for perhaps we should thus be better able to consider happiness also. Now the real politician[p] seems to be particularly engaged with this; for he wishes to render the citizens good and obedient to the laws; and of this we have an example in the legislators of the Cretans and Lacedæmonians, [Minos and Lycurgus,] and if there ever have been any other such. But if this enquiry belongs to the political science, it is evident that the investigation of it would be consistent with our original purpose. We must therefore[q] consider virtue, and evidently human virtue; for we have been tracing human good and human happiness; but we mean by virtue not that of the body, but that of the soul; and happiness also we call an energy of the soul.

2. But if these things are so, it is obvious, that the politician ought in a manner to know every thing that relates to

[p] The man whose professed end and business is πολιτικὴ: whereas Aristotle only considers πολιτικὴ, because he cannot separate ἠθικὴ from it.

[q] Read δή.

the soul; as he, who would cure the eyes, should know the whole body; and more so, as the political science is more honourable and excellent than the medical. And of medical men, those who are well educated, spend much labour on the knowledge of the body. So likewise the politician must consider the nature of the soul; but he must consider it for the sake of these things, and as far as is necessary to the objects of enquiry. For to investigate this matter with more accuracy, is perhaps more laborious than is required by the subject proposed.

3. But some things are spoken well enough concerning it even in our popular writings, and we must use them; such as that one part of it is irrational, the other rational. But whether these are divided in the same manner as the parts of the body and every thing divisible, or whether they are two only in definition, being by nature indivisible, as in the circumference of a circle, the convex and concave side, makes no difference for the present.

4. Of the irrational, one part resembles the common and vegetative power; I mean the cause of its being nourished and increased: for such a power of the soul[r] one would admit in all things that are nourished, even in embryos, and the same also in perfect animals; for it is more reasonable that this should exist in them than any other. Now the virtue of this appears to be common, and not human; for this part and this power seem to operate most in sleep; but the good and bad man are least distinguishable in sleep; whence they say that the happy for half their life differ in nothing from the miserable: and this happens reasonably; for sleep is the inaction of the soul, as to that from which it is termed good and bad, unless some emotions partially reach it [even

---

[r] It is evident from this that the Greek term ψυχὴ and the English term *soul* have not exactly the same signification attached to them: ψυχὴ seems to imply every thing distinct from the mere mass of matter of which man is composed: not only that spiritual and immortal part which is to survive the material, but all the properties active and passive possessed by the material. Thus ψυχικὸν σῶμα is opposed to πνευματικὸν in 1 Cor. xv. 44, 46: see also 1 Cor. ii. 14.

then], and for this reason the visions of the good become better than those of ordinary men. But of these things enough; and therefore the nutritive part must be rejected, since it is naturally destitute of human virtue.

5. There appears, however, to be another nature of the soul, which is irrational; but nevertheless partakes in a manner of reason; for we praise the reason of the continent and incontinent man, as well as that part of the soul which possesses reason; for it excites men rightly and to the most excellent deeds.

6. But there appears in them another part also naturally contrary to reason, which contends with and resists reason; for in fact, as the paralyzed members of the body, if we intend moving them to the right, on the contrary are torn away to the left, just so is it in the soul; for the impulses of the incontinent are towards the contrary. But in bodies we see that which bears itself contrary, but in the soul we do not see it; but perhaps we must nevertheless suppose that there is also in the soul something contrary to reason, opposing and bearing against it; but in what manner it is different does not matter.

7. But even this appears, as we have said, to partake of reason; this part, therefore, in the continent man is obedient to reason; and still more submissive perhaps is it in the temperate and brave; for in these every thing is concordant with reason. The irrational part then appears to be two-fold; for the vegetative by no means partakes of reason; but the part which desires and in short that which moves the appetite partakes of it in a manner, inasmuch as it is obedient to it. Thus too we say that a man pays regard to his father and friends, and not as he pays regard to the mathematical sciences *. But that the irrational part is somehow directed by reason, both admonition and every reproof and exhortation indicate.

* This sentence can scarcely be translated into English: λόγον ἔχειν generally means, as it is here rendered, *to pay regard to*, in which sense it may be applied to the advice of friends, or mathematical pursuits: but in the former case it may be taken literally, and a man may be said λόγον ἔχειν τοῦ πατρὸς, to employ the reason of his father.

8. But if we must say that this also possesses reason, that division of the soul which is rational will be also two-fold[t]; the one properly and in itself, the other as a something obedient to a parent.

9. But virtue also is divided according to this difference; for we call some of the virtues intellectual, others ethical; wisdom, and intelligence, and prudence, we call intellectual; but liberality and temperance, moral; for when speaking of the moral character of a man, we do not say that he is wise or intelligent, but that he is meek or temperate; but we praise the wise man also according to habit; but praiseworthy habits we call virtues.

---

[t] It might be concluded that there are three parts of the soul, the rational, and the two parts of the irrational. But as that part which disobeys reason sometimes also obeys it, and therefore some people have chosen to call it rational; Aristole allows them to subdivide both parts of the soul into two: first, the rational part, into that which is purely intellectual, and that which obeys reason: second, the irrational part, into that which opposes reason, and into the vegetative part. He acknowledges this four-fold division in the 6th book, c. 12, where he speaks τοῦ τετάρτου μορίου τῆς ψυχῆς.

ARISTOTLE'S ETHICS.

BOOK II.

CHAP. I.

That virtue is not innate, but acquired by custom.

1. VIRTUE being two-fold, the one part intellectual, the other moral; the intellectual for the most part derives both its origin and increase from discipline; hence it needs experience and time; but the moral comes to us from custom, whence also it has received the name [ἠθική], but little removed from the word *custom* [ἔθος].

2. From which likewise it is clear, that not one of the moral virtues is born in us by nature; for none of those things which exist by nature can be changed by custom; for instance, a stone naturally borne downward could not be caused by custom to tend upwards, not if a person accustomed it ten thousand times by throwing it upward, nor could the fire be made to tend downwards; nor can any of the things naturally produced one way be turned by custom to the contrary. The virtues then are produced in us neither from nature, nor contrary to nature, but after we have been naturally adapted to receive them, and perfected by custom.

3. Again[a], as many things as accrue to us from nature, we

---

[a] This is a good opportunity for mentioning the two senses in which the word δύναμις is used: it signifies, first, the mere capacity of acquiring a habit, which is implanted in us by nature: secondly, the faculty of performing an action, which is the natural consequence of the habit, and which is acquired by our own exertions. In those things, which are given by nature, as the senses, nature supplies at once both the capacity and the

first receive the powers of them, but afterwards produce the
energies; which is evident in the case of the senses; for we
have not from frequently seeing or frequently hearing received those senses, but, on the contrary, having the senses
we use them, but have not received them by using. But the
virtues we receive by first operating, as in the case of other
arts; for whatever we are to do when we have learnt, these
we learn by doing; as by building, men become builders,
and harpers by playing on the harp; so also by performing
just acts we become just, by doing temperate acts temperate,
by performing brave acts we become brave.

4. Moreover what is done in states adds its testimony to
this; for legislators render the citizens good, by accustoming
them; and indeed this is the wish of every lawgiver; but as
many as do not do this well, err; and in this respect polity
differs from polity, the good from the bad.

5. Again, every virtue is both generated and corrupted from
the same things, and through the same [b]; so also is it with
every art; for from harping both good and bad harpers are
produced, and analogously architects and all other artists;
for from building well, men will be good builders, but bad
from building ill; for if it were not so, there would be no
occasion for a master, but all would be born either good or
bad. Just so then is the case with the virtues; for by performing the acts of intercourse between man and man, we become some just, others unjust; by acting in dangers and
accustoming ourselves to be terrified or confident, some become brave, others cowards. So also is it with acts of desire

faculty, and the act may immediately take place. In those things which
are acquired, as moral virtues and arts, nature gives the capacity, but we
acquire the faculty by practice. Thus a man is born with the capacity of
being a statuary; but he must have practised a long time and even made
many entire statues in a rude and imperfect manner, before he can be properly said to have the faculty of making a statue. This capacity and this
faculty are both expressed by the same word δύναμις, and perplexities often
arise from not observing the distinction.

[b] Or, in other words, virtue and vice are both produced by a succession
of similar actions: for the expression, that virtue is corrupted, is equivalent to saying that vice is produced.

and anger; for some become temperate and meek, others intemperate and irascible; the one by being engaged with them in one way, the others by engaging in them another way.

6. And in one word therefore, from similar energies arise similar habits; wherefore it is necessary to produce energies of a certain quality; for the habits follow according to the different species of these. It makes then no small difference whether we accustom ourselves one way or the other immediately from our youth, but a very great or rather the whole difference.

CHAP. II.

As moral virtue depends upon actions, it is considered how each particular action should be performed.

1. SINCE then the present undertaking is not for the purpose of theory, as other discussions are; (for we do not speculate that we may know what virtue is, but that we may become good, since otherwise there would no advantage accrue from it;) it is necessary to consider the circumstances of actions, in what manner we are to perform them; for these are the causes of the habits also being of a certain quality, as we have before said.

2. Now to act according to right reason is too general a precept, and let it lie over for the present; but we will discuss that subject hereafter, both what right reason is, and what reference it bears to the other virtues.

3. But let this be previously agreed upon, that every treatise concerning practical things ought to be composed in outline, and not with accuracy, as we have also said in the outset; because reasonings are to be required according to the subject matter; but things belonging and conducive to actions have no stability, as neither have things conducive to health. But the general argument being of this nature, much more will the discussion of particulars be deficient in

accuracy ; for it does not come under any art or under any precept : but it becomes the individuals themselves, when in action, to observe what is suitable to the occasion, as is the rule in the medical and the pilot's art. But although the present discussion is of such a nature, (i. e. incapable of accuracy,) we must endeavour to make up for it.

4. In the first place then it must be noticed, that things of this kind are by nature apt to be corrupted by defect and excess, as we see in strength and health, (for it is necessary to use things obvious, as examples in things less known;) for exercises, which are excessive as well as those which are defective, destroy the strength. In like manner also liquids and eatables taken in too great or too small a quantity destroy the health ; but when taken in moderation, both produce and improve and preserve it. This then is the case with temperance and fortitude and the other virtues ; for he who flies from and is terrified at every thing, and sustains nothing, becomes timid ; and he that fears nothing altogether, but marches up to every thing, is rash. In the same manner he who takes his fill of every pleasure, and abstains from none, is intemperate ; but he who flies from all pleasures, as rustics do, is a kind of insensible character. For temperance and fortitude are destroyed by the excess and defect, but preserved by mediocrity.

5. But not only the origin, and increase, and corruption [of the virtues] proceed from and by the same things, but also their operations will be in the same things[c] ; for thus it is in other more obvious cases ; for instance, in strength ; for that is produced by taking much food, and submitting to many labours ; and the strong man is best able to do these things. So it is also with the virtues ; for by abstaining

[c] Or, in other words, the act which precedes and leads to the habit, and that which follows and flows from it, will be the same in kind. But, as is shewn in the following chapter, there will be this difference between them : the latter is accompanied with pleasure, the former is not : at least although the man may feel pleased that he has been obliged to do a virtuous act, yet if the habit is not formed, he will feel a certain degree of pain in resisting the suggestions of his passions.

from pleasures we become temperate, and having become temperate we are most able to abstain from them. In like manner also in fortitude ; for accustoming ourselves to contemn terrific objects, and to bear them, we become brave, and having become so, we shall be best able to endure terrific things.

CHAP. III.

That the pleasure or pain attendant on our actions is to be the test of our habits, whether they are formed to virtue or vice; and therefore that virtue and vice are conversant in pleasure and pain.

1. But we ought to make the pleasure or pain which attends actions, the indication of habits. For he who abstains from bodily pleasures, and exults in this very thing, is temperate; but he who is grieved in doing so, is the intemperate[d] : and he who endures dangers, and exults in doing so, or at least feels no pain, is brave ; but he who feels pain is a coward ; for moral virtue is conversant with pleasures and pains; for we act viciously by reason of the pleasure, and abstain from noble deeds by reason of the pain. Wherefore it is requisite, as Plato says, to be trained up in a particular manner immediately from our childhood, so that we may be pleased and pained by the things we ought; for this is right education.

2. Moreover, if the virtues are conversant with actions and passions, but pleasure and pain are consequent upon every passion and action, for this reason also virtue must be conversant with pleasures and pains.

---

d He who abstains from bodily pleasures without any struggle at all, merely from the force of habit, is *temperate*. He who abstains after some struggle, because his principle overpowers his passions, is *continent*. But he who abstains and is very sorry at being obliged to abstain, is *intemperate*.

3. The punishments also inflicted by means of these [pains] point out this; for they are a kind of remedies; but remedies are naturally applied by contraries [c].

4. Again, as we have also said before, every habit of the soul, by whatever it is naturally apt to become worse and better, bears its nature toward those things and about them; but they [the habits of the soul] become vitiated by means of pleasures and pains, by our pursuing and avoiding either those things which we ought not, or when we ought not, or in a manner we ought not, or in as many other ways as these things are divided by reason [f]. Wherefore some define the virtues to be certain apathies and tranquillities; yet not properly, because they assert it simply, not saying as is proper, and as is not proper, and when it is proper, and other provisos which are added [g]. Virtue therefore is admitted to be of this kind, conversant with pleasures and pains, apt to perform the best actions; but vice is the contrary.

4. These very things may be made yet clearer from those [arguments which follow]. For the objects of desire being three, and the objects of aversion being also three, the honourable, the advantageous, and the delightful; and the three contraries, the base, the disadvantageous, and the painful; in all these the good man succeeds, but the bad man errs, and particularly in the instance of pleasure; for this is common to all animals, and attends upon all the objects of choice; for both the honourable and the advantageous appear to be delightful. Further, pleasure is connected with

[c] Punishment is evidently a pain: therefore if punishments (like medicines) act by contraries, the vicious act, which required pain as a punishment, must have been caused by pleasure.

[f] i. e. in any of the seven other categories, which are in all ten: vide L. i. c. 6. note n.

[g] Some people, observing the influence which pleasure and pain had upon virtue and vice, conceived virtue and vice to be wholly inactive, and that pleasure and pain alone influenced the virtuous and vicious man: thus virtue and vice would each be an ἀπάθεια or ἠρεμία. But, says Aristotle, they ought to have added, that virtue, (even supposing it to be inactive) is influenced by pleasure rightly, vice wrongly.

the growth of each of us from our infancy; hence it is a difficult task to expunge that passion which has given a colour to life. Moreover, we measure our actions by the rule of pleasure and pain, some of us more, some less. On this account then it is necessary that the whole discussion should have a reference to these things; for it is of no mean consequence towards actions, whether we rejoice or feel pain properly or improperly.

5. Again, it is more arduous to contend against pleasure, than anger, which last Heraclitus speaks of as an arduous task; but both art and virtue are always engaged with the more difficult thing; for the good is more excellent in this [difficulty]. So that on this account also the whole business both of virtue and the political science is with pleasure and pain; for he who employs these well, will be a good man, but he who employs them badly, will be bad.

6. That virtue then is conversant with pleasures and pains, and that by whatever it is produced, it is both improved and vitiated by those same things when not performed in a similar manner; and that, from whatever it is produced, it also energizes about the same, let so much be said.

CHAP. IV.

An objection is started to the clause, that men become virtuous by performing virtuous actions, and that they are not necessarily virtuous in the performance of them; and an answer is given, by shewing the many requisites towards an action being good besides the mere act or performance.

1. But a person might doubt, how we say that men must become just by doing just actions, and temperate by acting temperately; for if they perform just and temperate acts, they are already just and temperate; as, if a person perform

grammatical or musical actions, they are grammarians and musicians [h].

2. Or is this not true even in the arts? For it is possible to do a thing grammatically, either from chance or at another's suggestion. He will therefore be a grammarian then only when he does a thing both grammatical and grammatically, that is, according to the art of grammar inherent in himself.

3. Moreover the case is not similar with the arts [i] as with the virtues; for the things produced by the arts contain the excellence in themselves. It suffices, therefore, that these should be done in a certain manner; but the things performed according to the virtues, are performed [for instance] justly or temperately, not if the actions themselves are of a certain cast, but if the doer performs them with certain dispositions; in the first place, if he performs them knowingly; next, if deliberately choosing them, and deliberately choosing them on their own account; and thirdly, if with a firm and immutable habit. Now these things are not reckoned among the requisites for the possession of the other arts, except the mere knowing. But to the acquisition of the virtues, the mere knowledge avails little or nothing, whereas the other requisites have not a little but the whole force; which [requisites] also accrue from frequently performing virtuous actions; for instance, just and temperate actions.

4. Actions therefore are called just and temperate, when they are such as a just or temperate man would do; but he is the just and temperate, not who merely does these things,

[h] The refutation of this objection is most complete: the objection appeals to the arts of grammar and music. Aristotle proves, first, that in those arts the case is not as the objector states: secondly, supposing it were so, he denies the analogy between the arts and virtue.

[i] And yet in the first and second chapters he argued analogically from the arts to the virtues. The case is this. There is an analogy in the production of arts and moral habits; for they are both produced by a succession of similar actions. But here the analogy ceases; and the difference between performing a moral act and a work of art is what is stated in the text.

but who also does them, as just and temperate men perform them. It is therefore rightly said, that the just character results from performing just actions, and the temperate from performing temperate actions, but from not doing these things no one would ever be likely to become good. But the multitude do not act thus, but flying to mere words, they fancy they are philosophers, and that thus they shall be worthy characters; acting something like the sick, who indeed attentively hear the physicians, but use none of their prescriptions. As therefore these will never have a good habit of body by thus taking care of it, so neither will those have a good habit of mind who thus philosophise.

CHAP. V.

That virtue is a habit.

1. In the next place we must consider what virtue is. Since then the things produced in the soul are three[k], passions, powers, and habits, virtue must be one of these. By passions I mean, desire, anger, fear, audacity, envy, joy, love, hatred, anxiety, emulation, pity, in short, those things which pleasure or pain follow; and by powers, those things by which we are said to be capable of these passions; for instance, by which we are capable of being angry, or pained, or feeling pity; but habits, by which we are well or ill disposed with respect to the passions; for instance, with

---

k Since *moral* virtue is the subject of discussion at present, he of course speaks of that part of the soul only, which sometimes obeys and sometimes disobeys reason; (vide l. i. c. ult.) the purely intellectual part is necessarily excluded. Now nothing is given by nature to the moral part, (if it may be so called,) except animal passions, and the power of acting in consequence of them: nor can any other effect be produced from following or subduing them, than a good or bad habit: i. e. there can be nothing in the *moral* part of the soul, except passions, capacities, (v. note u, to c. 1. of this book,) and habits.

respect to being angry, if we are vehemently or remissly so, we are badly affected; but if moderately, well; and so on with the rest.

2. Neither the virtues therefore nor the vices are passions; for we are not called worthy or vicious on the score of our passions, but we are said to be so on the score of our virtues or vices, and because we are neither praised nor blamed on the score of our passions; for neither he who is angry, nor he who is afraid, is praised; nor is he blamed who is simply angry, but he who is so after a certain manner; but we are praised or blamed on the score of our virtues and vices.

3. Again, we are enraged or terrified without deliberate choice; but the virtues are a kind of deliberate choice, or not without deliberate choice.

4. And in addition to these reasons, we are said to be *moved* according to our passions, but are not said to be *moved* according to the virtues or vices, but to be *disposed* in a certain manner[1].

5. For these reasons neither are they powers; for we are called neither good nor bad from being able simply to feel passion, nor are we praised or blamed. And farther still, we possess powers from nature, but we do not from nature become good or bad; but concerning this we have spoken before.

6. If then the virtues are neither passions nor powers, it remains that they are habits. What therefore virtue is in genus has been explained.

---

[1] An argument drawn from mere words may at first appear weak: it must be remembered however that words are only the signs of things, but they are signs universally agreed upon: consequently if men had conceived virtues and passions to be the same, they would not by universal consent have used different signs to express their effects.

CHAP. VI.

Virtue is a habit consisting in a mean.

1. IT is proper, however, not only to say thus, that it is a habit, but also what kind of a habit it is. We must say then, that every virtue causes the thing itself, of which it is the virtue, to be rightly formed, and brings to perfection the work of it; for instance, the virtue of the eye renders the eye and its work excellent; for by the virtue of the eye we see well. In a similar manner the virtue of a horse renders the horse excellent and proper for running, and bearing its rider, and standing the charge of an enemy. But if this be the case in all instances, then the virtue of man must be the habit, by means of which man becomes good, and by which he will produce his peculiar work perfectly.

2. How this will be effected we have shewn already[m]. And it may also be proved in this way, if we trace out what is its nature. Now in every thing continuous and divisible we may take a greater, a less, and an equal part; and that either in the thing itself, or with reference to ourselves; but the equal is a kind of mean between excess and defect. Now I call that the mean of the thing itself, which is equally distant from each of the extremes, which is one and the same in all things, but the middle with reference to us, that which neither exceeds, nor falls short of what is proper. But this is not one nor the same to all; for instance, if ten are too many, but two too few, they take six for a mean according to the thing; for [six] equally exceeds [two], and is exceeded [by ten]. But this is a mean according to arithmetical proportion; the mean, however, with reference to us is not to be thus assumed. For supposing the eating ten pounds is too much, but eating two pounds is too little, the master of the exercises will not prescribe six pounds; for perhaps this also may be too much or too little for him who

[m] Vide c. ii. of this book.

is to take the food; for to Milo it would be little, but to one who is a beginner in the exercises, much; so is it in the race and wrestling. Thus then every scientific man avoids excess and defect, but searches out for the mean, and makes this the object of his choice; the mean, not of the thing, but that which is referred to ourselves.

3. Now if every science brings its work to perfection in this way, by looking to the mean, and making the productions tend towards that; (whence men are accustomed to say of well-executed works, that it is impossible to take away from, or add any thing to them, inasmuch as the excess and defect destroy the excellency, but the mean preserves it;) and if good artists work, as we say, looking to this, but virtue as well as nature is more accurate and better than every art, virtue must certainly be a something tending to the mean. But I am speaking of moral virtue; for this is conversant with passions and actions; but in these there is excess and defect, and the mean; for instance, it is possible to be afraid, and be confident; and to desire, and abhor; to be enraged, and to pity; and, in short, to be pleased, and be grieved, both in excess and defect, and each manner not right. But the being moved by our passions at the proper time, and for proper reasons, and towards proper persons, and for a proper end, and in a proper manner, is the mean and the best, which is a quality of virtue. In like manner also in actions there is excess and defect, and a mean; but virtue is conversant in passions and actions, in which the excess is an error, and the defect is blamed, but the middle is praised and succeeds; and both these belong to virtue. Hence virtue is a certain mean, inasmuch as it tends to the middle. Again, it is possible to err in many ways; (for evil belongs to the infinite, as the Pythagoreans conjectured, but good to the finite;) but we can act rightly only in one way; wherefore also the one is easy, the other difficult; for it is easy to miss the mark, but difficult to hit it; and on this account excess and defect belong to vice, but the mean only to virtue; "For men are only in one way " good, but bad in various ways."

4. Moral virtue then is *a habit deliberately choosing, existing in a medium which refers to us, and is defined by reason, and as a prudent man would define it;* but a mean between two evils, the one consisting in excess, the other in defect; and farther, it is a mean, in that one of these falls short of and the other exceeds what is right, both in passions and actions, and that virtue both finds and chooses the mean. Wherefore, according to essence, and the definition, which explains the genus, virtue is a mean; but according to preeminence and excellence it is a summit.

5. But neither every action nor every passion admits a mean; for some as soon as named imply depravity, such as, malevolence, impudence, envy; and of actions, adultery, theft, murder. For all these and such like are named from their being themselves bad, but not the excess nor defects of them. It is impossible therefore at any time to be right in these, but we always must err. Nor does the good or the bad consist in things of this kind, in committing adultery with whom, or when, or how we ought, but the mere doing of any of these actions is to err. Similar to this would be the requiring a mean, and excess, and defect in doing an injury, and in acting the coward, and in being intemperate; for there would be in such a case indeed a mean of excess and defect, an excess of excess, and a defect of defect. But there is no excess and defect of temperance and fortitude, because the mean is in one point of view a summit, so neither is there a mean, nor excess, and defect of these, but in whatever manner they are performed there is an error; for, in short, there is neither a mean of excess and defect, nor excess and defect of the mean [o].

---

[n] I have translated μεσότης and μέσον by the same word *mean*, as I know of no separate terms which will express the difference. The difference however is plain: μέσον is the mean itself, or centre of any thing, μεσότης the act of being in the μέσον.

[o] This fifth section may be summed up by saying, there is a mean, excess, and defect in every thing, except in that which is itself a mean, an excess, or a defect.

CHAP. VII.

*By an induction of the particular virtues the truth of the general
proposition is demonstrated, namely, that virtue is a mean.*

1. It is necessary however that this should not only be
asserted universally, but it should also be applicable to particulars; for in discussions on actions, universal reasonings
are more unsubstantial, and particular ones more true; for
actions are engaged in particulars; and with these our po-
sitions ought to accord. We must therefore assume these
things from a sketch.

2. Now in fear and confidence, fortitude is the mean. Of
those who exceed, he who exceeds in absence of fear has no
particular name; (there are indeed many characters name-
less;) but he who exceeds in confidence, is audacious; he
again who exceeds in being afraid, but is deficient in being
confident, is timid.

3. Again, in pains and pleasures, not in all, however, and
indeed less in pains, the mean is temperance, the excess
intemperance. But those who are deficient in pleasures do
not often exist, wherefore neither have these obtained an
appellation; but let them be called the insensate.

4. In the giving and receiving of money, the mean is
liberality, but the excess and defect are prodigality, and illiberality. But men exceed and are deficient in these contrariwise; for the prodigal exceeds in expending, but is deficient in receiving money; on the other hand, the illiberal
exceeds in receiving, but is deficient in expending. For the
present, we speak in outline and summarily, being contented with going thus far; but we shall discuss them more
accurately at a future time.

5. In the case of riches, there are also other dispositions;
the mean is magnificence; for the magnificent man differs
from the liberal; for the former is conversant with great
expences, but the latter with small; but the excess is a
want of taste, and a vulgarity in profusion, and the defect

parsimony; but these [dispositions] differ from those which relate to liberality; in what however they differ will be hereafter explained.

6. In honour and dishonour, the mean is magnanimity, the excess is what is called haughtiness; the defect, pusillanimity.

7. But in the same manner as we have said that liberality is related to magnificence, differing only in that it is conversant with small things, thus also a certain disposition has a relation to magnanimity, which is engaged in great honour, itself being conversant with small; for it is possible to aspire after honour as we ought, and more and less than we ought. Now he who exceeds in his desires is said to be ambitious, but he who is deficient, unambitious, but the middle has no peculiar name. The dispositions also have no name, except that of the ambitious man, ambition; whence the extremes claim as their right the middle place. And we indeed sometimes call the middle ambitious, sometimes unambitious; and sometimes we praise the ambitious, sometimes the unambitious. But from what cause we do this will be explained in the course of the following treatise; but now let us speak concerning the rest, according to the manner we have set out with.

8. In anger there is also excess and defect, and a mean; but these being nearly anonymous, as we call the middle character mild, we will call the mean mildness; and of the extremes, let him who exceeds be the wrathful, and the vice wrathfulness: and let him who is deficient be a certain dispassionate character, but the defect dispassion.

9. There are also three other means, having indeed some similarity to each other, but different from each other; for all of them are conversant with an interchange of words and actions, but they differ because the one is engaged in the truth which is in those actions, the others in what is pleasant; and this latter part consists in amusement, part in all the affairs of life. We must therefore speak concerning these, that we may the more clearly see, that in all cases the mean is laudable, but that the extremes are neither right nor laud-

able, but reprehensible. Of these also the greater part are anonymous; but we must attempt, as in the other cases, to give them appellations, for the sake of perspicuity, and that we may be easily followed.

10. As to truth then, the middle character is a kind of truth-telling person, and the mean may be called truth; but pretence, when carried to excess, may be termed arrogance, and he who possesses it, arrogant; but that which leans to defect, may be called dissimulation, and the person a dissimulator.

11. With respect however to pleasure in amusement, the middle character is the facetious, and the disposition facetiousness; but the excess is scurrility, and he who possesses it, a scurrilous man; but he who is deficient, a kind of rustic character, and the habit may be called rusticity.

12. Now concerning the other pleasure, that in the affairs of life, he, who pleases in such a way as is proper is friendly, and the medium is friendliness; he who exceeds, if for no advantage to himself, is a fawner, but if for his own advantage, he is a flatterer; and he who is deficient, and in all things unpleasant, is contentious and morose.

13. There are likewise means in the passions, and in things attendant on the passions; for modesty is not a virtue, but still the modest man is praised; for in these, the one character is called middle, but he who exceeds, being, as it were, confounded, is the man who is abashed at every thing; and he who is deficient [in modesty], or who has it not at all, is the impudent, but the middle character is the modest.

14. Again, indignation is the mean between envy and malevolence, and these are conversant with the pain and pleasure, which arise from what happens to our neighbours; for the indignant man is pained at those, who are undeservedly prosperous; but the envious man exceeding the former, is pained at all who do well; but the malevolent man is so far short of feeling pain at the misfortunes of other men, that he even feels pleasure at them. But there will be an opportunity for these things elsewhere: with respect to justice however, since the term is not used in one way only, at a

future opportunity, we will divide it, and speak concerning each of its parts, how they are means; in like manner also we shall treat concerning the rational virtues.

CHAP. VIII.

How the extremes are opposed to the mean and to each other.

1. Now there being three dispositions, two of which are vices, one in excess, the other in defect, and there being one virtue, the mean, each in some manner are opposed to each; for the extremes are contrary both to the mean and to each other, and the mean is contrary to the extremes. For as the equal with reference to the less is greater, but with reference to the greater, less; so the middle habits compared with the defects are excessive, but compared with the excesses are deficient, as well in passions as in actions; for the brave compared with the timid appears rash, but compared with the rash he appears timid. In like manner also the temperate compared with the insensate is intemperate, but compared with the intemperate is insensate; the liberal man compared with the illiberal is prodigal, but with the prodigal, he is illiberal; wherefore also the extremes drive the mean each to the other, and the timid calls the brave audacious, but the audacious man calls him timid, and analogously in the other cases.

2. Now these being thus opposed to each other, the extremes have a greater contrariety to each other than to the mean; for they are more widely separated from each other than from the mean; as the great is more remote from the small, and the small from the great, than both from the equal. Again, there appears a certain similarity in some extremes to the mean, as in rashness to fortitude, and in prodigality to liberality; but between the extremes and each other there is the greatest dissimilarity; but things very

distant from each other are defined to be contraries; so that things the more distant are also the more contrary.

3. But in some things the defect, in other the excess is more opposed to the mean; for instance, to fortitude is opposed not rashness, which is the excess, but timidity, which is the defect; to temperance, not insensibility, which is the defect, but intemperance, which is the excess.

4. And this happens for two reasons; one indeed from the thing itself; for from that one extreme being nearer and more similar to the mean, we oppose to it not that extreme, but rather the contrary; for instance, since rashness seems to be more similar and nearer to fortitude, but timidity more dissimilar, we rather oppose this latter; for things the more distant from the mean seem to be the more contrary to it.

5. This then is one cause for the thing itself: but another cause is from ourselves; for to whichever extreme we are somehow naturally more inclined, this appears more contrary to the mean; for instance, we are ourselves naturally more inclined to pleasures, wherefore we are more easily borne to intemperance, than to orderly conduct. We call those then more contrary, to which the propensity is greater; and on that account intemperance being an excess is more contrary to temperance.

CHAP. IX.

How we are to arrive at the mean in action.

1. THAT ethical virtue therefore is a mean, and how it is so, and that it is the mean between two vices, the one consisting in excess, the other in defect, and that it is of such a nature, because it is a thing tending to the mean, which is in passions and actions, has been sufficiently discussed. Whence also it is a difficult task to be virtuous; for in every thing, to find the middle is a task; for instance, to find the centre of a circle is not in the power of every one, but of the scientific man. Thus also to be angry is in every one's

power, and easy; so also is the giving and spending money; but to do it with propriety as to the person, the quantity, the time, the motive, and the manner, is not in the power of every one, nor is it easy; for in these particulars is situated the good, the rare, the laudable, and the noble.

2. Hence it is necessary, that he who would attain the mean, should first recede from that which is more contrary; as Calypso also advises,

> Far from the smoke and waves steer off the ship P.

For of the extremes the one is more erroneous, the other less. Since then it is excessively difficult to attain the mean, as the next best thing q, according to the proverb, we must take the least of two evils; but this will be best done in the way we have mentioned.

3. It is likewise necessary to mark the extremes to which we ourselves are more easily inclined; for different men are naturally inclined to different vices: this will be known from the pleasure and pain which attends us. But we ought to draw ourselves away to the contrary; for by removing ourselves far from error, we shall arrive at the mean; which those do, who straighten crooked pieces of wood.

4. In every case, however, we must particularly guard against the delectable and pleasure; for we are not unbiassed judges of it. In the same manner, therefore, as the Trojan chiefs were affected towards Helen, we also ought to be affected towards pleasure, and in all cases to speak their sentiment; for by dismissing it as they did Helen, we shall err the less. By doing these things then, (to sum up all,) we shall be most able to obtain the mean.

5. This is perhaps difficult, and especially in particulars; for it is not easy to define how, and with whom, and on what account, and how long a time it is right to be angry: for we

---

P The smoke and waves represent Charybdis, which Ulysses was told to shun as the greater of two evils.

q That this is the meaning of the proverb κατὰ τὸν δεύτερον πλοῦν, may be seen from Polybius, l. viii. c. 2. v. 6. ed. Schweigh. where it occurs.

sometimes praise the defective in anger, and call them meek ; sometimes again we praise those who are exasperated, and we entitle them the manly ; but he who deviates a little from rectitude is not blamed, whether it be to the more or the less, but he who proceeds far ; for such a character cannot escape notice. But for what degree and what quantity of anger any one is reprehensible, is not easy to determine by precept, neither is it easy in any object of sense ; but things of this nature depend upon particulars, and the judgment of them rests with sense.

6. Thus much, therefore, is manifest, that the middle habit is in all things laudable ; but it is necessary to incline sometimes to excess, at other times to defect ; for thus we shall most easily attain the mean and the right.

ARISTOTLE'S ETHICS.

BOOK III.

CHAP. I.

Concerning the circumstances which determine the quality of actions[r]. And first, of the voluntary and involuntary.

1. NOW virtue being conversant with passions and actions, and praises and censures taking place in voluntary things, but in involuntary pardon, and sometimes even pity [being granted], it is perhaps necessary for those who contemplate virtue to define the *voluntary* and *involuntary*. It will be useful to legislators also, in the distribution of rewards and punishments.

2. But those actions appear to be involuntary which are done by compulsion or through ignorance; and the compulsatory is that, the principle of which is external, being of such a nature, as that the agent or the patient contributes nothing; as if, for instance, the wind, or men, who are masters of any one, should carry him to any place.

3. But as to those things which are done through fear of greater evils, or for the sake of something noble; for in-

[r] It was asserted in book ii. chap. 4. that the mere act or doing of a thing does not determine the character of the action, but that the agent must be actuated by certain dispositions; we see also in chap. 6. that προαιρετική forms part of the definition of virtue; hence, these things being of such material consequence, it was necessary that they should be more fully discussed, which is done in the first five chapters of this book.

stance, supposing a tyrant should command a person to do any base action, having the parents and children of that man under his power, and that, if he did it, they should be spared, but if he did it not, they were to die; such cases as these carry with them a doubt, whether they are voluntary or involuntary. Some such question as this arises in the case of throwing things overboard in storms; for, simply speaking, no one voluntarily throws his own goods overboard; but all endued with common sense do it for the safety of themselves and the rest of the crew. Such actions therefore are of a mixed character; but they are more similar to voluntary actions, for they are objects of choice at that particular time when they are performed; but the end of an action is according to the particular time; and therefore we must speak of the *voluntary* and the *involuntary* at the time when a man performs the action. But he performs it voluntarily; for the principle of moving the instrumental parts in such actions is in himself; but the doing or not doing of those things is in his own power, the principles of which is in himself. Such things therefore are voluntary; but, simply considered, they are perhaps involuntary; for no one would choose any of such things on its own account.

4. But in such actions as these, men sometimes are even praised, when for the sake of great and noble rewards, they endure any thing disgraceful or painful; but when they do the contrary, they are censured; for to endure the most disgraceful things with a view to no noble or moderate good is the part of a base man. To some actions praise indeed is not granted, but pardon, when a man may have done what he ought not to do, on account of such things as surpass human nature, and which no one could bear. Some things perhaps we should not allow ourselves to be compelled to do, but we should rather die, having suffered the most dreadful evils; for the causes which compelled the Alcmæon of Euripides to kill his mother appear ridiculous. But it is sometimes difficult to determine, what is to be chosen in preference to what, and which of two evils is to be endured; and it is still more difficult to stand firm by our decisions;

since for the most part the evils which are expected are disagreeable, and the things we are compelled to do are disgraceful. Hence, both praises and censures are given to
those who act, or act not from compulsion.

5. What actions then are to be called compulsatory? Are
they those simply when the cause is in externals, and the
agent contributes nothing? But things, which are of themselves involuntary, and yet are eligible at the present time
and in preference to something else, and the principle of
which is in the agent, in themselves indeed are involuntary;
but at the present time and in preference to those other things
they are voluntary; but they are more similar to voluntary
actions; for actions depend upon particulars; and these are
voluntary. But it is not easy to make out what things are
to be chosen in preference to others, for there are many va-
rieties in particulars.

6. But if any one should say, that things pleasant and
noble are compulsatory, (because, as they are external, they
do compel,) all actions would thus be compulsatory; for all
men do all things for the sake of these; and those, who do
things by compulsion, and unwillingly, act with pain; but
those who act under the influence of the pleasant, act with
pleasure. It is therefore ridiculous for a man to accuse things
external, and not himself, who easily falls a prey to things
of this kind; and to consider himself as the cause of his
noble actions, but delectable things [or pleasure] as the cause
of his base actions. It appears therefore that the compulsatory is that, the principle of which is external, the person
compelled contributing nothing.

7. But every thing which is done from ignorance, is not
therefore voluntary; but that is involuntary, which is attended with pain and repentance; for he who does any thing
from ignorance, but is not at all grieved at the action, has
certainly not done it willingly, inasmuch as he knew it not;
nor yet on the other hand unwillingly, as he is not pained by
it. Of those therefore who act from ignorance, he who
repents of it seems to be unwilling; but he who repents not,
since he is another character, may be denominated not will-

ing ; for since he is different from the other, it is better
that he should have a name of his own.

8. And also to act *from ignorance* appears to be a different
thing from acting *ignorantly*[b]; for he, who is drunken or enraged does not appear to act from ignorance, but from some
other of the above-mentioned causes, and yet not knowingly,
but ignorantly. Every vicious person therefore is ignorant
what things he ought to do, and consequently what he ought
to abstain from ; and from a defect of this kind men become unjust and altogether wicked. But an action ought to
be called involuntary, not if a person is ignorant of what is
advantageous ; for ignorance in the deliberative choice[c] of
a thing is not the cause of the action being involuntary, but
is the cause of depravity ; nor is the ignorance of universals
[to be called involuntary], for men are censured for this ;
but the ignorance of particulars, in which and about which
action is engaged ; for towards these there is pity and pardon ; for he, who is ignorant of any of these [particulars],
acts involuntarily.

9. Perhaps then it would not be amiss to define these, what
and how many they are ; they are these then, namely, the
person who acts, and the thing done, and the circumstances
of the action ; sometimes also there is the thing with which,
for instance, the instrument ; and the thing on account of
which, for instance, of safety ; and the manner in which a
thing is done, for instance, gently or vehemently. All these
things therefore no man can be ignorant of, unless he is in-

---

[b] One may be called ignorance of the principle ; the other, ignorance of
the fact : thus if a man has killed another, and pleads ignorance of the
crime of murder, he is not excused ; but if he was ignorant of any particular circumstance which caused the act, he is considered to have acted
involuntarily, and is excused. But this particular ignorance is sometimes
inexcusable, as is explained at the end of chap. 8. book v.

[c] For every person is supposed to be by nature capable of deliberating
upon the best means for obtaining any end, i. e. of forming a προαίρεσις :
consequently if a man pleads ignorance in this choice of means, his own
neglect or vicious course of life must have caused that ignorance : and the
action which follows must be considered entirely voluntary.

sane ; but it is plain that he cannot be ignorant of the agent ; for how can he be ignorant of himself? A man however may be ignorant of what he does ; for instance, men, who have said what they ought not, allege that the words escaped them, or that they were ignorant of their being secrets, as Eschylus did of the mysteries ; or wishing to shew an instrument, a man may let it fly, as the man did the cata-pulta. A person also may fancy, like Merope, that a son is an enemy; and that a sharp-pointed spear is blunted, or that a stone is a pumice ; and one striking a person with a view to his safety, may kill him ; and wishing to shew a person how to box, as they do who spar, may strike him. Now ignorance being in all these particulars in which ac-tion is concerned, he who is ignorant of any one of these seems to act unwillingly, and especially in the particulars of greatest consequence ; but those seem of greatest conse-quence, in which the action consists, and the cause of the ac-tion.   Consequently a deed according to such ignorance being called involuntary, it is still farther necessary, that it should be painful and repented of.

10. But the involuntary being that which is compulsatory, and that which is done-from ignorance, the voluntary would seem to be that, the principle of which is in the person himself, knowing the particulars in which the action takes place.

11. For perhaps it is not well said, that things done by anger or desire are involuntary. For, in the first place, [if it were so,] no other animal would act voluntarily, nor would children.   In the next place, of those things which we do from desire or anger, do not we do any voluntarily ? Or do we the noble actions voluntarily, but the base actions involuntarily ? Or is not that ridiculous, since the cause of both is the same ? And perhaps it is absurd to call those things involuntary which we ought to desire ; but it is our duty to be angry at some things, and to desire some things ; as, for instance, health and learning ; and, indeed, involuntary things seem to be painful, but the objects of desire are pleasant. And again, in what do the errors committed by reason or

passion differ with respect to their being involuntary? for both are to be avoided[d]; and the irrational passions do not seem to be less human; but some actions of man proceed from anger and desire. It would be absurd then to consider these as involuntary.

CHAP. II.

By negative argument we trace the definition of deliberate choice; or, in other words, the genus of προαίρεσις being given, viz. τὸ ἑκούσιον, those species of it are enumerated, which are not προαίρεσις. Then the difference between προαίρεσις and each of these being added to the genus, we are able to define the species προαίρεσις.

1. The voluntary and involuntary being defined, it follows that we should pursue the subject of deliberate choice; for it seems to be very closely attached to virtue, and to be a better test of moral character than actions[c] are. Deliberate choice certainly seems to be a voluntary thing, yet not the self-same, but the voluntary is more extensive: for both children and other animals partake of the voluntary, but not of deliberate choice; and things suddenly done we denominate voluntary, but we do not say they are according to deliberate choice.

2. But those who call it desire, or anger, or will, or a certain opinion, do not appear to speak rightly.

3. For deliberate choice is not common to irrational beings, but desire and anger are; and the incontinent man acts from desire, but not with deliberate choice; on the con-

---

d If it were true that whatever is done through anger or desire, is involuntary, then an error committed through anger would be involuntary, and consequently would differ from an error in deliberation; for in the latter case the action cannot be called involuntary: but there is really no difference, since they are both equally to be avoided: consequently the error committed through anger is not involuntary.

c Vide book x. c. 8. sect. 2.

trary, the continent acts with deliberate choice, but not from desire. And desire is opposed to deliberate choice, but desire is not opposed to desire. And desire is formed upon the pleasant and the painful, but deliberate choice is neither formed upon the painful nor the pleasant. Still less then is it anger; for things done from anger seem least of all [to be done] according to deliberate choice.

4. Nor yet indeed is it will, though it nearly resembles this; for there is no deliberate choice of impossibilities; and if any one should say that he deliberately chooses such things, he would appear to be an idiot; but will applies to impossibilities; as, for instance, to immortality. And the will is engaged in those things which are by no means to be performed by the person himself, who wills : for instance, that a certain actor, or prizefighter, may be victorious; but no one deliberately chooses things of this kind, but as many only as he supposes may be effected by himself. And again, the will rather belongs to the end, but deliberate choice to those things which conduce to the end ; for instance, we wish to be in health, but we deliberately choose the means by which we may obtain it : and we wish indeed to be happy, and express our wish ; but to say, we deliberately choose happiness, has no propriety; for deliberate choice seems to be entirely conversant with the things that are in our power.

5. Neither therefore can it be opinion ; for opinion seems to be conversant with all things ; and no less with things eternal and impossible, than with the things in our own power; and it is divided into the false and true, not into the good and evil ; but deliberate choice rather into the latter.

6. Perhaps then no one ever asserts it to be the same with opinion in general [f]; but neither is it the same with a particular opinion; for by deliberately choosing good or evil,

---

[f] i. e. Deliberate choice, considered generally and abstractedly, might perhaps not be the same as opinion taken abstractedly ; but still it might be argued, that each particular act of deliberation was only the forming an opinion.

we become of a certain character; but not by forming an opinion. And we deliberately choose to obtain, or avoid, or something of that kind; but we form an opinion of what it is, or to what it is advantageous, or in what manner; but we do not at all form an opinion of taking or rejecting a thing. And deliberate choice is praised for its being as it ought, than for being successful[g]; but opinion, for its being true. And we deliberately choose those things which we best know to be good; but we have our opinion of those things which we do not at all know. And the same persons do not appear deliberately to choose the best things, and have their opinion of them; but some appear to have a just opinion of what is better, but through depravity to choose the things which they ought not. But whether opinion precedes or follows deliberate choice does not matter, for we do not investigate that point; but whether it is the same with a particular opinion.

7. What then or what species of thing is it, since it is neither of the things mentioned? It certainly appears to be something voluntary; but every species of the voluntary is not the object of deliberate choice, but that only which has been first deliberated upon; for deliberate choice is attended with reason and discursive judgment. Its name [προαίρεσις] seems to suggest that, as being [πρὸ ἑτέρων αἱρετὸν] eligible in preference to other things.

---

[g] A person is praised, if he chooses those means which he is convinced are morally good, without it being considered, whether they are most likely to ensure his success. Ὀρθῶς in this place has no relation to moral rectitude, but to eventual success; in which sense it is properly applied to opinion, but not to προαίρεσις. See book vi. c. 9. δόξης δ' ὀρθότης ἡ ἀλήθεια.

CHAP. III.

The genus of πϱοαίϱεσις (*or rather of the* πϱοαιϱετὸν) *being given,*
viz. τὸ ἑκούσιον, *it remains to give the difference, viz.* βούλευσις,
deliberation. This chapter therefore explains the subject-mat-
ter and the process of deliberation.

1. BUT do men deliberate upon all things, and is every
thing the subject of deliberation, or are there some things
upon which there is no deliberation? But perhaps that is to
be considered as a subject of deliberation, not upon which
any idiot or madman would deliberate, but upon which a
person of sound intellect would. But concerning things
eternal no man deliberates, as concerning the world, or concerning the diagonal and side of a square, because they are
incommensurate; nor indeed concerning things which are
in motion, but always existing after the same manner, whether
it is by necessity, or nature, or from any other cause, as, for instance, the seasons[h], and risings of the sun; nor concerning
things which are different at different times, such as drought
and rain; nor about things depending upon chance, such as
the finding of a treasure; nor yet upon all human affairs; for
instance, no Lacedæmonian *deliberates* how the Scythians
may best regulate their state; for none of these things could
be effected by us.

2. But we deliberate upon things, which can be effected
by ourselves; and these indeed are all that remain [after
what we have already excluded]: for the causes of all actions
seem to be nature, necessity, and fortune; and besides these
intellect and every thing which operates by man himself[i].
But each particular man deliberates upon those things, which
may be effected by himself. And concerning the perfect and
self-sufficient sciences there is no deliberation; for instance,

[h] More properly perhaps the solstices or equinoxes.

[i] And as the three first have been excluded as causes of subjects for
deliberation, the last, viz. intellect, is the only one which remains.

concerning letters, for we do not doubt how we are to form the letters. But whatever things are done by us, but not always in the same manner, concerning such we deliberate ; for instance, concerning things belonging to the medical art, and the art of gaining money, and concerning the pilot's art more than the gymnastic art, inasmuch as it has been less determined by laws : so also concerning the rest ; and we deliberate more in the arts than the sciences ; for we are more divided in opinion concerning them. But deliberation exists upon things which happen generally, but are obscure as to the event, and in which there is something indefinite. And in matters of importance we employ counsellors, distrusting ourselves as insufficient to determine them.

3. But we deliberate not concerning ends, but upon the things contributing to the end ; for neither does a physician deliberate whether he still cure, nor a rhetorician whether he shall persuade, nor a politician whether he shall establish good laws, nor does any other character deliberate upon the end ; but having proposed some end, they examine in what manner and by what means it may be obtained. And if it appears, that it is to be obtained by means of many things, they examine by which of those it may be obtained in the easiest and noblest manner ; but if it is to be effected by one medium, they deliberate in what manner it will be by that, and by what [medium], that [medium] itself [may be effected], until they arrive at the first cause [k], which is the last in the investigation ; for he, who deliberates seems to investigate and analyze in the manner described, as he would analyze a diagram. Every species of enquiry however does not appear

---

[k] We wish to attain the grand end happiness, and we thus deliberate : How are we to attain happiness ? By energizing according to a habit of perfect virtue. How may we be possessed of a habit of virtue ? By virtuously performing virtuous actions. In what manner are virtuous actions thus performed ? By preserving the mean and avoiding the extremes in all the concerns of life. How are we to observe the mean ? By avoiding that to which our nature is prone : which, though we arrived last at it in the enquiry, is the first thing to be accomplished by us in our search after happiness.

to be a deliberation ; for instance, mathematical enquiries are not; but every species of deliberation is an enquiry, and the last clause in the analysis is first in production. But should they meet with an impossibility, they desist ; for instance, if there is occasion for money, and it is impossible to procure it ; but if it appear possible, they attempt to obtain it. But those things are possible, which can be effected by ourselves ; for things effected by means of friends are in a certain respect by means of ourselves; for the principle is in ourselves[1]. Sometimes instruments are sought for, sometimes the use of them, so also in other things ; sometimes the cause through which, at other times how, or in what way. Man then, as has been said, seems to be the principle of actions; and deliberation takes place upon things to be performed by him ; but actions are for the sake of other things[m]. Hence the end can not be the subject of deliberation, but things which conduce to the end ; neither surely can particulars ; as, whether this thing is bread, or whether it is baked or made as it ought ; for these things are the province of sense, but if a man shall always be deliberating, he will go on to infinity.

4. But the subject of deliberation and that of deliberate choice are the same, except that the subject of deliberate choice has been already determined ; for that which is preferred after deliberation is the subject of deliberate choice ; for every one ceases enquiring how he may do a thing, when he has reduced the principle to himself, and to that part of himself which presides ; for that is the part which deliberately chooses. This is moreover clear from the ancient polities, which Homer has introduced into his poems ; for the chiefs announced to the people what they had themselves deliberately chosen[n].

[1] For we gained the friend by some action of our own, and he loves us for our own sakes.

[m] Deliberation is upon action : actions have always some ulterior end in view : consequently the end itself, which has nothing ulterior, cannot be the subject of deliberation.

[n] The kings in the ancient governments formed a deliberate choice: so does the governing principle in man: hence every action originated with

5. Now since the subject of deliberate choice is a thing deliberated upon, and something desired, which is in our own power, deliberative choice must be a desire of the things in our own power attended with deliberation; for having determined upon a thing after deliberation, we form our desire according to the deliberation. Let so much be said in outline concerning deliberative choice, both concerning what it is engaged in, and that it belongs to things which conduce to ends.

CHAP. IV.

Whether the object of will be a real or apparent good.

1. THAT will belongs to the end has been proved; but to some it appears to belong to [the end which is] real good, to others, apparent good. But to those, who assert that the object of the will is the *summum bonum*, it happens that that thing is not an object of the will, which he wills, who does not choose rightly; for if it were an object of the will, it would be also good; but it may be if chance would so have it bad. But to those, on the other hand, who say that the object of the will is apparent good, [this error is incidental,] that there is not in nature an object of will, but to every man what appears to be such: and a different thing presents itself to different persons, and, if chance would have it so, contraries.

2. But if these systems do not please, we must therefore say, that simply and in reality *the good* is the object of will; but to individuals, apparent good. Consequently to the good man, that which is really good is the object, but to the depraved, according as it may happen; as is the case with

the kings; so does it with the governing principle in man: having been decided by the kings, it was executed by inferior agents; so is it in man: the intellect decides; the senses and members execute.

bodies, to such as are established in health, things are salubrious, which are in reality such; but to such as are diseased, something different. So is it also with things bitter, and sweet, and hot, and heavy, and each of the rest; for the worthy man judges of every thing rightly, and in each case the truth presents itself to him; for in every habit there are some things peculiarly honourable and pleasant. And perhaps the worthy man is most different from other characters in this, that he sees the truth in all things, being as it were the rule and measure of them; but with the multitude the deception appears to exist through pleasure, for, though not a good, it appears to be so. They therefore choose what is pleasant, as a good, but fly from pain, as an evil.

CHAP. V.

That virtue and vice are voluntary; and particularly vice.

1. SINCE therefore the end is an object of will, but things conducing to the end are objects of deliberation, and deliberate choice, the actions conversant with these must be according to deliberate choice, and voluntary; but the energies of the virtues are conversant with these. Virtue therefore is also in our power, and in like manner vice also; for in whatever to act is in our power; not to act is also in our power; and in whatever case we can desist, we can also act. Wherefore, if the doing of a thing, when honourable, is in our power, the not doing it, when base, will be in our power; and if the not doing an action, when honourable, is in our power, the doing of it, when base, is also in our power. But if the doing things excellent and things base is in our power, as well as the not doing them; (but this is tantamount to being good and bad;) to be worthy and depraved will be in our power.

2. But such a sentiment, as that " No man is willingly

depraved, or unwillingly happy," is partly false and partly true; for no man is unwillingly happy; but depravity is voluntary; or we must question what has been already laid down, and we must assert, that man is not the principle or creating cause of actions, in the same manner as he is of children. But if these things are evident, and we cannot reduce them to any other principles than those in our power, those things, the principles of which are in our power, are themselves also in our power, and are voluntary °.

3. But to these things testimony seems to be added, both privately by individuals, and by legislators themselves; for they chastise and punish those who perpetrate villainous actions, as many as do them not by compulsion, or from ignorance, of which they are not the cause; but they honour those who act well; as if they would animate the latter, but repress the former. But surely, in such things as are neither in our power nor voluntary, no man animates another to action, as it would be nothing to the purpose to be persuaded not to be hot or cold, or hungry, or any such thing; for we shall not the less suffer these things. For indeed they punish a man for the ignorance itself, if he appears to be the cause of the ignorance; thus the penalties are doubled for the intoxicated; for the principle is in the man himself; for he has the power of not becoming intoxicated; but this is the cause of his ignorance. And they punish such as are ignorant of any particulars in the laws, which they ought to know, and which are not abstruse; so also in other things, which men seem to be ignorant of through negligence, since the being not ignorant of them was in their power; for they have the power of paying attention.

4. But perhaps a person is of such a constitution as not to

° This argument is taken from the process of deliberation mentioned in the last chapter; where it was stated, that we do not cease to deliberate and begin to act, till we have found some means, which is immediately in our own power; i. e. till we have brought the principle or beginning of the action *to* ourselves: consequently the action, which follows, must proceed *from* ourselves, and be voluntary.

have been in the habit of paying attention; but men themselves are the causes of their being such, by living dissolutely; and men are themselves the causes of their being unjust, or intemperate, the former by acting dishonestly, the latter by spending their lives in drinking, and other vices of that description; for energizing in any mode renders men of such and such habits. This is obvious from those who are trained for any contest, or action; for they persevere in energizing. Now to be ignorant that by energizing in any thing [similar] habits are produced, is the character of one thoroughly insensate. Again, it is absurd, that he who does unjust actions does not wish to be unjust, or that he who acts intemperately is unwilling to be intemperate: but if any one does those actions, from which he will be unjust, not ignorantly, he will be unjust unwillingly.

5. Not that he will cease being unjust, if he should wish, and become just; for neither can the sick become healthy, though, most probably, he voluntarily became diseased by living intemperately, and disregarding his physicians. Then indeed it was in his power not to be diseased, but no longer, after having abandoned himself; as it is impracticable for a person who has flung a stone to recall it; but at the same time to throw and pelt it was in his power; for the principle was in his power; thus also the unjust and intemperate were at liberty in the outset not to become such; hence they are voluntary; but having become so, it is no longer in their power not to be so.

6. But not only the vices of the soul are voluntary, but in some persons the vices of the body also, which are those that we censure; for no one censures those who are naturally deformed; but those who are so through want of exercise and inattention to themselves. The case is the same with debility, and deformity, and mutilation; for no one would reproach a man blind by nature, or from disease, or a blow, but would rather pity him; but every one would censure a person blind from sottishness, or any other intemperance. Of the vices then attached to the body, those in our own power are censured, but not those which are not in

our power. But if this is right, in other cases [P] also those vices which are censured must be in our power.

7. But if any one should say, that all aspire after what appears good to them, but are not directors of the faculty, by which they see good; but that of whatever character each is, such also the end appears to him; if in a certain respect every one is to himself the cause of his habit, he will also be in a certain respect the cause of this faculty.

8. But supposing that no man is the cause of his committing vice, but that he does those things from ignorance of the end, fancying that through such means the best good will be his; and if the pursuit of the end is not spontaneous, but he must be born with it as with sight, by which he will judge rightly, and choose the real good; and if that man is of a good natural disposition, in whom this is innate in a perfect manner; (for he will have that which is the greatest and most noble, and which it is impossible to receive or learn from another, otherwise than it comes by nature, and that this should be excellently and finely implanted in us by nature, must be perfect and real goodness of disposition;) if, I say, these things are true, why will virtue be more voluntary than vice? for the end, whether by nature or by whatever means, equally is placed in view to each, both to the good and the bad in the same way; and referring other things to this, they act according to their different habits.

9. Whether then [q] the end, whatever it is, does not present itself to each by nature, but there is something in his own power; or whether the end be natural, but because the worthy man performs the rest, i. e. the means, voluntarily,

---

[P] The argument is this: it is true that only those bodily failings are censured, which are voluntary: therefore the converse is true, that when bodily failings are censured, they are voluntary: applying this analogy to moral conduct, when moral failings are censured, they are voluntary.

[q] This is a continuation of the last argument: he had there shewn, that if nature gives the ends, then virtue would be as involuntary as vice: (which is not what the objectors wish to prove.) He now argues, that granting their assertion to be true, that nature gives the ends, still as the means are in our power, vice must be voluntary.

therefore virtue is voluntary, vice also must be no less voluntary ; for free-will is possessed in an equal manner by the bad man, in the *actions*, whatever it be in the *end*. If then, as has been said, the virtues are voluntary, (for we are in a certain respect the cooperative causes of habits, and because we are of certain qualities, we propose an end of the same character,) the vices also must be voluntary; for they are under similar circumstances.

10. We have now spoken generally concerning the virtues, stating the genus in outline, that they are means, and that they are habits, and by what they are produced, and that they are apt to perform the same things, and that of themselves, and that they are in our power, and voluntary, and in such a manner as right reason shall prescribe. But actions and habits are not voluntary in one and the same manner ; for we have power over our actions from beginning to end, being conscious of particulars, but of habits we are masters of the beginning only; but the accession of particulars is not known to us, as it is not in diseases; but because it was in our power to use the particulars in this or that manner, at first, on this account the habits are voluntary. Resuming therefore our discussion, let us speak concerning each of the virtues, what they are, and on what things they are engaged, and in what manner; at the same time it will become evident, how many in number they are. And first concerning fortitude.

CHAP. VI.

What those cases are in which fortitude is most shewn.

1. THAT fortitude is a mean conversant with fear and confidence, has been already observed. But we evidently fear those things which are objects of fear; and these are, in one word, evils; hence they also define fear to be the

expectation of evil. We fear then all evils, as disgrace, poverty, disease, a friendless state, and death[r].

2. But the brave man does not appear to be conversant with all evils; for it is a duty to fear some things, and it is noble; and not to dread them is base, as, for instance, infamy; for he who fears that, is a worthy and modest man; but he who fears not disgrace, is impudent. But this character by some is called brave, by metaphor; as he possesses something similar to the brave man; for the brave man is also a certain fearless person. But perhaps it is no duty to fear poverty, or disease, or, in fine, all such things as are not generated from vice nor from ourselves; but still, he who is fearless in these circumstances, is not brave. But we apply the term to this character also from its similitude; for some, who are timid in the dangers of war, are liberal, and behave with firmness under the loss of money. Nor if a man fears insult upon his children and wife, or envy, or any such evil, is he therefore a coward; nor, if he feels confidence when about to be flogged, is he brave.

3. With what species then of fearful things is the brave man conversant? Is it not with the most fearful? for no man is more patient of dreadful evils. But death is the most fearful of all things; for it is the boundary of life; and nothing further appears for the dead, either good or evil. But it would seem, that the brave man does not shew himself in death under all circumstances; for instance, not if it were in the sea, or in diseases. In what kinds then? Is it not in the noblest deaths? But such are deaths in war; for they happen in the greatest and noblest danger. The honours conferred by states and monarchs are also consonant with these sentiments. He then would be called properly brave, who is fearless in a noble death, and in such things as when they bring death are sudden. And of this kind particularly are the dangers of war.

[r] It is said in the Rhetoric, (book 2. concerning fear,) that men do not fear death: but the author is there speaking of death as a *distant* evil, in meditating upon which the passion of terror is not raised: he is here considering it as present, in which the habit of fortitude is displayed.

4. Not but that the brave is fearless also by sea, and in diseases; but not in the same manner as seamen; for the former despair of their fafety, and indignantly bear a death of this kind; but the latter are well supported with hope from their experience. Besides, brave men act with fortitude where there is strength necessary, or where to die is noble; but in deaths of this kind there is neither.

CHAP. VII.

The characters of the brave, the audacious, and the timid, described.

1. But the terrible is not the same to all; but we say, that there is something [terrible] even beyond [the fortitude of] man; this therefore is terrible to every one endued with intellect. But things tolerable for man differ in magnitude, and in being more or less terrible; so also is it with things which inspire confidence. Now the brave man is undaunted, as a man; he will therefore fear such things as the above; but he will endure them as is right, and as reason dictates, for the sake of what is noble; for that is the end of virtue. But it is possible to fear these things in a greater and less degree, and even to fear things which are not terrible, as if they were so. But one error arises from not bearing what we ought[s]; another from not bearing it in a proper manner; another, not at a proper time, or something of this kind; the same is also the case with the things which inspire confidence.

2. He, therefore, who endures and is terrified at those things which he ought, and for a proper reason, and in the manner, and at the time that is proper, and he who feels confidence in the same way, is a brave man; for the brave

---

[s] The text is probably corrupt here: but this seems to be the meaning of the passage: or perhaps we should read ἡ μὲν, ὅτι οὐχ οὗ δεῖ.

man suffers and acts according to the importance of the thing, and as reason prescribes. But the end of every energy is that which is agreeable to the habit; and to the brave man the habit of fortitude is a noble thing; such also is the end; for every thing is defined by the end. Consequently, the brave man, for the sake of what is noble, endures and performs things incident to fortitude.

3. But of those who exceed, he who exceeds in fearlessness has no particular name : and it has been said by us already, that many characters have no particular name : but a person, if he feared nothing, neither an earthquake, nor inundations, as they say of the Gauls, must be in a manner mad or insensible of pain.

4. He, on the other hand, who exceeds in being confident in things terrible, is audacious ; moreover the audacious appears to be arrogant, and a pretender to fortitude. As therefore the former really is with respect to things terrible, such does this character wish to appear ; consequently in whatever he is able, he imitates him. Hence also many of them are audacious cowards; for being audacious in these things, they do not endure things terrible.

5. He again, who exceeds in being terrified, is timid; for the [circumstances of fearing] the things, which are not proper, and in the manner that is not right, and all such [failings], are attendant on him ; he is also deficient in confidence ; but he is more conspicuous, when he shews his excess in [not bearing] pain. The timid therefore is a kind of despairing character; for he fears all things : but the brave is the contrary : for to be confident is the province of one full of hope.

6. It appears then that both the timid, and audacious, and the brave man, are conversant with the same things ; but they are differently affected towards them ; for the two former exceed and are deficient ; the latter is situated in the medium, and acts as he ought ; and the audacious, though precipitate and eager before dangers, in the dangers themselves shrink away; but the brave are ardent in actions, but before are placid. As has been said therefore, fortitude is a medium

conversant with things inspiring confidence, and fear, in such cases, as we have mentioned: and it chooses and endures them because it is honourable or because it is base not to do so.   But to die, in order to fly poverty, or love, or any thing painful, is not the part of a brave, but rather of a timid man; for to fly things toilsome is effeminacy; and this character does not endure it because it is honourable, but to escape the evil.   Fortitude, therefore, is something of this nature.

CHAP. VIII.

We proceed to mention other kinds of courage which are similar to fortitude, but are inferior either as to the principle or the manner.

1. THERE are, moreover, other kinds of fortitude spoken of under five divisions[t]: and first, political fortitude[u]; for it is most similar to the former; for citizens appear to endure dangers on account of the punishments and disgraces inflicted by the laws, and on account of honours.   And for that reason, those [nations] appear to be most brave, among whom the timid are in disgrace, and the brave honoured. Such heroes Homer introduces; as for instance, Diomed and Hector, who says, " Polydamas will first cast reproaches " upon me:" and Diomed; " For Hector shall sometime " say haranguing the Trojans, The son of Tydeus fled from " me."   This kind of courage is most similar to that before mentioned, because it owes its origin to virtue; for it owes it to a sense of shame, and a desire of what is noble; namely,

---

t The tests for trying these five kinds of fortitude are, whether the motive is the καλὸν; whether the several acts are performed εἰδότως, προαιρουμένως, and βεβαίως.   Vide book ii. c. 4.

u By political fortitude is meant that of native troops, as opposed to that of mercenaries.

[a desire] of honour[x], and the avoiding of disgrace, which is
shameful.   Under the same head one would arrange those
also, who are impelled to dangers by their leaders; but they
are inferior, inasmuch as they do not thus act from the influence of shame, but of fear; and to escape not what is disgraceful, but what is painful; for their superiors compel
them, as Hector does;

> Whom I find crouching, slinking from the fight,
> That covert shall not save him from the dogs.

And their marshals do the same, even flogging them, if they
retreat.   Those also who draw up troops before trenches and
the like, effect the same; for all use compulsion; but a man
should be brave not from compulsion, but because it is honourable.

2. Experience in particulars seems also to be a kind of
fortitude; whence Socrates was even of opinion that fortitude
was a science.   Different men have this in different matters;
but in warlike affairs, mercenary soldiers have it; for there
seem to be many empty terrors in war, which these most see
at one view.   On that account they appear brave, because
other men know not of what kind these terrors are : again
from their experience they are most able to assail and not
suffer, and to guard themselves, and to strike, being able to
use their arms, and bearing such arms as would be most
powerful both to attack and to defend.   They fight therefore
as it were armed with unarmed men, and as well trained
wrestlers with common persons; for indeed in such contests,
not the most brave are most fit for the struggle, but those who
are most powerful, and have their bodies in best order.   But
mercenary soldiers become timid, when the danger overwhelms
them, and when they fail in numbers, and ammunition; for
these fly first : but troops actuated by political courage die
maintaining their post, which was the case also at the Her-
mæus; for to such flight is disgraceful, and death is more
eligible than such security : the others also in the onset en-
countered the danger, as being superior; but having known

---

[x] We are accustomed to translate καλὸν and τιμὴ by the same word,
honour : we here see the difference between them.

their danger, they fly, dreading death more than disgrace. But the brave[y] man is not such.

3. And some refer anger to fortitude; for those also seem to be brave, who are borne on by anger, just like wild beasts, on their assailants; and because the brave are irascible; since anger is a great incentive to dangers: hence Homer says, " He added strength to his anger;" and, " He roused " his courage and anger;" and, " Pungent fury flowed " through his nostrils;" and, " His blood boiled;" for all these expressions seem to point out the excitation and impulse of the mind. The brave therefore act for sake of what is noble; and anger cooperates with them; but beasts act from pain; for it is from their being wounded or terrified; since if they are in a wood or in a marsh, they do not come on. It is not therefore fortitude, that things incited by pain and anger rush upon danger, foreseeing none of the formidable circumstances; since thus even asses would be brave, when they are starving; for, though beaten, they do not desist from grazing; and adulterers also perform many daring acts through their lust. Those consequently are not brave, which are impelled to danger by pain or anger. But the fortitude, which proceeds from anger, seems to be most natural, and by adding deliberate choice, and a proper motive, to be real fortitude. Men also when enraged feel pain, but having avenged themselves they are delighted; but those who are spirited on these accounts are contentious, but not brave; for they do not act with a view to what is noble, nor as reason dictates, but by the force of passion; however they have some similarity.

4. Neither in fine are the sanguine brave; for they are confident in dangers, because they have conquered many people at many times; but they are similar, because both are confident: now brave men are confident for the above mentioned reasons; but these, because they fancy that they are superior, and shall suffer nothing in return. Those also that are intoxicated do the same thing; since they become

[y] Vide Thucydides, l. v. c. 72.

elated with hope; but when things similar [to their hopes] do not happen to them, they fly; but it was said to be the character of the brave man to endure things which are and appear formidable to man, because it is noble to endure, and base not to endure. Hence it appears the part of the braver man to be fearless and undisturbed in sudden terrors, rather than in such as were foreseen; for it is more from habit, or even because it is less from preparation: for things which are foreseen, a person might even choose deliberately from reasoning and reason; but things which are sudden, [must be chosen] from habit.

5. Those also who act from ignorance, appear brave, and are not far removed from those elated by hope; but they are inferior, inasmuch as they have formed no conception [of the evil]; but the others have: hence also the latter stand firm for a certain time; but the former having been deceived, if they know that the fact is different from what they suspected, fly; which the Argives experienced when they fell in with the Lacedæmonians, taking them for Sicyonians. We have stated therefore what kind of character the brave have, and those who appear to be brave.

CHAP. IX.

That fortitude is rather an endurance of pain than abstinence from pleasure; consequently that the brave man feels pain from the means, though from the glory of the end proposed he cheerfully endures it.

1. Now fortitude being engaged with confidence and fear, is not equally engaged with both, but rather with things terrific: for he who is unruffled in these, and when engaged in them conducts himself as he ought, is the brave man, rather than he, who thus conducts himself in things which inspire confidence. Men therefore, as has been said, are

called brave from their enduring painful things; hence fortitude is also very painful, and is justly praised; for it is more difficult to endure things painful, than to abstain from pleasures. Not but that the end which belongs to fortitude may appear to be pleasant, but to be obscured by surrounding objects: as is the case likewise in gymnastic contests; for to boxers, the end for which they contend is pleasant, viz. the crown and honours; but to be beaten, (at least if they are made of flesh,) is bitter and painful, and so is every labour; but because these are many, the end, for the sake of which they contend, being small, appears to possess nothing pleasant. Consequently, if the case is the same with fortitude, death and wounds will be painful to the brave man, and against his will; but he will endure them because it is noble, or because not to endure them is base. And by how much the more he possesses every virtue, and the more happy he is, by so much the more will he be pained at death: for life is most valuable to such a man, and he is knowingly deprived of the greatest goods: now this is painful; yet the person is no less brave: and perhaps even more so, because he chooses that which is honourable in war, in preference to the other goods. In fine, to energize with pleasure is not possible in all the virtues, except as far as it is connected with the end. But nothing perhaps hinders mercenary soldiers, who are not thus formed, from being best, but those may be so, who are less brave, and have no other good in possession: for these are prepared for dangers, and exchange their lives for inconsiderable gain. Concerning fortitude therefore let so much be said; but to conclude at least in outline what it is, is not difficult from what has been said.

CHAP. X.

Of temperance : that it is a mean conversant with pleasures; not all, however, but the pleasures of taste and touch only.

1. NEXT to this virtue, let us speak concerning temperance; for these seem to be the virtues of the irrational parts[z]. That temperance therefore is a mean conversant about pleasures, has been mentioned by us; for it is engaged with pains in an inferior and dissimilar manner; in these intemperance also shews itself. Let us now therefore determine, with what kind of pleasures it is conversant.

2. Let the pleasures then of the soul be divided from those of the body; such as ambition, love of learning; for out of these, every man is delighted with that of which he is fond, the body being not at all affected, but rather the mind; but those engaged in such pleasures are not called either temperate or intemperate. In like manner, neither are those called so, who are engaged in as many other pleasures as are not bodily; for we call the lovers of fables, and newsmongers, and those who spend their days in pursuit of trifles, talkative, but not intemperate; nor those who are pained at the loss of money or friends.

3. Temperance then must be conversant with the pleasures of the body; nor yet with all these; for those who are delighted with the pleasures of sight, such as colours, and figures, and drawings, are neither called temperate nor intemperate; although it should seem to be possible to be delighted with these also, both in the degree that is right, and in excess and defect. So is it also in the pleasures of hearing; for no man calls those intemperate, who are excessively de-

---

[z] Of those virtues which are formed by bringing the irrational parts, i. e. the passions, under the obedience of reason, fortitude, and temperance are the best.

lighted with music, or acting; nor those who are delighted
within bounds, temperate; nor those delighted with scents,
except by accident; for those who are delighted with the
scents of apples, or roses, or perfumes, we do not denominate intemperate; but rather those [who are delighted with
the scents] of balsams and meats; for the intemperate are
delighted with these, because by means of them a recollection
of the objects of their desire is formed in them.   Now one
may see other men also, when they are hungry, delighted
with the scents of meats; but to be delighted with such
things is characteristic of the intemperate man; for these
to him are the objects of desire.   Nor indeed is there pleasure to any other animals by means of these senses, except
by accident; for dogs are not delighted with the scent of
hares, but the eating of them; but the scent causes the sense
[of taste].   Neither is the lion delighted with the voice of the
ox, but the eating of it; but he perceives by the voice that
he is near, and hence he appears to be delighted with the
voice: in like manner he is not delighted from seeing or
finding a stag or a wild goat, but because he shall have food.
In fine, temperance and intemperance are engaged with
such pleasures as other animals also participate in; hence
they appear slavish and brutal; and these are the touch and
taste.

4. Indeed, they appear to use even the taste but in a
small degree, or not at all; for the province of the taste is
the judgment of savours; which those do who try wines,
and season food: now the intemperate are delighted very
little, if at all, with these savours, but with the enjoyment
which is produced entirely by the touch, both in meats and
drinks, and in those pleasures which arise from love. Hence,
one Philoxenus, the son of Eryxis, who was an epicure,
wished he had a neck longer than that of a crane, as being
delighted with touch, (which by the bye is the most common of the senses,) in which intemperance is situated: and
it would seem to be justly ignominious, since it exists in us
not as we are men, but as we are animals.

5. In short, to be delighted with, and very fond of, such

things is brutal; for the most liberal of the pleasures of the touch are excepted[a], such as the pleasures produced in gymnastic exercises by friction and heat; for the touch of the intemperate man is not extended to all the body, but to certain parts of it.

CHAP. XI.

Desires divided into common and peculiar. It is shewn how temperance is a mean, and intemperance an excess, in each of those classes.

1. OF desires, however, some appear to be common, others peculiar and adventitious; for instance, the desire of food is natural; since every one, when in want of it, desires dry or moist food, and sometimes both : the young and vigorous man desires the joys of love, as Homer says ; but every one does not desire this or that food, nor the same food. Hence it appears to depend upon ourselves ; not but that it has something natural also ; for different things are pleasing to different persons, and some things are more pleasing than others to some persons.

2. In natural desires then few err ; and that to one side, namely, to excess ; for to eat or drink common food, till there is excessive fulness, is to exceed in quantity the measure of nature ; for natural desire is the supplying of a deficiency. Hence such persons are called gluttons, as supplying that beyond what is becoming : those, who are perfect slaves to appetite, become such.

3. But in peculiar pleasures many err, and that in many ways : for men being called lovers of such and such things, either from their being delighted with what they ought not, or in being excessively pleased, or as the multitude is de-

---

[a] It certainly puts intemperance in a worse point of view to shew that it does not enjoy the most liberal pleasures even of touch.

lighted, or in the manner that is not proper, or with a view to what is not proper ; in all these the intemperate exceed ; for they are both delighted with some things which they ought not, because they are detestable ; and if it is proper to be delighted with any pleasures of that kind, they are delighted more than is proper, and as the multitude is delighted. That excess then in pleasures is intemperance, and that it is reprehensible, is evident.

4. But as to pains, a man is not called temperate by enduring them, as in fortitude ; nor intemperate by not enduring them ; but he is intemperate, in being pained more than he ought at not meeting with pleasures ; and indeed pleasure to him causes pain ; he on the other hand is temperate, in not being pained at the absence of pleasure, nor in being restrained from it. The intemperate man therefore desires all pleasures, or the chief of them ; and is so led by desire, as to choose these in preference to all other things ; hence also he is pained, both when missing his object and when desiring it : for desire is accompanied by pain ; but it seems absurd that a man should be pained for sake of pleasure.

5. But those who fall short with regard to pleasures, and are delighted with them less than is right, are not frequently in being : for such an insensibility is not human ; for even other animals discriminate food, and are delighted with some kinds and not with others. But if to any body nothing is pleasing, and no one thing differs from another, he must be very far from being human ; but this character has no name allotted him, because it does not frequently occur.

6. But the temperate man is moderate towards these things ; for he is not pleased with the things which the intemperate man is especially delighted with, but rather is disgusted with them ; neither at all with things which he ought not, nor excessively with any such pleasure ; nor is he pained by their absence ; neither does he feel desire, or at least only moderately, nor more than he ought, nor when he ought not, nor, in short, any thing of this kind. But whatever things tend to health, or a good habit of body, being

pleasant, these he desires moderately and as he ought; and
other pleasant things he desires, as long as they are no impediment to these, nor are contrary to what is noble, nor
beyond his means; for he who is thus affected, loves such
pleasures more than they deserve; now the temperate man
is not such, but is such as right reason warrants.

CHAP. XII.

That intemperance is more voluntary than cowardice, consequently
more reprehensible. That our desires ought to be obedient to
reason, as a child ought to his governors.

1. But intemperance seems more voluntary than cowardice; for the former arises from pleasure, but the latter from
pain, of which the one is eligible, the other an object of
aversion. And indeed pain confounds and destroys the nature of him who feels it, but pleasure does no such thing.
Consequently it is more voluntary; hence it is also more
disgraceful; for it is more easy to be accustomed to these
things; since there are many such in life; and customs are
formed without danger; but in things that cause terror it is
otherwise.

2. Timidity likewise would appear to be voluntary not in
the same manner with particular acts [of timidity]; for the
habit itself is free from pain; but particular acts confound a
man through pain, so that he even throws away his arms,
and behaves indecently in other respects: whence also they
seem compulsory. But with the intemperate it is the contrary; for particular acts are voluntary; since he desires
and longs after them; but [the habit], as a whole, is less
voluntary; for no man desires to be intemperate.

3. But we apply also the name of intemperance to childish errors; for they have a certain similarity; but which is

named from the other, matters not for the present subject. It is clear however that the latter [derived its name] from the former[b]; nor does it appear to be badly transferred; for it is expedient, that the thing, which desires what is base, and has luxuriant growth, be corrected: but of this nature particularly are desire, and a child; for children live under the influence of desire, and the desire of what is pleasant is predominant in them. If therefore it be not docile, and under the management of its superior, it will spread to a great extent; for the desire of that which is pleasant is insatiable, and comes from all quarters to the foolish man; and the energy of desire increases every thing allied to it; and should those desires be great and strong, they even drive out reason. Hence it is necessary, that they should be moderate and few, and in nothing be opposite to reason; but we call such a thing docile and corrected: for as it is right that a child should live according to the mandate of his preceptor, so likewise should the part of the soul, which desires, live according to reason. Hence it is necessary that the part of the temperate man, which desires, should accord with reason; for the *honestum* is the aim of both; and indeed the temperate man desires the things which he ought, and as he ought, and when he ought; just so does reason also ordain. Let these things then be explained by us concerning temperance.

b It is clear that the name of intemperance is properly and primarily applied to bodily desires, and from thence in a borrowed sense to childish errors.

ARISTOTLE'S ETHICS.

BOOK IV.

CHAP. I.

Concerning liberality, and its extremes, illiberality and prodigality.

1. IN the next place let us speak concerning liberality. It seems to be a mean about wealth; for the liberal man is praised not in warlike concerns, nor in those cases in which the temperate [is concerned], nor yet in judicature, but for the giving and receiving of property; and rather in the giving. But we call all those things property, the value of which is measured by money.

2. Moreover, prodigality and illiberality are excesses and defects about property. And we charge illiberality always upon those who are more solicitous than is right concerning their property, and sometimes by combination we apply [the term] prodigality to the intemperate; for we denominate the incontinent and those expensive upon intemperance, prodigals; hence these seem to be the most depraved; for they have at the same time many vices. They are not however appositely designated; for a prodigal will be one who has one certain vice, the wasting of his property; for the prodigal is he who is ruined by himself; but the reduction of one's property seems to be a certain destruction of the person, as life is preserved by means of that. In this sense then we take prodigality.

3. Now whatever there is any use for, it is possible to use both well and ill; but riches are of the number of

useful things; now that man best uses any thing, who has the virtue attendant on it; and consequently he will use riches in the best manner who has the virtue conversant in wealth; and this is the liberal man. But the use of wealth seems to be the expenditure and giving of it; but the accepting and preserving it seems rather a possession : hence it appears more the province of the liberal to give to those whom he ought, than to receive whence he ought, and not to receive whence he ought not; for it is more the part of virtue to benefit than be benefited, and more to perform noble actions than not to perform mean actions. It requires indeed no proof, that to benefit and to perform noble actions attend upon giving; but that to be benefited or not to do a base action attend upon receiving. And thanks [are due] to the giver, not to him who does not receive; to him praise also is rather due. And again, the not receiving is easier than giving; for men less willingly dispose of their own than they abstain from receiving what is another's. And again, those who give are called liberal; but those who do not receive, are praised, not for liberality, but just as much for justice; but those who receive are not praised at all. But of those who are loved for their virtue, the liberal are beloved nearly in the highest degree; for they are useful; and this [use consists] in the giving. But actions according to virtue are noble, and for the sake of the noble; and therefore the liberal man will give for the sake of the noble, and give rightly; for he will give to whom he ought, and how much, and when, and all other [provisos] attendant on right giving : and that with pleasure, or without pain; for that which relates to virtue is pleasant, or void of pain, but least of all painful. But he who gives to those to whom it is not right, or not for the sake of the noble, but for some other reason, shall not he denominate liberal, but some other character. Nor the liberal who gives with pain; for he would choose riches in preference to a noble action; but this is not the character of the liberal. Nor will he again receive whence he ought not; for such a receiving is not the mark of one who does not value riches. Neither is he at all apt to ask favours;

for it is not the part of one who confers favours, to receive favours easily; but he will receive whence he ought; for instance, from his own possessions, not as being noble, but as necessary, that he may have means of expending. Nor will he neglect his own affairs, wishing indeed by means of these to support others. Nor will he give to persons indifferently, that he may have to bestow on whom he ought, and when, and where it is noble. Moreover, it is also [the peculiarity] of the liberal man to be extremely excessive in the giving, so as to leave the lesser part for himself; for the not having regard to himself is the character of the liberal man. Now the term liberality is applied with reference to the property [of the giver]: for the liberal does not consist in the number of the things given, but in the habit of the donor; and this gives according to the property. And nothing hinders, but that he who gives the smaller quantity may be more liberal, if he gives not of smaller means. But those men seem to be more liberal who have not gained their property, but have received it from others; for they are inexperienced in want; and all men are more fond of their own productions, as are, for instance, parents and poets. It is not easy then for the liberal man to be rich, being neither disposed to receive, nor to preserve wealth, but to dispense it, and not valuing it on its own account, but for the sake of giving. Hence also an accusation is laid against fortune, because those who are most worthy of riches, are least rich. But this happens not unreasonably; for it is impossible that he should possess wealth who does not study how he may obtain it; as neither can it be in other things. Nevertheless he will not give to those to whom he ought not, nor when he ought not, in any such ways as are improper; for he would then no longer be acting according to liberality; and having expended upon these objects, he would not have wherewithal to expend upon objects which are proper; for, as has been said, he is liberal who spends according to his property, and upon objects which are proper; but he who exceeds is prodigal. Hence we do not term kings prodigals; for it does not seem an easy task for them in gifts and expences to exceed the quantity of their property. Liberality then being a mean engaged in the giving and receiving of wealth, the liberal man will both give to and expend upon proper objects, and in proper quantities, equally in small and great things; and that with pleasure. He will also receive whence he ought, and as much as he ought; for the virtue being a medium engaged in both, [i. e. giving and receiving,] he will perform both as is right; for a corresponding receiving attends a just giving; but that which does not correspond is contrary. Those things therefore which are consequent, subsist together in the same subject; but contraries plainly cannot. But if it should happen to him to expend beyond what is proper and honourable, he will be pained, yet moderately, and as he ought; for it is a characteristic of virtue both to be pleased and pained with the things we ought, and in the manner we ought. Moreover, the liberal man is communicative in pecuniary affairs; for as he does not regard wealth, he may even be injured: and he is more hurt if he has not spent something which it was his duty to spend, than vexed if he has spent something which it was not his duty to expend: and he is no admirer of [penurious persons, such as] Simonides.

4. But the prodigal errs in these things; for he is neither pleased nor pained at proper objects, nor in the manner that is proper. But this will be more clear to us as we proceed. Now we have said, that prodigality and illiberality are excesses and defects; and that in two things, in giving and receiving; for we place expending also under the head of giving. Prodigality therefore exceeds in giving, and in not receiving, but is deficient in receiving; illiberality is deficient in giving, and excessive in receiving, yet in small things only. The components therefore of prodigality are not altogether compatible; for it is not easy for him, who receives from no source, to give to all; since property rapidly fails those private individuals who give [largely]; who also appear to be prodigals. Again, such a character as this would seem to be in no small degree better than the illiberal; for he is easily reformed both by age and distress, and may arrive at the medium; for he possesses the pro-

perties of the liberal ; since he both gives and does not receive, yet neither as he ought, or well.   If then he were to
become accustomed to this, or should in any other way be
changed, he would be a liberal man ; for he would give
to those to whom he ought, and would not receive whence
he ought not.   Hence he also appears not to be depraved
in his moral character ; for it is not the mark of a villainous
or ignoble person to be excessive in giving and not receiving, but of a silly man.   Now he who is in this manner prodigal, appears to be much better than the illiberal,
both for the above-mentioned reasons, and because the one
benefits many, the other no one, not even himself.   But
most prodigals, as has been mentioned, also take whence
they ought not, and are in that view illiberal.   But they become greedy to receive, because they wish to spend, but are
not able to do that easily ; for their means shortly fail them.
They are therefore compelled to procure them elsewhere ;
at the same time, since they have no regard whatever for
what is noble, they receive thoughtlessly, and from every
source ; for they have a violent desire of giving ; but how
or whence makes no difference to them.   Wherefore neither
are their gifts liberal ; for they are not noble, nor for the
sake of that same noble, nor as is proper ; but sometimes
those who deserve to be in poverty, they make rich, and will
give nothing to the virtuous in morals, and yet much to
flatterers, or those who procure them any other pleasure.
Hence also the most of them are intemperate ; for spending
their property freely, they are also expensive on intemperate
pleasures ; and because they do not live by the canon of
what is noble, they incline to pleasures.   The prodigal then
being left without a guide, transgresses in these things ; but
were he to meet with attention, he may arrive at the medium and the becoming.

5. But illiberality is incurable ; for old age and every in-
firmity seem to render men illiberal ; and it is more conge-
nial to men, than prodigality ; for the great mass of mankind
is more fond of money, than apt to give.   Moreover it is

very widely extended, and is multiform; for there appear
many species of illiberality; since, consisting of two things,
the deficiency in giving, and excess in receiving, it does not
come to all in its entire state, but sometimes is separated;
and some [illiberal] men exceed in receiving, others are deficient in giving. For those who come under such appellations as these, as stingy, closefisted churls, all are deficient in
giving; yet they do not desire the property of others, nor
wish to receive it, some indeed through a certain sense of
justice and awe of disgrace; for some of them seem to be,
or at least say they are, careful of their means, that they may
never be compelled to do a shameful action. Of these also
the split-straw, and all that class, has been denominated from
the quality of not giving to any one being excessive in them.
Others again refrain from property not their own through
fear, considering it not easy for a man to take the property of
other men, and that others should not take his. They are
content therefore neither to receive nor give. Others again
exceed in receiving, by taking from every quarter and every
thing: such as those who work at illiberal trades, and pan-
ders, and all that class, and usurers, and those who purchase
small gains at a dear rate; for all these receive whence they
ought not, and a quantity which they ought not. But the
baseness of gain appears to be common to these; for all of
them endure disgrace for the sake of gain, and that a paltry
gain. For those who take great things whence they ought
not, and such as they ought not, we never call illiberal, as
tyrants, who sack cities and sacrilegiously rifle temples, but
rather we call them villains, and impious, and unjust. Nevertheless the gamester, and the highwayman, and the robber,
are among the illiberal; for they are addicted to base gain;
since for the sake of gain both the last toil, and undergo insults: and the one class endures the greatest dangers, for the
sake of what they may get; the others gain from their friends,
to whom it is their duty to give. Both these therefore wishing to gain whence they ought not, are addicted to base gain:
and consequently all such receivings are illiberal. Justly
then is illiberality said to be contrary to liberality; for it is

both a greater evil than prodigality, and men are more apt to err in this than in the prodigality, which we before described. Concerning liberality therefore and its opposite vices let so much be said.

CHAP. II.

Concerning magnificence, which is a virtue in shewy expences, as liberality is in common ones, and its extremes, parsimony and illiberal profusion.

1. It would seem to follow next that we should discuss magnificence : for this also seems itself to be a certain virtue engaged in wealth ; it does not indeed, as liberality, extend to all actions attendant on wealth, but to those only, which are sumptuous. But in these it exceeds liberality in magnitude ; for, as the name itself suggests, it is a becoming sumptuousness in greatness. Magnitude however is a relative term : for the same expenditure does not become a trierarch[a] and a president of games. The becoming therefore is referred to the person who gives ; the object, on which he spends ; and the sum, which is spent. Still he, who expends with propriety in small or in moderate things, is not called magnificent ; such as, " Often have I bestowed " on the wandering beggar ;" but he [who spends with propriety] in great things is the character : for the magnificent is certainly liberal ; but the liberal is not consequently magnificent. And of such a habit the defect is called parsimony ; but the excess, a vulgar and inelegant profusion ; and all such vices, as do not exceed in magnitude in cases where greatness is proper, but which are gaudy in things not becoming. But we shall speak concerning these at a future period.

---

[a] Those citizens, who, from their wealth, had the expensive offices of the state laid upon them in Athens, were called λιτουργοὶ: the principal offices were τριηραρχία, χορηγία, ἑστίασις.

2. Now the magnificent is similar to the scientific man; for he is capable of tracing out the becoming, and of expending vast sums with elegance: for, as we have said in the beginning, a habit is defined by the operations, and by those things, of which it is the habit. Consequently the expences of the magnificent are vast and becoming: consequently his works are also such; for thus the expenditure will be great, and suitable to the work. Wherefore it is right that the work should be worthy the expence; and the expence equal to the work, or even surpassing it. The magnificent man then will thus expend for the sake of what is noble; for this motive is common to all the virtues; and moreover [he will spend] with pleasure and amply, for a strict account of expences is parsimonious. And he will rather consider, how a deed may be performed most nobly and becomingly, than at what expence, and how at the least expence. It is necessary then that the magnificent man should be liberal; for the liberal man also will expend what is right, and that in the manner that is right; but in these things whatever is great refers to the magnificent, for instance, the greatness of the expence[b]. Though liberality is conversant with the same things as magnificence, magnificence even with equal expence will produce a more magnificent work; for the virtue of possession and production is not the same; for a possession should be most valuable and precious, as gold; but a work should be vast and noble; for the display of such a thing is admirable: but the magnificent is admirable. And the virtue of a work is magnificence in magnitude. But there are some expences which we call honourable, such as those which belong to the gods, offerings, and building of temples and sacrifices: in like manner also expences relating to every thing divine, and whatever is done from an ambition of patriotism; for instance, if in any state they should think it their duty to furnish splendid spectacles, or triremes, or even to entertain a whole city at a feast. In all cases however, as we have said, respect is had to the agent, as to who he is,

---

The passage is corrupt.

and what his means are ; for the expence ought to be worthy
of the means, and to become not only the work, but also
the performer.   Hence a poor man cannot be magnificent ;
for he has not the means of spending much in a becoming
manner; but he who attempts it is silly; for he attempts
it inconsistently with his rank and with propriety : but
whatever is right, is according to virtue.   Such expence is
becoming to those, who have had such means in possession
through themselves, or from their ancestors, or those with
whom they are connected ; also to the nobly born and renowned, and such characters ; for all these have magnitude
and dignity.   In the most perfect sense therefore such is the
magnificent man, and in such expences consists magnificence,
as we have said; for these are the greatest and most honourable.   But of private expences, those are magnificent,
which are incurred once ; such as a marriage-feast, and
whatever is of that class, and whatever the whole city is
earnestly occupied about, or those who are in dignified situations : also expences incurred in the receiving and dismissing of noble strangers, in gifts and remunerations; for
the magnificent is not lavish on himself, but on the public.
But gifts have some similarity to offerings.   Moreover it is
the province of the magnificent man to furnish his house in
a manner suitable to his wealth ; for this also is a kind of ornament ; and rather to be expensive on those works, which
are lasting; for these are the most honourable; and in all
cases to preserve fitness ; for the same things are not suitable
to gods and men, nor in temples and sepulchres.   And of
expences, each is great in its own class : and that is most
magnificent, which is great in a great work : but in any particular instance, what is great in that.   And greatness in
the work is distinct from greatness in the expence; for a
ball or very beautiful jug has the magnificence of a child's
gift; yet the price of it is small and illiberal.   On this account it is the duty of a magnificent man, to act magnifi-
cently in whatever genus of things he may be acting ; for
such magnificence is not easily surpassed, and is done with

a due reference to the expence. Such therefore is the character of the magnificent.

3. But he, who exceeds and is vulgarly profuse, exceeds, as has been explained, in spending inconsistently with what is right; for in things requiring small expence he expends much, and is unbecomingly splendid; for instance, feasting his club companions with the pomp of a marriage-feast; and being manager of the chorus at a comedy, he introduces them in purple on their entrance, as the Megarensians do. And all these things he will do, not for the sake of what is noble, but to display his wealth, and fancying that by such means he shall be admired; and where it is his duty to expend much, he expends little; but where he ought to spend little, he is profuse.

4. But the parsimonious man will be deficient in every thing, and having expended the largest sums, he will ruin the honour of the deed in a trifle; putting off whatever he is to do, and reckoning how he may spend least; and this, bewailing and suspecting that he is doing every thing more sumptuous than he ought. These habits, then, are vices: nevertheless they do not bring reproach on men, because they are neither injurious to one's neighbours, nor very unseemly.

CHAP. III.

Concerning magnanimity, and its extremes, pusillanimity in defect, vanity in excess.

1. But magnanimity seems from the very name to be conversant with great things. But with what kind of things it is conversant, let us first ascertain. It makes no difference, whether we consider the habit, or the man who acts according to the habit. Now he appears to be the magnanimous

man, who, being worthy, thinks himself worthy of great
things; for he, who does this without desert, is a fool : but
of those who act according to virtue, no one is a fool or an
idiot.   He therefore, who has been just described, is magnanimous; for he, who is worthy of small [honours], and thinks
himself worthy of the same, is modest, but not magnanimous; for magnanimity consists in magnitude, as likewise
beauty does in a large body : for small men are elegant and
well-formed, but not handsome.   He again, who thinks
himself worthy of great things, being unworthy, is vain;
but every one is not arrogant, who thinks himself worthy of
more than he is : but he, who thinks himself worthy of less
than he deserves, is pusillanimous, whether he is worthy of
great things, or of moderate things, or even of little things,
if he thinks himself worthy of still less; and he, who is really
worthy, of great things, would seem to be most [pusillani-
mous]; for what would he have done, if he had not been
worthy of such things?

2. The magnanimous therefore is as to magnitude at the
summit; but in observing propriety he is in the mean; for
he thinks himself worthy of that, which is according to his
desert; but the others exceed and are deficient.   Consequently, if being worthy, he thinks himself worthy of great
things, and especially if of the greatest, he must be especially
conversant with one thing.   What that is must be collected
from its value; now value is spoken of with reference to
exterior goods.   But we must lay that down as greatest,
which we attribute to the gods, and which men of consequence most aspire after, and which is the prize in the most
noble contests; of this kind is honour; for this is the greatest of external goods.   Therefore the magnanimous man is
conversant with honours and dishonours, just as he ought.
And indeed without argument the magnanimous are evidently
engaged with honour; for great men especially think themselves worthy of honour; but it is according to their desert.
But the pusillanimous man is deficient both with respect to
himself, and in reference to the claim of desert in the magnanimous man; but the arrogant exceeds with respect to him-

self; not so however with reference to the magnanimous man.

3. But the magnanimous man, if he is really worthy of the greatest things, must be a most excellent character; for the better man is always worthy of the greater honour, and the best man of the greatest. It necessary follows then, that a man truly magnanimous must be good; and what is great in each virtue would seem to be the duty of the magnanimous: and it would by no means fit a magnanimous man to fly wringing his hands, or to commit an injury; because, what inducement can he have to commit base actions, to whom nothing seems great? Indeed, if we consider particulars, a man magnanimous without being good would appear perfectly ridiculous. Nor can he by any means be worthy of honour, if he is vicious; for honour is the reward of virtue, and is allotted to the good. Magnanimity therefore appears to be as it were a kind of ornament of the virtues: for it renders them greater, and does not exist without them. For this reason it is arduous to be in reality a magnanimous man: for it is impossible to be so without perfect virtue.

4. The magnanimous man therefore is especially conversant with honours and dishonour. And with great honours, and when conferred by worthy men, he will be moderately pleased, as if he only obtained what was his own, or even less; for there cannot be an honour adequate to perfect virtue. Not but that he will receive them, in that they have no greater to confer on him; but the honours presented by indifferent persons, and for trifles, he will altogether contemn; for he is not deserving of these: so likewise he will despise dishonour; for it cannot be justly applied to him. The magnanimous man therefore is for the most part, as we have said, engaged with honours. Nevertheless he will conduct himself moderately with respect to wealth also, and power, and every prosperous and adverse fortune, in whatever manner they may happen. And neither in prosperity will he be too elated, nor in adversity too dejected; for he does not even so behave with respect to honour, which is a thing of the greatest value; for dominion and

riches are eligible on account of honour; since those who possess them wish to be honoured on their account. Consequently to whomsoever even honour itself appears trifling, to him all other things surely are so; hence they also appear to be supercilious.

5. However successes seem to contribute to magnanimity; for the nobly born are thought worthy of honour; as also they who are in power, or are rich, for they are in a superior state; but every thing that has a superiority in any good is more honourable. Hence such things as these render men more magnanimous; for they are honoured by some. But in reality the good man alone is to be honoured; yet he who possesses both these is thought more worthy of honour; but those who possess such goods without virtue, neither justly think themselves worthy of great things, nor are properly called magnanimous; for this cannot properly be without perfect virtue. But men who are supercilious and insolent, and possess these external goods, become depraved; for without virtue it is not easy to bear successes with a good grace; now being not able to bear them, and fancying that they are superior to other men, they despise them; yet act themselves as chance directs; for they imitate the magnanimous, though they are unlike him; and this they do in whatever they are able. They do not therefore perform actions suitable to virtue, but they despise others.

6. The magnanimous man justly despises others: for he has a correct opinion of things; but the multitude is right or wrong by accident. Moreover he is not apt to expose himself to small dangers, nor is he a lover of danger, since he thinks but few things to be of consequence; but he courts great dangers; and when in the danger, he is prodigal of life, as if life were altogether of no value. And he is always inclined to do a kindness, but when he receives one, he is ashamed; for the former is the part of a superior, the latter of one who is surpassed. And he is apt to return more than he received; for thus he, who began, will be his debtor, and will be the person benefited. They seem moreover to re-

member those, whom they may have benefited, but not so
those, by whom they have been benefited ; for he who is benefited is the inferior of him who confers ; but he wishes to be
the superior : and the one circumstance they hear with pleasure, but the other with pain. Hence also it is that Thetis does
not recount her good services to Jupiter, nor the Lacedæmonians to the Athenians, but those cases, in which they had
been benefited. It is moreover the character of the magnanimous to beg nothing or barely any thing of any one, but
readily to supply the wants of others. And in his behaviour
to men of consequence and affluence, to be great ; but to the
middle class, moderate ; for to surpass the former is difficult and dignified, but to surpass the latter is easy ; and to
be august among those is not ungentlemanly, but to be so
among the lower class, is vulgar, just as displaying strength
upon the weak. And not to eager for what is held honourable, or for those things in which others are chief.
And to be inactive and slow, except where the honour or en-
terprize is great ; and to be active in few things, but these
great and renowned. It is moreover requisite, that he should
be an open enemy and an open friend ; for to be concealed
is the part of one who is afraid. And to attend more to
truth than to opinion. Also to speak and act openly ; for
that is the part of one, who contemns others ; hence he uses
freedom of speech [c] ; [for this is the part of one who asserts
his liberty of speaking ; hence he is a contemner of others,]
and a lover of truth, except what he speaks in irony : but he
is ironical to the vulgar. And it is his character also not to
be dependent upon any one, except upon a friend ; for that
would be servile : hence all flatterers are mercenary ; and
abject persons are flatterers. Nor is he given to admiration ;
for nothing is great to him. Nor is he mindful of injuries ;
for it is not the province of the magnanimous to recollect
any thing, especially injuries, but rather to overlook them.

---

[c] There is evidently some corruption here : I should wish to leave out
what is between the brackets, and to read the Greek, καταφρονητικοῦ γὰρ·
διὸ παῤῥησιαστικὸς καὶ ἀληθευτικός.

Nor does he speak of men; for he will speak neither of himself, nor of another; since he studies neither to be praised himself, nor how others may be blamed. Neither again is he apt to praise; on which account he is no slanderer, not even of his enemies, unless it be because of an insult. And in necessary or trifling concerns, he is least of all apt to whine and beg; for to behave so in these matters is the character of him who takes great pains about them. And he is apt to possess things noble and unproductive, rather than such as are lucrative and advantageous; for that is more the part of an independent person. Moreover, the motion of the magnanimous man appears to be slow, his voice deep, and his expression stately: for he is not apt to hurry, who studies but few things; nor impetuous, who thinks nothing great; but shrillness of voice and hurried step arise from these causes. Such then is the magnanimous.

7. But he who is deficient is pusillanimous; and he who exceeds is vain. Neither indeed do these appear to be wicked; for they are not injurious to others, but they are under an error; for the pusillanimous, being worthy of good things, deprives himself of what he is worthy; and he appears to have a kind of depravity from his not thinking himself worthy of good things; and he appears also to be ignorant of himself; for otherwise he would aspire after those things of which he is worthy, especially if they are goods. Not that such men appear to be fools, but rather sluggish. Moreover such an opinion seems to render them still worse; for every man desires those things, which are according to his desert; and they also withdraw themselves from noble actions and professions, as if they were unworthy of them; and in like manner, from external goods. But the vain are foolish and ignorant of themselves, and that openly; for they make an attempt at things honourable, as if they were deserving, then they are exploded; they also adorn themselves with fine clothes, and by a dignified appearance, and such things; and wish that their successes should be public, and speak of themselves as if they were to be honoured on this account. But pusillanimity rather than vanity is opposed to magnanimity;

because it more frequently exists, and is worse. Magnanimity therefore, as we have said, is engaged in those honours which are great.

CHAP. IV.

Concerning an anonymous virtue conversant with small honours, which is called ambition, or want of ambition, according to the nature of its object.

1. BUT there seems to be another virtue engaged with this subject, as was stated in our first [sketch], which would seem to be related to magnanimity in the same way that liberality also is to magnificence; for both these retire indeed from what is great, but in moderate and small things they dispose us as is proper. Now as in the receiving and giving of money there is a mean, and excess, and defect; so also in the desire of honour there is the desiring it more than is proper, and less, and whence it is proper, and in the manner that is right; for we blame the ambitious man, as one aiming after honour both more than he ought, and whence he ought not; and the unambitious, as one determined not to be honoured even for noble actions. Sometimes indeed we praise the ambitious as heroic, and a lover of what is noble; but the unambitious, as moderate and temperate, as we have also said at the first. It is however evident, that since a man is styled a lover of any thing in more ways than one, we do not always apply the term ambitious to the same thing; but in praising him, we refer to his being more ambitious than the vulgar; but in blaming him, to his being more so than he ought. Now the mean having no particular name, the extremes appear to contend for it, as a vacant place; but in whatever there is excess and defect, there is also a mean. But men desire honour both more than they ought, and less; consequently there is also the desiring it, as is proper. In

short, this habit is praised, being an anonymous mean engaged with honour. It appears when compared with ambition, to be want of ambition ; when compared with want
of ambition, ambition; when compared with both, it appears to be in a manner both : but this seems to be the case
in the other virtues also. Here however the extremes are
apparently opposed, because the mean is not named.

CHAP. V.

Of meekness, which is a mean between hastiness of temper, and
an anonymous defect. This virtue regulates the passion of
anger.

1. MEEKNESS is a mean in anger. Now the mean and
perhaps the extremes also having no peculiar names, we
place in the mean meekness, which inclines to the deficiency,
which also has no peculiar name. But the excess may be
·called a certain hastiness ; for the passion is anger; but the
things which produce it are many and various.

2. He therefore who is roused to anger by just causes,
and at proper objects, and moreover in the manner that, and
when, and as long as is proper, is praised. Such a man
would be the meek, if indeed meekness is praised ; for the
meek man is generally undisturbed, and not led by his passion ; but feels indignation, as reason would dictate, and for
such motives, and for such a time. But he appears to err
rather towards the defect ; for the meek is not apt to revenge, but rather to forgive. But the defect, whether it is
a certain want of proper spirit, or whatever it may be, is
blamed ; for those who are not moved to anger by causes
which they ought, seem to be foolish, as are they who are
not moved as they ought, nor when, nor by proper objects :
for they appear not to feel, nor be pained ; and, not being
moved to anger, they appear to be incapable of defending

themselves; but that a man when personally insulted should
bear it, and overlook his friend's being so, is slavish.

3. Now the excess exists in all possible ways; for there
is the being angry with those with whom it is not proper,
and from causes that are not proper, and in a greater degree, and quicker, and for a longer time than is proper.
Not indeed that all these faults exist in the same person;
for that could not be; since the evil both destroys itself, and
if it comes all at once, it becomes intolerable. The irascible
then are roused to anger quickly, and with things which are
not proper, and from causes that are not proper, and more
than is proper; but they are soon assuaged, which is indeed
the best quality they possess. But this happens to them, because they do not confine their anger, but return it on their
enemy; by which means they are easily seen, because of their
impetuosity, after that they are calm. But the furious are impetuous in excess, and irascible towards every thing, and on
every occasion; whence also the name was derived. But the
bitterly angry are difficult to appease, and are angry for a long
time; for they confine their anger: but there comes a cessation, when they have revenged themselves; for revenge allays
the anger, producing pleasure instead of pain. But as long
as this does not take place, they carry a weight [on their
minds]; for since it is not open, no one expostulates with
them; but for the anger to subside of itself needs time.
But such characters are most annoying to themselves and
their best friends. But we call those severely angry, who
fret at those things at which they ought not, and more, and
for a longer time, than they ought, and will not be recon-
ciled without revenge or punishment.

4. But we oppose the excess more particularly to mildness, ince it is more frequent; for to revenge an injury is
more human. And for society the severe in anger are the
worse kind. Moreover what was before asserted, is obvious
also from what has just been said; for it is not easy to define the points how, and with whom, and for what reasons,
and how long a time, a man should be angry, and up to
what point a man does right, or errs. For he who errs a

little is not blamed either for his excess, or his deficiency ; for sometimes we praise those who are deficient, and call them meek ; and we call those who are angry manly, as being capable of governing. But how far, and how a man errs, so as to be blameable, is not easy to define in precept ; for the deciding of this depends upon particulars, and upon sense. But so much at least is clear ; that the middle habit is praiseworthy, by means of which we are angry with proper objects, and from proper causes, and in a proper manner, and all that ; but the excesses and defects are reprehensible ; and when erring only a little, slightly reprehensible ; proceeding to a greater degree, more blameable ; but if to a very great degree, they are strongly reprehensible. It is evident therefore, that we must adhere to the middle habit. Let the habits therefore which are engaged with anger be so far discussed.

CHAP. VI.

In the pleasures of society, there is an extreme which may be called litigiousness, which is the deficiency ; another, the excess, is flattery ; and an anonymous mean, which is something similar to friendship.

1. But in intercourse and society and a communication of words and actions, some men appear to be fawners ; who praise every thing with the view of pleasing, and act adversely in nothing, but in short who think that it is their duty to be inoffensive to those whom they meet ; those again, who are the opposite to these, opposing every thing, and having not the least caution of offending, are called morose and contentious.

2. That therefore the above-mentioned habits are blameable, requires no proof : and that the mean of these is praiseworthy, according to which a man will assent to what

he ought, and as he ought, and in a similar manner will be dissatisfied. Now no name has been assigned it; but it is most like friendship ; for he, who is according to this middle habit, is just such a character as we generally call a worthy friend, after he has added affection for us. But it differs from friendship, because it is without strong feeling and affection towards those, whom he has intercourse with ; for he does not assent to each circumstance as he ought, from loving or hating the person ; but because he is of this kind of disposition ; for he will do this equally by those whom he does not, and those whom he does know; and by his associates and those he does not associate with, except in each case as far as is suitable to himself; for it is not fit to respect, or on the other hand to give pain to, familiars and strangers in the same manner. It has been therefore asserted universally, that he will have intercourse with men in such a manner as is proper; but referring to the noble and advantageous, he will aim at not giving pain, or at pleasing. For indeed he seems to be engaged with the pleasures and pains, which occur in our intercourses with men ; but as many of these pleasures as it is either not honourable or injurious that he should contribute to, he will feel indignant at, and will choose rather to give pain. And should the pleasure bring disgrace, and that not small, or injury upon the person, who thus pleases, but the contrary brings but little pain, he will not receive it, but will be indignant. But he will associate differently with men of consequence, and common persons, and with those who are more or less known to him ; in like manner also with respect to the other distinctions, allotting to each what is suitable. And generally choosing to give pleasure, and dreading to give pain ; but following the circumstances, which happen, if they are greater ; I mean, what is honourable and advantageous ; and for the sake of great pleasure to ensue, he will give a little pain.

3. The middle character then is such ; but it has no peculiar name. But of that character which contributes pleasure, he, who aims at being pleasant for no other end, is fawning ;

but he, who does so that some advantage may accrue to him, in money, or those things which are obtained by money, is a flatterer. He again, who is dissatisfied with every thing, we have said is morose and contentious. But the extremes appear to oppose each other, because the medium is anonymous.

CHAP. VII.

Concerning the observer of truth, or veracious, who is the middle character, and the extremes, arrogant and dissemblers, which are conversant with nearly the same subjects as the characters last treated of.

1. ALMOST with the same subjects is the medium of arrogance engaged; this also is anonymous. However it is not wrong to discuss such like habits; for we may be more acquainted with what belongs to manners, by treating the virtues individually; and we should believe that the virtues are means, if we were conscious that it is so in all of them. Now in society, those who have intercourse with men with a view to pleasure or pain, have been mentioned. But let us speak concerning those who are observant of truth, and those who are false, both in words and actions, and pretension to character.

2. The arrogant therefore seems to pretend to things illustrious, and which he does not possess, and greater than he does possess. The dissembler, on the other hand, [seems] to deny what he possesses, or render them less; but the middle character, being a certain self-same in every thing, is a man of veracity both in his life and his words, allowing those things to belong to him which he does possess, and neither greater or less. Both of these things however may be done for the sake of something, or for nothing. But such as a man is, such things does he speak and do, and so does he

live, unless he acts for the sake of something. Of itself
however falsehood is base and reprehensible; and truth,
noble and laudable. Hence also he, who is observant of
truth, being a middle character, is laudable; but those who
are false, are both indeed reprehensible; though the arrogant
is the more blameable.

3. Let us then speak concerning each; and first, of the
character observant of truth; for we are not talking of him,
who observes truth in compacts, or in things which relate to
justice or injustice: for these things would belong to another virtue; but of him, who, when nothing of this kind
is concerned, is observant of truth both in words and in his
life, because he is such in habit. But such a man must appear to be a worthy man; for the lover of truth, and he who
speaks the truth in matters in which it makes no difference,
will still more be observant of truth in cases where it makes
a difference; for he will dread a falsehood, as base, which
he had already dreaded in itself; but such a character is
praiseworthy. But he will rather lean to what is less than
the truth; for this appears more fitting, because excesses
are intolerable.

4. He, again, who pretends to greater things than he possesses for the sake of nothing, is similar to a depraved man:
for, [otherwise,] he would not have been delighted with a
falsehood; but he appears more a vain than a bad man. If
however it is for the sake of something, he who is so for the
sake of glory or honour, is not very reprehensible, such as
is the arrogant; but he, who is so for the sake of money, or
those things which produce money, is more mean. But the
arrogant man does not derive his character from his capa-
bility of being so, but from his deliberate choice; for he is
arrogant by habit, and because he is of that character, as
is the liar also; the one delighting in the falsehood itself,
the other desiring glory or gain. Those therefore who are
arrogant for the sake of glory, pretend to those things,
which praise or congratulation attends; but those who are
arrogant for the sake of gain, pretend to those things, the
enjoyment of which goes also to their neighbour, and which

may be kept a secret when they do not exist, as the being a physician, or prophet, or philosopher. Hence most men pretend to such things, and are arrogant in such; for the qualities we have been describing are in them.

5. But the dissemblers speaking less than the truth appear more amiable in manners, for they do not seem to speak for the sake of gain, but to avoid fastidiousness. These men especially deny [the possession of] illustrious things; as Socrates did. But those, who pretend they do not possess things small and obvious, are called meanly cunning, and are truly despicable. And sometimes this appears to be arrogance; for instance, the dress of the Lacedæmonians; for both excess and a great deficiency is arrogant. But those, who moderately use dissimulation, and who use it in things which are not too common and obvious, appear to be well-bred men. But the arrogant appears to be opposed to the observer of truth; for he is the worse character.

CHAP. VIII.

Of the medium in relaxation and social conversation, which is called facetiousness; the extremes of which are scurrility and rusticity.

1. THERE being also relaxation in life, and in that a spending of time in jesting, there seems to be here also a certain just intercourse, and a speaking the things which are proper, and in a proper manner; in the same manner also we may hear them. There is a distinction also between the speaking among such and such persons, and listening to such persons. But it is evident, that there is in these things also an excess as well as defect of the mean. Those then who exceed in the ludicrous, seem to be buffoons and vulgar, always itching after the ludicrous, and rather aiming at

raising a laugh, than speaking decent language, and not
paining the person jested upon. But those, who can neither
themselves speak any thing ludicrous, and are dissatisfied
with those who thus speak, appear to be rustic and morose.
But those, who jest elegantly, are termed facetious, as it
were, well-turned; for there appear to be in the moral character such motions as these: for as bodies are judged of
from their motions, so also are manners. Now the ludicrous
being redundant, and most men being delighted with jest,
and satirizing more than is proper, buffoons are also called
facetious, as being genteel men; but that they differ, and
not a little, is clear from what has been said.

2. But good taste also is a proprium of this middle habit.
But it is the character of the man of good taste to speak and
hear such things, as are adapted to a good and liberal man;
for there are some things proper for such a man to speak
and hear by way of jest. And the jesting of the liberal man
differs from that of the slavish, and again that of the educated from that of the uneducated. This a person may also
see from the old and new comedies; for in the one obsce-
nity was the ludicrous; in the other the delicate hint: and
these things make no little difference as to decency. Is then
the man who jokes properly, to be defined by his speaking
the things which become a liberal man? or by his not
giving pain to the hearer, or by his giving him pleasure?
or is not a thing like this indefinite? for different things are
disgusting as well as delightful to different persons. Moreover he will hear the same kind of things; for whatever
things a man endures to hear, these he also appears to do.
Consequently he [the middle character] will not do every
thing; for a joke is a kind of invective; but legislators forbid some kinds of invective; they ought perhaps to forbid
lampooning also. Consequently the gentlemanly and liberal man will thus behave, being, as it were, a law to himself. Such an one therefore is the middle character, whether
he is called the man of taste, or facetious.

3. But the buffoon is overpowerd by the ludicrous, sparing
neither himself nor others, if he can raise a laugh; and

speaking such things as a gentleman would not speak at all, and some things which he would not hear.

4. On the other hand, the rustic is useless in such meetings : for contributing nothing himself, he is dissatisfied with all. But relaxation and jesting appear to be necessary in life. The three last mentioned means therefore are media in common life ; and they are all engaged with a communication of certain words and actions, but they differ, because one is conversant with truth, the others with what is pleasant. And of those conversant with pleasure, the one is engaged with jests, the other in the intercourses of the rest of life.

CHAP. IX.

That shame is no virtue, as was generally maintained, nor
a mean.

1. WE ought not to treat of shame, as of a virtue, for it is more similar to a passion than a habit. It is defined however to be a certain dread of disgrace ; and its effect is nearly the same as the fear, which is engaged with dangers : for those who are ashamed blush ; but those who dread death are pale. Both consequently appear to be in a manner bodily ; which appears to be rather characteristic of a passion than a habit.

2. But this passion is not adapted to every age, but to youth ; for we consider it just, that persons of that age should be bashful, because living under the influence of passion they err in many things, but are checked by shame. And we praise the bashful among young men ; but no man would praise an old man, because he is bashful ; for we suppose that it is not right he should do any thing upon which shame would be consequent ; for neither is shame the characteristic of a good man, if indeed it arises from the com-

mission of base actions : for he ought not to perform such.
But whether some things are in reality shameful, others in
idea, differs not ; for neither are to be committed ; so that
they ought not to feel shame.   Moreover it is the character
of a depraved man to be such, as to commit any base action ;
but that a person should be so affected, as to feel shame if he
commit any such, and on that account fancy himself to be
worthy, is absurd ; for shame is attendant on voluntary
actions ; but a worthy man will never voluntarily commit
base actions. But shame may upon certain suppositions be a
worthy feeling ; for if the good man did such things, he
would be ashamed ; but this is not in the virtues ; but if
impudence is vile, and not to be ashamed at committing
shameful deeds, the being ashamed, when doing such things,
is not the more worthy.

3. Neither is continence a virtue, but something mixed ;
but we will treat of this at a future place.   But now let us
speak concerning justice.

ARISTOTLE'S ETHICS.

BOOK V.

CHAP. I.

Of justice, and its contrary, injustice. Justice and injustice are divided into universal and particular. Universal justice explained.

1. BUT let us investigate justice and injustice, with what actions they happen to be conversant, and what kind of mean the habit of justice is, and between what things the principle of justice[d] is a medium. And let our investigation be according to the same method with that of the subjects before treated of. We see then all men willing to call justice a habit of that kind, by which men are wont to practise just things, and by means of which they do perform justice, and wish what is just; in the same manner also of injustice, [that it is the habit], by means of which men do injuries, and wish what is unjust. Wherefore let thus much be laid down by us first in outline: for the case is not the same with the sciences and faculties as with habits[e]. For a

---

[d] A distinction should carefully be observed throughout this book between the habit of justice, δικαιοσύνη, and the principle of justice, τὸ δίκαιον: the former is a μεσότης, the latter a μέσον.

[e] The above definition is not sufficient, because one term of it, τὰ δίκαια, requires explanation as much as δικαιοσύνη, the term defined: also in describing moral habits, we must give a different definition for two con-

faculty and science seems to be the same in contraries ; but the same habit does not belong to contraries ; for example, from health the contrary actions are not performed, but those alone which indicate health ; for we say that a man walks healthfully, when he walks as a healthy man would.

2. Frequently, therefore, a contrary habit is found out from its contrary, and frequently habits [are known] from their subjects[f] ; for supposing a good habit of body is well known, a bad habit also becomes well known ; and from things which create a good habit the good habit [is known], and from this, those things which create a good habit ; for if a good habit of body be firmness of flesh, it is necessary that a bad habit of body be softness of flesh ; and that which produces a good habit is that which is creative of firmness in the flesh.   It follows, also for the most part, that if one of the two [contraries] have more significations than one, the other likewise has more than one signification : for instance, if the just has more, so also has the unjust[g]. Now the term justice, as well as injustice, appears to have more than one signification ; but, because their homonymy is near[h], it is not observed, and not clear, as it is in things widely separated ; for the difference in that case is great, namely, a difference of species : for instance, the Greek term κλεὶς is predicated ho-

---

trary habits, such as justice and injustice ; which is not required in describing a science : for instance, whatever is the definition of the science of medicine, a good or bad physician lays claims to it : so also the definition of rhetoric comprehends the orator and the sophist.   This makes it more difficult to define a moral habit ; though there is one advantage, that by taking the direct opposite of any definition, we know the contrary habit.

[f] Τὰ ὑποκείμενα means every thing connected with the habit : thus if we understand what τὸ δίκαιον is, we shall know what the habit is, δικαιο-σύνη, which is conversant with it.

[g] If the term *just* is applied to different characters, so probably is the term *unjust.*

[h] i. e. because the different significations closely resemble each other. An homonymous term is what we otherwise call an equivocal term, i. e. one which is applied to many things in different significations.   Thus (as will be shewn in section 3.) δίκαιος is an equivocal or homonymous term, applied in significations somewhat different to the νόμιμος and the ἴσος.

monymously, both of that bone which is under the neck of animals, and of a key by which they lock doors.

3. Let us then discover how many significations the unjust man admits of[i]. Now the illegal, and the avaritious, and the unequal man, appear to be unjust; hence it is obvious, that the just man will be the observer of the law, and the equal man. Justice then is what is lawful and equal; injustice is the unlawful and the unequal.

4. But since the unjust man is also avaritious, he will be so with respect to goods; yet not all goods, but such as prosperity and adversity is concerned with; which are in themselves always goods, but to individuals not always so. Now men wish for and pursue these things; yet they ought not; but rather to pray, that those things which are in themselves goods may be good to them also, but to choose the things which are good to them. But the unjust man does not always choose the greater part, but even the smaller in things absolutely bad. But because he thinks that the lesser evil is in one view a good, and avarice is a desire of more good, on that account he appears to be avaricious. The unjust man is also unequal: for this comprehends the other, [viz. avarice,] and is common to both. He is also illegal; for this, that is illegality, or in other words inequality, comprehends every injustice, and is common to all injustice.

5. Now since the illegal man was said to be unjust, and the legal just, it is obvious, that all things legal are in one view just; for the things defined by the legislative power are legal; and we say that each of these is just. But the laws treat of all things, aiming either at what is advantageous to all men in common, or to the best, or to those in power, or according to virtue, or some other such rule. Hence in one view we call those things just which are productive and preservative of happiness and its parts to the political society.

---

i The second section contained rules for discovering moral habits, which rules are applied in this and the following sections to the habit of justice: for ἀδικία is known from its subject matter τὸ ἄδικον, and from ἀδικία is known its contrary δικαιοσύνη.

But the law enjoins the doing the works of the brave man, such as, not to desert one's post, nor to fly, nor throw away one's arms; and the works of the temperate man, such as, not to commit adultery, nor offer violence to any one; and the actions of the meek, as not to strike, nor revile; so also throughout the other virtues and vices, encouraging the one, and forbidding the other; in a proper manner, the law which is properly enacted; but that which is hastily drawn up, badly.

6. This justice therefore is perfect virtue: not simply so however, but relatively[k]. And on this account justice appears frequently to be the most exalted of the virtues, and neither morning dawn nor the evening star are so wonderful. And we say in a proverb, "Every virtue is collected in justice." And it is especially perfect virtue, because it is the use of perfect virtue; and it is perfect, because he who possesses this is able to use virtue not only in himself, but toward another also; for many are able to use virtue in their private concerns, but in their dealings with others they cannot. And for that reason the saying of Bias seems to be good, that a public office will prove a man; for he who bears a public office is necessarily engaged with other men, and is in society. For this very same reason also justice alone, of the virtues, appears to be another man's good, because it is applied to another; for it performs the things advantageous to another, either his superior or the public. He therefore is most depraved who applies his villany to himself and his friends; but he is best, not who applies his virtue to himself, but he who does it to another; for this is a difficult task. This justice therefore is not a part of virtue, but the whole of virtue; nor is its opposite, injustice, a part of vice, but all vice. In what however virtue and this justice differs, is evident from what has been said: for it is the same in substance, but its essence is not the same; since,

---

[k] Not that justice is the only virtue, which is relative; for liberality, magnificence, and several others are so also: but if on account of the excellent nature of justice, we choose to call it perfect virtue, we must add that it is relative.

inasmuch as it refers to another, it is justice; but in that it is a habit of a certain kind, it is simply virtue[1].

CHAP. II.

That there is a particular justice and injustice. Particular justice divided into distributive and corrective.

1. BUT we are in search of the justice which is a part of virtue; for there is òne of that kind, as we have said; so also of the injustice which is a part of vice. A proof that such exists is this; he who performs any other act of depravity, acts unjustly, but is not at all avaritious; for instance, he who threw away his shield through cowardice, or who has spoken ill of another through asperity, or has not assisted another with his wealth through illiberality; but when he covets more than his share, it is frequently in pursuance of none of these vices; nor surely is it in pursuance of all, but of some one particular vice; for we blame him also on the score of injustice[m]. There is certainly then another kind of injustice, as it were a part of universal injustice, and

---

[1] The substance of this chapter is briefly this. Justice (δικαιοσύνη) is that habit by which men wish and do what is just (τὸ δίκαιον.) Then if we substitute νόμιμον and ἴσον for δίκαιον, justice will be that habit, by which men wish and do what is legal and equal. Then if we adopt the explanation of the term νόμιμον, as given in section 5, justice will be that habit, by which men consult the happiness of the community, and practise every virtue. This definition results from a consideration of only one of the former terms, viz. νόμιμον: the other, ἴσον, is discussed in the next chapter, and furnishes another definition of justice.

[m] According to the description of justice and injustice contained in the last chapter, if a man performed any act of vice, he would be unjust, because he violates the law. But if we look to facts, we see a man perform an act of vice, and he is not necessarily called unjust: there must therefore be a kind of injustice distinct from the former, which attends upon every particular vice: and the truth is, that when a man performs an act of vice for the sake of gain, he is then, and then only, called unjust.

something unjust as a part of what is universally unjust and contrary to the law. Again, if one man should commit adultery for the sake of gaining, and should receive something in addition, and another through his desire should do the same, having given of his own, and being a loser by it; the latter would seem to be intemperate rather than avaricious, but the former unjust, and not intemperate; it is then obvious that it is so because he did it for the sake of gain. Again, in all other unjust deeds there is a reference made still to some particular vice; for instance, if a man has committed adultery, [it is referred] to intemperance; if he has deserted his comrade, to cowardice; if he has struck any body, to anger; but if he has gained by it, it is referred to no other vice than to injustice. So that it is clear that there is a certain other particular injustice besides the universal, synonymous with it, because the definition is in the same genus; for both virtually exist in being relative[n]; but the one is conversant with honour, or wealth, or safety, or, if we could include all these things under some one term, with that; and under the influence of the pleasure which arises from gain; but the other is conversant with all the things with which the upright man is conversant. That therefore there are more justices than one, and also that there is a certain other justice besides the whole of virtue, is evident; but we must understand what it is, and of what nature.

2. The unjust therefore has been divided into the illegal, and the unequal; and the just into legal and equal. In the illegal then the first mentioned injustice is situated. But[o] since the unequal and the illegal are not the same, but different, as a part to the whole; for every thing unequal is illegal, but every thing illegal is not unequal; the unjust also and injustice in the one are not the same with those in

---

[n] The same definition of wishing and doing to another what is legal and equal applies to both; but universal justice is more concerned with obeying the law, particular justice with observing equality.

[o] I cannot make any sense of the received text, and have therefore adopted the reading of Muretus.

the other, but different; these indeed are as parts, those as wholes; for this injustice is a part of universal injustice ; so also is this justice a part of that justice. Wherefore we must also treat of justice and injustice, which are particular, and of the just and unjust in like manner. The justice there-fore and injustice, which are arranged under entire virtue, the one being the application of the whole of virtue to other men, the other of [universal] vice, may be dismissed. And it is evident in what manner the just and unjust which at-tends on these are to be distinguished ; for almost the whole of things legal are the same things as are enjoined by uni-versal virtue ; for the law enjoins us to live according to each virtue, and forbids our living according to each vice. But the things productive of universal virtue are those legal things, which have been enacted for the discipline of the community. But concerning discipline in particulars, by means of which a man is properly good, whether it belongs to the political science, or some other, must be determined at a future time P. For perhaps it is not the same thing to be a good man and a good citizen in every sense.

3. Of particular justice and the just which is attached to it, that is one q species, which is engaged with the distribu-tions either of honour, or wealth, or of those other things which are divisible among such as partake of the benefits of the state : for in these things it is possible to have an un-equal and an equal share compared with one another; an-other species is that which is corrective in the dealings be-tween man and man. Of this there are two parts ; for of those dealings some are voluntary, some involuntary. The

---

P Vide book x. c. ult.

q In c. 1. sect. 3. justice was defined to be a habit, by which men wish and do what is legal and equal : and by explaining the term legal, (νόμιμον,) we obtained a description of universal justice. The other term, (ἴσον) enables us to describe particular justice: so that universal justice is that habit, by which men wish and do what is νόμιμον: particular justice, that habit, by which they wish and do what is ἴσον. But as the term equality admits of two senses, viz. an equality between two things, and an equality of ratios, particular justice will also be divided into two kinds.

voluntary are such as these, for instance, selling, buying, lending, bail, borrowing, pledging, hiring; but they are called voluntary, because the principle of these dealings is voluntary. Of the involuntary, some are clandestine, such as theft, adultery, poisoning, prostitution, kidnapping, assassination, false witness; others compulsatory, as blows, bonds, death, plundering, maiming, libelling, aspersion.

CHAP. III.

That all justice is in proportion: and distributive justice in geometrical proportion.

1. BUT since the unjust man is unequal, and injustice is unequal, it is evident that there is also a certain mean of the unequal, and that is the equal; for in whatever action there is the greater and the less, there is also the equal. If then injustice is unequal, justice is equal; which is clear to all men, even without demonstration. But since that which is equal is a mean, justice also must be a kind of mean. But the equal is in two things at least; it is therefore necessary, that justice, being a mean as well as equal, should be both in reference to something and be between some persons; and inasmuch as it is a mean, [it is a mean] between certain things; and these things are the more and less; but in that it is equal, it is an equality of two things; but in that it is just, [it is just] to certain persons. It is necessary then, that justice should consist of four things at least; for the objects, to whom it happens to be just, are two; and the subjects, in which the affairs take place, are two.

2. Also the equality will be the same, of the persons and of the things in which the just consist[r]; for as the things in

---

[r] There will be an equality of ratio between one person and one thing, and the other person and the other thing: or the ratio of Ajax to his reward will be the same as that of Achilles to his reward.

which the just consists are to each other, so are those persons also to whom it is just; for if the persons are not equal, they will not have equal things. But hence arise quarrels and accusations, when either equal persons have and are allotted unequal things, or unequal persons have equal things. This is further evident from the consideration of merit; for all allow that in distributions justice ought to be according to a kind of merit. All however do not assert that merit is the same thing; but the members of a democracy think it is liberty[s]: those of an oligarchy, either riches, or birth; but of an aristocracy, virtue. Justice therefore is a kind of proportion; for proportion is the property not only of arithmetic, but of number universally; for proportion is the equality of ratio, and is in four terms at least.

3. That disjunctive[t] proportion therefore is in four terms, is obvious; so also is continuous; for it uses one term as two, and mentions it twice; for instance, as the line A is to the line B, so is the line B to the line C; the line B, therefore, is repeated twice; so that if the line B is laid down twice, the proportionate terms will be four. But justice is also in four things at least, and the ratio is the same; for the persons, and the things in which the justice is, are correspondently divided. Consequently, as the term A is to B, so will C be to D; and therefore alternately, as A is to C, so is B to D. So that the whole also bears a ratio to the whole[u], which indeed the distribution conjoins; and if they

---

[s] That is, in a democracy he is considered to have most merit, and to desire the honours of the state, who has contributed most to liberty: in an oligarchy, the rich or the well-born obtain the honours of the state: in an aristocracy, the virtuous.

[t] Disjunctive proportion is this, A is to B, as C to D: continuous proportion is this, A is to B, as B to C.

[u] By the whole is meant the person and his reward united. In numbers or letters the proportion is evident: nor will it be less so if we take the real terms in question: first, Ajax is to Achilles, as Ajax's reward is to Achilles' reward: secondly, alternately, Ajax is to his reward, as Achilles is to his reward: thirdly, Ajax when rewarded is equal to Achilles when rewarded; which last is called the composition of ratios; and if this composition is not equal, the distribution is not just.

are put together in this manner, it conjoins them justly. Consequently the connection of the term A with C, and of B with D[x], is the justice which takes place in distribution; and justice is a mean, that is, of that which is contrary to proportion; for proportion is a mean; and justice is proportion. But mathematicians call such a proportion as this geometrical; for in geometrical proportion the whole proves also to be to the whole, as each part is to each[y]. But this proportion is not continuous; for the person and the thing cannot become one term in number.

4. This justice therefore is in proportion: but the unjust is that which is contrary to proportion; it becomes then partly more, partly less. Which is indeed the case with actions; for he who injures has more, but he who is injured less of the good. But in evil, the contrary happens; for the lesser evil comes into the account of good, compared with the greater evil; for the lesser evil is more eligible than the greater; but the eligible is good, and the more eligible is the greater good. This then is one species of what is just.

CHAP. IV.

Of corrective justice, which is similar to arithmetical proportion, and is used in reducing the loss and gain to an equality in voluntary and involuntary dealings.

1. BUT the remaining species is the corrective, which exists in the voluntary and involuntary dealings between man and man. Now this justice has a different form from the former; for the justice which is distributive of common property is always according to the proportion just described; for if there is made a distribution out of public money, it will be made according to the same ratio, which the services contributed have to each other, and the unjust the opposite to this just, is contrary to that proportion.

[x] Here A and B are taken for the two persons, C and D for the two things.

[y] The reason therefore why distributive justice is in geometrical proportion, is because in distributing we may compound the ratios.

2. But justice in contracts is a kind of equality, and the unjust is unéqual; yet not according to the above proportion; but to arithmetical proportion[z]; for it matters not, whether a worthy man has cheated a bad man, or a bad man a worthy one; nor whether a good or bad man has committed adultery; but the law looks only to the difference of injury, and treats them as equal, whether the one injures and the other is injured, or whether the latter should do, and the former suffer harm. Whence the judge endeavours to reduce to equality this injustice, as being unequal; for indeed when one is struck, but the other strikes, or when one kills, but the other dies, the suffering and action are divided into unequal parts; but he endeavours by a penalty to equalize them, by subtracting from the gain. For to speak generally, we use the term gain in such cases as these, although it is not exactly appropriate to some, as for instance when it is applied to the person who struck, and loss to him who suffered; but when the suffering has been calculated, the one is called loss, the other gain. So that the equal is a mean between the greater and less. But the gain and the loss are, one greater, the other less in a contrary manner; the greater share of good, and the less of evil is gain, the contrary is loss: between which, equality was said to be a mean, which we call justice. So that corrective justice must be the mean between loss and gain.

3. Hence also when men disagree, they fly to the judge; and to go to the judge is to go to justice: for the judge will be as it were justice embodied; and they search after a judge as a mean; and some call them [μεσίδιοι] mediators,

[z] The reason therefore why corrective justice is in arithmetical, and not geometrical proportion, is because the persons are here not taken into consideration, as they are in distributive justice: but the only object of the judge is to make the two things themselves, and not their ratios, equal. For instance, the buyer is to his money, as the seller is to his commodity: or a person robbed is to his loss, as the robber is to the penalty: here the money and the commodity, the loss and the penalty, are made respectively equal; but as no notice is taken of the relative state of the parties, the ratios cannot be compounded, and consequently it cannot be geometrical proportion.

supposing that, if they find the medium, they will find what is just. Justice then is a certain mean, if the judge is so. But the judge equalizes, and, as if a line were divided into unequal parts, he takes off that quantity, by which the greater division exceeds the half, and adds it to the lesser division; but when the whole is divided into two equal parts, they then say that each has his own, when they receive what is equal. But the equal is the mean of the greater and less, according to arithmetical proportion[a]. On this account also it is named δίκαιον, because it is equally divided; as if one were to say δίχαιον, and the judge δικαστὴς were called δίχαστὴς; for two things being equal, if a part were taken from the one, and added to the other, the latter exceeds by these two parts; for if it had been subtracted, and not added to the other, the latter would have exceeded by one part only; consequently it exceeds the mean by one part, and the mean exceeds that from which the part was taken, by one part. By this then we shall know what we ought to take away from him who has more, and what to add to him that has less; for by how much the mean exceeds the lesser part, so much we are to add to him who has less; and the part by which it is exceeded we must take away from the greatest. Let the lines AA, BB, CC, be equal to each other; from AA, let AE be subtracted, and added to CC, namely, the part CD; thus the whole line DCC exceeds the line AE by CD and CF; consequently it exceeds BB by CD[b].

```
A        E        A
B        '        B
C        F        C        D
                  '
```

[a] That is, if twenty pounds are divided between two persons, one of whom has taken twelve, the other eight pounds; they go to the judge, who draws an arithmetical mean between the two quantities, and gives each of them ten pounds.

[b] Let AA and CC represent two persons, each of whom possess ten pounds, and let BB represent the ten pounds: now let ~~BB~~ rob AA of four pounds and take it to himself: then CC exceeds AA by eight pounds and BB by four pounds.

This moreover is the case with other arts ; for they would be subverted, unless the thing acted upon received the same in substance, quantity, and quality, as the thing acting produced. But these terms, loss and gain, came from voluntary exchange; for the having more than his own property is called gaining, but the having less than at the onset [c] is called losing ; as in buying and selling, and such other contracts as the law has granted liberty in. But when neither more nor less but the very same things are produced, they say that they have their own, and neither lose nor gain by them. So that justice is a mean between a certain gain and loss in involuntary dealings, namely, the having an equal part both before and afterwards.

CHAP. V.

Whether the giving like for like is justice: that simple retaliation is not consonant with distributive or corrective justice, but a proportionate return after the goods have been first made equal: that money is this common standard of measure.

1. But retaliation seems to some to be simply justice, as the Pythagoreans maintained ; for they defined justice simply to be that which was retaliated upon another. But retaliation does not coincide with either distributive [d] or corrective justice ; though they even wish to assert that this was the justice of Rhadamanthus, " If a person should suffer " the things he has committed, upright justice would fol- " low :" for in many parts it disagrees ; for instance, if a magistrate has struck any one, it is not right he should be struck in return ; and if a person has struck a magistrate, he

[c] The state which the parties were in before any intercourse took place answers to the mean in numbers or lines.

[d] He does not explain why an exact retaliation cannot take place in distributive justice : in fact, the thing is evident : for if a general wins a victory, the state cannot go out and reward him by winning one for him in return.

deserves not only to be struck, but even to be severely punished [e].   Again, there is a great difference, whether an action is voluntary or involuntary [f].

2. But in commercial intercourse that kind of justice which makes a return by proportion and not by equality, keeps the parties together.   For by proportionate returns being made, a state stands united; for either men seek to return an injury, otherwise there appears to be slavery if they do not retaliate; or they desire to return a benefit, otherwise there is no remuneration: but by remuneration they stand united.   Hence they also place the temple of the Graces in a conspicuous situation, that there may be retribution; for this is the property of gratitude [g]: for a person ought to serve in return him who conferred the kindness, and to shew the first kindness again himself.   But diagonal conjunction produces the retribution which is according to proportion: for instance, let the builder of a house be A, a shoemaker B, the house C, the shoe D.

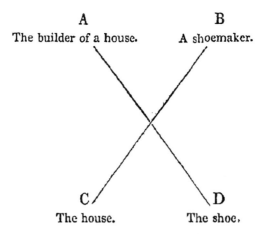

A
The builder of a house.

B
A shoemaker.

C
The house.

D
The shoe.

[e] And yet it was said in section 2. of the last chapter, that the persons are never taken into consideration: but there is no contradiction between the two passages; for they are not considered, when they are before the judge, but only so far as to hinder a person from taking the law into his own hands.

[f] Which difference was destroyed if retaliation were allowed in every case.

[g] This sentence is unintelligible in English, from the circumstance of the Greek word χάρις signifying grace and gratitude.

It is necessary then that the builder receive from the shoe-maker his work, and himself return his own work to the other. If therefore there be at first that equality which is according to proportion, and then a mutual return is made, and what was said above will exist; but, if not, there is no equality, nor will the state remain united; for nothing pre-vents the work of the one from being better than that of the other. In short, it is therefore necessary that these should be equalized; this, moreover, is the case with other arts; for they would be subverted, unless, how far soever, and howsoever the agent acted, the thing acted upon received the same, and just so far, and just in the same manner. For so-ciety is not made up of two physicians, but of a physician and husbandman, and, in short, of different persons, and those not equal; but it is necessary that these be equalized. Hence it is necessary, that the things, of which there is ex-change, should in some manner admit of comparison.

3. For which purpose money has been introduced, and is become in a manner a measure; for it measures all things; consequently it measures both excess and defect; and there-fore, how many shoes are equal to a house, or to food. It is necessary therefore that whatever proportion the builder of a house bears to a shoemaker [h], so many shoes should answer to a house, or food; for, if this is not done, there will be neither exchange nor intercourse. But this will not be, un-less they are in some manner equal. It is necessary, then, that all things should be measured by some one measure, as has been before said; and this is in reality the demand, which connects all things; for if men were in want of no-thing, or not equally so, either there would be no exchange, or at least not the same. But coin has been made by com-pact a kind of substitute for demand; and on that account it has this name νόμισμα, because it exists not by nature, but by law (νόμῳ,) and it is in our power to alter, or render it useless.

h i. e. the proportion of the labour, expence, &c. should regulate the exchange: the persons themselves are of course not considered, as was stated above.

4. So that there will be retaliation, when the things have been equalized. So that, as the husbandman is to the shoemaker, so is the work of the shoemaker to that of the husbandman. But it is necessary to apply them to the scale of proportion, when they are to be exchanged; for, if not, the one extreme will have both excesses[i]. But, when they have their own, they are in this manner equal and capable of commerce, because this equality can take place between them. Let A be the husbandman, the food C, the shoemaker B, his work when made equal D.

A
The husbandman.

B
The shoemaker.

C
The food.

D
The work of the shoemaker
equalled to the food.

But, if it were not possible to have such mutual retribution, there would have been no society. But that the demand, being as it were some particular thing, is the tie [of society,] is evident from this, that men, when they do not stand in need of each other, either both or one of the two, do not exchange; as when one man wants what the other has, for instance, wine, they grant an exportation of corn. It is necessary then that this should be equalized. But for the use of a future exchange, if nothing is wanted at this time, the coin is as it were a pledge to us, that, when it is wanted, the thing will be to be had; for it is necessary that the thing be ready for him to receive who brings this. This moreover is liable to the same objection; for it is not always of the same value; at the same time it is more likely to be stable. Hence it is necessary that all things should be valued; for thus there will always be exchange: and if that, then commerce. Consequently money, as a measure rendering things commensurate, equalizes them; for, if there had been no exchange, there would have been no com-

---

i i. e. the work which he gives will be too little; that which he receives will be too great.

merce; nor exchange, if there had not been equality; nor
equality, if there had not been a common measure. In
reality, it is impossible for things differing so much to become
commensurate; but with regard to the demand, it is sufficiently possible. Consequently there must be one certain
[standard]; and this from universal compact. Hence it is
called νόμισμα; for this renders all things commensurate;
for all things are measured by money. Let a house be A,
ten pounds B, a bed C; A then is the half of B, if a house
is worth or equal to five pounds; but let the bed C be the
tenth part of B; it is clear then how many beds are equal to
a house, namely, five. But that exchange was thus, before
coin was used, is evident; for it makes no difference whether five beds, or the value of five beds, are given for a
house.

5. What therefore injustice is, and what justice, has been
discussed. But these things being determined, it is evident,
that acting justly is the mean between injuring and being
injured; for the one is the possessing more than is just, the
other less. Now the habit of justice is a mediocrity, not in
the same manner with the former virtues [k], but because it is
so in a mean [l]; and injustice belongs to the extremes. And
justice is the habit in which a just man is said to be apt to
practise that which is just from deliberate choice, and fit to
distribute justly both between himself and another man, and
between two other persons; not in such a manner, as [to
allot] the greater share of the eligible to himself, and the
less to his neighbour, and the contrary of what is hurtful;
but allotting that equality which is according to proportion;
in like manner also between two different persons. The
habit of injustice, on the other hand, is practical of what is
unjust; and this is the excess and defect of what is profitable
or injurious contrary to proportion. Wherefore injustice is
excess and defect, because it belongs to excess and deficiency;

k The difference between the habit of justice (δικαιοσύνη) and all the
other virtues is, that δίκαιον, the subject matter of δικαιοσύνη, is itself a
mean.

l Which mean is the δίκαιον.

as to the person himself, the excess of what is in itself profitable, and the defect of what is injurious : and between
other men, the whole act is similarly unjust; but the viola-
tion of proportion leans to whatever side chance directs.
And of unjust action, the less is to be injured; the greater,
to injure. Concerning justice and injustice, what is the nature of each, let it be discussed in this manner : in like
manner also of the just and unjust universally.

CHAP. VI.

The question is proposed, in what way a man must commit an
act of injustice, in order to be called unjust : which leads to a
distinction between abstract and political justice.

1. BUT since it may happen, that he who does an unjust
action is yet not unjust, by perpetrating what kind of unjust
deeds is he consequently unjust in each species of injustice ?
is it, for instance, by doing it as a thief, or adulterer, or as a
robber would do it ? Or will there be no difference in that
respect ? for a person may have connection with a woman,
knowing who she is, yet not originally from deliberate choice,
but through passion. He therefore acts unjustly, but is not
an unjust man; for instance, he is not a thief, yet he has
stolen ; nor an adulterer, yet he has committed adultery ;
and in like manner in the other crimes.

2. But it must not escape us, that the object of our enquiry is both abstract justice, and political justice[m]; but

---

[m] This distinction of abstract and political justice is necessary in order
to answer the above question. For if we judge a man by abstract justice,
he must be pronounced unjust, when he barely performs an act of injustice : but as such a decision will often be erroneous, we must not consider the nature of the act abstractedly, but we must look to political
justice, and observe when a man is rewarded or punished for his actions,
as that will decide, when he is really and habitually just or unjust.

this last takes place amongst those, who have society together to the end that they may have a sufficiency, they being free and equal, either by proportion, or according to number[n]. So that as many as have not this, have not political justice towards each other, but a species only of justice, and that by similarity. For justice exists amongst those, with whom there exists law also towards each other; but law exists where injustice is; (for judgment is the determination of what is just and unjust,) and among whomsoever there is injustice, there is also among these the doing unjust actions; but where the acting unjustly is, there is not always injustice. But this [the acting unjustly] consists in the distributing to one's self the greater share of things simply good, and the less of things simply bad. Hence we do not suffer man to rule, but reason; because he does this for himself, and becomes a tyrant. But he who rules is the guardian of justice; and if of justice, of equality also. But, since there appears to be no greater good accruing to him, at least if he is a just man; (for he does not allot to himself the greater share of what is simply good, unless the proportion comes to him; on which account he acts for another, and consequently they say that justice is another man's good, as has been mentioned also before.) Some reward then must be presented; and this is honour and distinction; but all those to whom these things are not sufficient become tyrants.

3. But the justice between master and servant, and between father and child, is not the same with these, but similar; for there is not injustice simply towards a man's own property; but the slave, and the child, as long as he is of a certain age, and is not separated, is as a part of himself; but no man deliberately chooses to hurt himself. Hence there is no habit of injustice towards a man's self. Consequently there is no political injustice, nor justice: for it was stated to be according to law, and among persons with whom law

[n] That is, either actually equal, as in a pure democracy; or having an equality of rights, but a distinction of ranks.

naturally existed; but these were they, who had in possession an equality of ruling and being ruled. Hence there exists justice rather towards a wife than towards children and slaves; for this is economical justice; but this also is different from political justice.

CHAP. VII.

Political justice divided into natural, and legal.   A definition of the terms used in speaking of justice and injustice.

1. But of political justice, one kind is natural, the other legal. The natural, which has the same power everywhere, and is not just from its being or not being decreed. The legal, which at first, whether it was enacted in this or the other way, made no difference, but after they have constituted it, it does differ; as the ransoming of prisoners for a mina, or the sacrificing a goat and not two sheep: again, as many laws as men enact on particular occasions, such as sacrificing to Brasidas and things agreed upon by public edicts.

2. But all [just] things appear to come to be such, [i. e. legal,] because that which subsists by nature is immoveable, and has the same power every where; as, the fire burns both here and with the Persians; but they see that just things are moved. Now this is not so, yet it is in a certain degree; nevertheless with the gods perhaps it never is so; but with us there is something moveable even by nature, but not every thing. But at the same time there is a certain justice by nature, and a certain other not by nature. Now which of the things capable of change is just by nature, and which is not so, but legal and enacted by compact, if both are equally moveable, is plain; and the same distinction will apply in other things°. For by nature the right hand is the better;

° The point most insisted on in this chapter is, that there is a natural justice, although even that is in some cases liable to change: and the chief argument is, that an exception does not overturn a general rule.

nevertheless it is possible that some should have the use of both hands equally. But things which are just from compact and utility are similar to measures; for the measures of wine and corn are not in all places equal; but where men buy, they are larger; where they sell, smaller[p]. In like manner also just things which are not natural, but human, are not the same in every place; since neither is the form of government the same; but one only is every where according to nature, namely the best.

3. But of things just and legal, each bears the same reference to actions, as universals to particulars; for the things done are many; but each of the former, viz. justice and injustice, is one: for they are universal. But an injury and injustice differ; so do a just action and justice; for injustice exists by nature, or compact. But this, when put in practice, is an unjust action; but before it was committed, it was not so yet, but unjust; and in a similar manner also is a deed of justice. Moreover the common act is called rather δικαιοπράγημα; but δικαίωμα is the correction of an unjust action. But how many and what are the species of each of these individually, and what things they are conversant with, must be investigated at a future time.

CHAP. VIII.

We return to the question proposed in chap. 6. and from a consideration of the voluntary and involuntary, we conclude that, to constitute a man just or unjust, it is necessary that the deeds be accompanied with deliberate choice.

1. Now just and unjust things being what were mentioned above, a man does unjustly and acts justly, when he does

[p] It is difficult to understand this remark: perhaps the meaning is, that in importing countries the measures are larger, in exporting countries they are smaller.

them voluntarily; but when he acts involuntarily, he neither acts unjustly, nor acts justly, except by accident; for they do such things, as *happened* to be just or unjust. But an unjust and just deed are determined by the voluntary and involuntary; for, when the thing is voluntary, it is blamed at the same time also, it is then an unjust action. So that it will be something unjust, but not yet an unjust action, unless the voluntary is added to it.

2. But I call that voluntary, as was stated before, which being amongst the things in his own power, a man does knowingly, and not ignorant of the person whom he acts upon, or the thing with which, or the thing for the sake of which; for instance, whom he strikes, and with what, and for the sake of what, and all those things, not from accident, nor by compulsion; as if a person seizing a man's hand should strike another with it; but the blow was not voluntary, for it was not in his power. But it may be that the man struck was his father, and that he knew that he was a man or one of those present, but was ignorant that he was his father. In like manner let the same distinction be made with regard to motive, and the whole action. But that which is unknown, or which, though not unknown, yet is not in the power of him who acts, or is done by compulsion, is involuntary; for we both perform and endure many of the things which come to us by nature knowingly, none of which are either voluntary or involuntary, as, to grow old, or to die. But accident takes place both in unjust things and just: for should a person restore a deposit unwillingly and through fear, he cannot be said either to do just things, or practise justice, except by accident. So also we should say, that he who by compulsion and unwillingly does not restore a deposit, injures and performs unjust things by accident. But of things voluntary, we do some with deliberate choice, others without deliberate choice; with deliberate choice, as many as we do having first deliberated; but without deliberate choice, as many as we do not having first deliberated.

3. Now there being three kinds of harm in the intercourse of men, those accompanied with ignorance are errors, when

a man does these things neither to the person, nor in the manner, nor with the instrument, nor from the cause that he conceived, for he thought either that he should not strike, or not with this instrument, or not this person, or not for this end, but an event followed, not with the motive he thought; for instance, he did it, not that he might wound, but that he might prick him; or not this person, or not in this manner. When therefore the harm follows unintentionally, it is a misfortune; but when it happens not unintentionally, yet without maliciousness, it is an error [q]; for a man errs, when the principle of the cause is in himself; but is unfortunate, when the principle is exterior. When however he does it knowingly, yet not having previously deliberated, it is an unjust deed; for instance, such things as befal men through anger and other passions, which are necessary or natural; for hurting and erring in these, they injure indeed, and the deeds are unjust; nevertheless they are not for those reasons unjust men, nor wicked; for the harm was not done through villany. But when it is done from deliberate choice, he is unjust and vicious. Hence things proceeding from anger are rightly judged not to proceed from forethought; for it is not he who acts from anger that is the principle, but he who irritated him. Moreover the question is not concerning the thing being done or not, but concerning the justice of it; for anger is roused at the appearance of injustice. For it is not as in dealings of commerce that they dispute concerning the fact, when one of the parties must be vicious [r], unless they do so from forgetfulness; but being agreed as to the fact, they dispute whether it is just. But he, who plots the harm, is not ignorant. So that the one person

---

[q] If A throws a stone at B, meaning only to hit him, but happens to kill him, it is an error. But if he throws the stone into the air, to make an experiment, or for any other cause, and it happens to fall upon B and kill him, it is a misfortune.

[r] If A says that he lent B a sum of money, and B denies it, one of them must be vicious, unless they forget: for either A must have said what was not true, or B must have denied what was true.

thinks he is injured, the other thinks he is not. But if he
hurts from deliberate choice, he injures; and in such unjust
actions as these a man injuring is consequently unjust, when
it is contrary to proportion, or equality. In like manner is
a man just also, when he practises justice with deliberate
choice; but he practises justice, if he only does it willingly.
But of involuntary actions some are pardonable, others unpardonable; for as many things as men do amiss not only
ignorantly, but also through ignorance[s], are pardonable;
but as many things as are done, not through ignorance, but
ignorantly, yet through a passion neither natural nor human, are unpardonable.

CHAP. IX.

To constitute an injury it must be a harm inflicted against a
man's will. That he who distributes the greater share to an-
other is the person who does the injury. That it is no easy task
to be just, though to act unjustly is in our power.

1. BUT one might doubt, whether the question concerning
being injured, and injuring, has been satisfactorily discussed.
First, whether the case is, as Euripides has said absurdly
enough, " I have killed my mother; the story is short, I
" willing killed her willing; or I was not willing and she was
" willing." For the question is, whether it is thus true, that
a person is injured voluntarily or not? or rather is it not altogether involuntary, just as injuring is altogether voluntary,
and consequently that it is altogether in the one way or the
other, as injuring is also altogether voluntary; or is it partly
voluntary, partly involuntary? In a similar manner may we
enquire concerning receiving one's due; for to practise jus-

---

[s] For the distinction between doing a thing through ignorance and ignorantly, see book iii. c. 1. sect. 8.

tice is altogether voluntary. So that it is reasonable, that as to being voluntary or involuntary, the receiving an injury and receiving one's due are similarly opposed in each. It would indeed appear absurd as to receiving one's due, if it were all voluntary; for some receive their due not willingly. Since one might question this also, whether every one who has suffered an unjust deed, is injured; is it not the same with receiving as with doing? for it is possible in both to obtain what is just by accident. But it is equally plain, that it is the same also in unjust things: for to perform unjust things is not the same with doing an injury; nor the suffering what is unjust the same with being injured. So is it also in practising justice and receiving one's due; for it is impossible to receive an injury, when there is no one who injures; or to receive one's due, when there is no one who does justice.

2. But if injuring is simply to hurt any one willingly, and willingly means knowing both the person, and the instrument, and the manner, but the incontinent man willingly hurts himself; then he might willingly be injured, and it would be possible for a man to injure himself. But this is one of the matters of dispute, whether it is possible for a man to injure himself. Again, a man willingly may through his incontinence be hurt by another willing; so that it would be possible for a man to be injured willingly. Or is the above definition not true, but must we add to hurting a man, knowing both the person, and the instrument, and the manner, its being also contrary to the other person's will? A person, therefore, is hurt willingly, and suffers unjust things; but no one is willingly injured; for no one wishes it, not even the incontinent; but he acts contrary to his will; for no man wills what he does not think to be good; but the incontinent does what he does not think that he ought to do. But he, who gives away his own, as Homer relates that Glaucus did to Diomed, "Golden for brazen armour, "the value of a hundred beeves for the value of nine," is not injured: for the presenting them is in his own power; but to be injured is not in his power, but there must be a

person who injures. Concerning the being injured, therefore, that it is not voluntary, is evident.

3. But of the questions we proposed, there are yet two to be discussed: whether he who has distributed the greater share beyond a man's worth, or he who receives it, injures; and whether it is possible for a man to injure himself. For if what was said first is possible, and he who distributes is the injurer and not he who possesses the greater part, if any one allots more to another than himself knowingly and voluntarily, this man injures himself; which moderate persons seem to do; for the equitable man rather takes the less part. Or is the matter not simply thus? for, it may happen, that he covets the greater share of some other good; for instance, of glory, or of what is in itself honourable. Again, this question is also solved from the definition of injuring; for he suffers nothing against his own will. So that he is not injured, at least not through this; but, if any thing, he is hurt only. Moreover, it is evident, that he who distributes injures, but not he who receives the greater part; for it is not the man to whom the injustice happens to come that injures, but he in whom is the doing this voluntarily; but this is in the person whence the principle of the action originates, which is in the distributer, not in the receiver. Again, since to act admits of several meanings, and it is possible that inanimate things kill, as the hand, and a slave at the command of his master; these things do not injure, but perform unjust things. Again, if a man has decided ignorantly, he does not injure according to legal justice, nor is his judgment unjust; yet he is in a certain manner unjust; for legal justice and the first sort [t] are different. But if he has knowingly decided unjustly, he is also himself desirous either of favour, or vengeance. Just therefore as when a person is party in an unjust action, so he who on these accounts judged unjustly, receives a greater share; for in the latter case

---

[t] In c. 6. sect. 2. justice was divided into abstract and political: by the *first sort* is meant the abstract, according to which a man would be unjust merely from doing an act which was in itself unjust without any intent.

he who adjudges the field, does not receive the field, but money.

4. But men are of opinion that to injure is in their power, and therefore that to be just is easy. But it is not so; for to have connection with the wife of a neighbour, and to strike a neighbour, or give money with one's hand, is easy and in their power; but to do these things thus and thus disposed is neither easy nor in their power. And in like manner to know just things and unjust they think is nothing clever, because it is not difficult to under-stand the things concerning which the laws treat; but these things are not just except by accident; but acted and dis-tributed in a certain manner they are just things. But this is a greater task than to know what things are wholesome; since there also it is easy to know honey, and wine, and hellebore, and burning, and cutting; but how it is necessary to apply these to healing, and to whom, and when, is as much a task, as being a physician. And for this same reason men suppose that to injure is no less the action of the just man : because the just man is no less but even more able to do each of these things : for he is able to have connection with a woman, and to give blows, and a brave man may throw away his shield, and turning away run to any side. But to be timid and unjust is not merely the doing these things, (except from accident,) but it is to perform these things disposed in a particular manner ; as also to physic and to heal is not merely the cutting or not cutting, or the administering or not administering medicines, but the doing this in a certain manner. But just things exist among those, with whom there is a participation of things in themselves good ; they have also excess and defect in them. For to some beings there is no excess of goods, as perhaps to the gods ; to others no particle is beneficial, as to the incurable and wicked, but all are noxious ; but to others they are goods to a certain extent : on this account the good is human.

_____'. X.

*Concerning equity, which is a superior kind of justice situated in
the breast of the good man, whereby he rectifies the general
terms of the law, and applies them in a softer sense to particular cases.*

1. It now follows that we speak concerning equity and
the equitable, how equity has a reference to justice, and the
equitable to the just thing; for to those who examine this
subject, it neither appears as simply the same, nor as different in genus. And sometimes we praise the thing which
is equitable, and the man of that character; so that in praising we even transfer to other things instead of the term
good the term equitable, thereby shewing that it is better.
Sometimes again it appears absurd to us when we follow
the reasoning, that the *equitable* being something beyond the
just is praiseworthy; for either the just is not equitable, or
the equitable is not just, if it is a different thing; or if both
are good, they are the same.

2. The doubt therefore concerning the equitable arises
almost entirely from these things. Now all these are in a
certain view right, and in no respect contradictory to one
another; for the equitable, inasmuch as it belongs to one
sort of justice, is a better species of justice, and not as being
any other genus, is it better than justice. The just and the
equitable, therefore, are the same; and both being excellent,
the equitable is better [u]. But this creates the difficulty, that
the equitable indeed is just, yet not the just according to the
law, but the rectification of the legal justice. And the reason is this, that every law speaks universally; but concerning some things it is impossible to speak correctly and universally. In whatever things then it is necessary to speak
universally, and it is impossible it should be correctly, the

[u] The comparison can in fact never be made whether justice or equity
would decide the same cause best; for equity is only called in where justice cannot be applied.

law assumes the general case, though it is not ignorant of the defect. Nor is it therefore less right; for the fault is not in the law, nor in the legislator, but in the nature of the thing; for, from the first the matter of the subjects of action is of this kind. When, therefore, the law expresses itself universally, and something turns out in these matters besides the universal, then it is right, where the legislator is deficient, and erred by speaking universally, to rectify that which was omitted, which indeed the legislator, if he were present, would thus have said; aud if he had known it, he would have enacted accordingly.

3. Hence it is justice, and better than a certain kind of justice; not better than that which is abstractedly just, but than the defect which arises from its being abstract. And this is the nature of the equitable, the rectification of the law where it is deficient from being universal; for this is the reason that all things are not according to law, because it is impossible that a law should be enacted concerning some things. So that there is need of a decree; for of the indefinite, the rule also is indefinite, as of a Lesbian building ˣ the rule is leader; for the rule is altered to suit the figure of the stone, and is not fixed; and so is a decree, to suit the circumstances. What, therefore, the equitable is, and what sort of justice it is, and better than what kind of justice, is clear. It is moreover evident from this, who the equitable man is: for he who is apt deliberately to choose these things, and ready to perform them, and who is not strictly just on the worse side, but ready to make allowances, though he has the law to support him, is equitable; and this habit is equity, being a species of justice and not a different kind of habit.

ˣ That style of building is here alluded to, in which the stones were not put together, so as to form one even surface, but each stone alternately projected and retired.

CHAP. XI.

The question of a man being able to injure himself is considered both in universal and particular justice.

1. WHETHER it is possible for a man to injure himself or not, is evident from what has been said; for one part of justice is that which is ordained by the law in reference to the whole of virtue; for instance, the law does not command a man to kill himself; but, what it does not command, it forbids. Again, when a person hurts another contrary to the law, not hurting in revenge, he injures willingly; and he acts willingly, who knows both the person, and the instrument, and the manner. But he who cuts his own throat through rage, perpetrates that willingly contrary to right law, which the law permits not. Consequently he injures; but whom? is it not the state, and not himself? for he suffers voluntarily; but no man is injured voluntarily. Hence also the state punishes him, and a certain disgrace is attached to him who has destroyed himself, as to one who injures the state. Again, with respect to a man being unjust, who only commits an act of injustice, without being entirely depraved, [i. e. in particular injustice,] it is not possible for a man to injure himself; for this head of injustice is different from the other; for the unjust man is in a manner depraved, in the same manner that the timid man is; not as having the whole of depravity. So that neither in this injustice does he injure himself; for the same thing might at the same time be subtracted from and added to the same person; but this is impossible; but it is necessary that the unjust and just should always exist between more persons · than · one. Again, injuring is voluntary, and from deliberate choice, and an act of aggression ʸ: for he who, because he has suffered, repays the same, appears

---

ʸ If A injures B, the act of A must precede any act of B: but if A injures himself, it cannot be said that the act of A precedes the act of A, for there is only one act.

not to injure; but he who hurts himself both suffers and performs the same things at the same time. Besides, it would then be possible for a man to be injured willingly. And besides these things, no man commits an injury without its being one of the particular acts of injustice; but no man commits adultery with his own wife, nor breaks through his own wall, nor steals his own property. But on the whole that a man should injure himself is refuted, according to the definition concerning being voluntarily injured.

3. It is moreover obvious, that both are bad things, the being injured and injuring; for the one is to have less, the other to have more than the mean; which is like what is salutary in the medical art, and what in the gymnastic art is productive of a good habit of body. But at the same time to injure is the worst of the two; for to injure was stated to be joined with viciousness, and to be blameable; and that viciousness either perfect and simply so, or that which is nearly so; for every thing voluntary is not attended by injustice; but the being injured is without viciousness and injustice. In itself therefore to be injured is a less evil; but by accident nothing prevents its being the greater evil. But that has nothing to do with art; but art calls a pleurisy a severer disease than a stumble; and yet the other by accident may become the greater, if it should happen to a person stumbling to be taken by the enemy, in consequence of his fall, and to be slain.

4. But by metaphor and similitude, there is indeed no justice between a man and himself, but between certain parts of himself. Not, however, every kind of justice, but that between master and slave, or the economic; for in this manner the part of the soul possessing reason is distinct from the irrational[z]. To which men consequently refer, and think that there is injustice from a man towards himself, be-

---

[z] See book i. c. 13. sect. 7. where it was said that the irrational part of the soul obeys the rational, like a child obeys its father: so that when a child commits an act of injustice against its father, it is considered to be like the irrational part opposing the rational.

cause it is possible in this sense to suffer something contrary to their desires. As therefore the governor and governed have a certain justice between themselves, so also have these parts. Concerning justice, therefore, and the other moral virtues, let a discussion be made in this manner.

ARISTOTLE'S ETHICS.

—◆—

BOOK VI.

—◆—

CHAP. I.

*He proves the necessity of explaining the nature of right reason;
and, for this purpose, divides the rational part of the soul into
the scientific, (ἐπιστημονικὸν,) and the reasoning or ratiocina-
tive part (λογιστικόν.)*

1. BUT since we have before observed that it is necessary
to choose the mean, not the excess, nor the defect; and
since the mean is as right reason directs, let us discuss this
subject more fully. For in all the habits already described,
as well as in other things, there is a certain mark, to which
he, who possesses reason, looks, and is thereby more intent
or remiss [in exertion]; and there is a certain boundary of
the means, which we say are between excess and defect,
being according to right reason [a]. Now [simply] to say so is
true indeed, but not at all perspicuous: for in other pursuits in which science is employed, it is a truth to say, that
it is not fit to labour or relax, too much or too little, but
moderately, and as right reason [directs]. But a man having
received this alone, would not know any thing the more:
for instance, [he would not know] what things ought to be
applied to the body, if any one was to say, that they are

---

[a] It is reason only which can settle the boundaries of the mean: i. e.
declare how far it can go without running either into excess or deficiency.

those which the medical art prescribes, and as one who possesses this [art] would. Hence it is necessary in treating of the habits of the soul also, that not only this be spoken with truth, but that it be also explained what right reason is, and what are the bounds[b] by which it acts.

2. The virtues of the soul then we have already divided, and some we have said belong to morals, others to intellect. Those then which belong to morals we have thoroughly examined ; and as to the others, having first spoken of the soul, let us proceed to treat of them. It has indeed been before observed, that there are two parts of the soul, one possessing reason, the other void of reason. And now a similar division of the part possessing reason must be made ; and let it be laid down, that those parts which possess reason are two, the one being that by means of which we contemplate those things whose principles cannot be otherwise than they are ; the other that whereby we contemplate those things which are contingent : for in [contemplating] things different in kind, it is necessary that the part of the soul also which is naturally formed for each be different in kind : if at least it is by similitude, and connection[c] [with objects], that they possess the knowledge of them. Let one of these parts then be termed the scientific, the other the reasoning part, for to deliberate and to reason are the same thing. But no one deliberates about those things which cannot exist otherwise. Wherefore of that part of the soul which possesses reason, the reasoning [or ratiocinative] part is one. We must see therefore what is the best habit of each of

---

[b] The meaning of the word ὅρος here is somewhat doubtful. I consider it as referring to the definition of moral virtue in book ii. c. 6. where it was said that the mean (μισότης) is ὡρισμένη λόγῳ, καὶ ὡς ἂν ὁ φρόνιμος ὁρίσιι : for there are two things which require explanation in that definition : first, what is to decide the limits of the mean ? which we are told is reason : secondly, to whom are we to look to see what *right* reason is ? and we are told to look to the prudent man.

[c] i. e. if the faculty which contemplates is in any way connected with the thing contemplated.

these.   For this is the virtue of each ; but [every] virtue [is best known] by reference to its peculiar work [d].

_____

CHAP. II.

The best work or ἔργον of each part is found to be truth; for it is truth which makes the ordinary work of each perfect.

1. Now there are three things in the soul, which influence action and truth [c], [viz.] sense, intellect, desire ; but of these, sense is the *principle* of no moral action : and this is evident from brutes having sense, but yet partaking of no moral action.   What, however, affirmation and negation are in the discursive power [of the soul], that pursuit and aversion are in desire.   So that since moral virtue is a habit joined with deliberate choice, and deliberate choice is desire attended by deliberation, it follows that reason must be true, and desire

[d] As the reasoning part of the soul has been divided into two parts, right reason must reside in one of them : and it must necessarily be the virtue or excellence of that part : we must therefore find the virtue, or (which is the same thing) the best habit of each part : but every habit is formed, and may therefore be known, by some particular work ; and the best habit will be known by discovering what is the best work, or ἔργον of that in which the habit resides : we must therefore find the best work, or ἔργον, of each part of the soul : for the best work will give us the best habit of each ; the best habit will give us the virtue of each ; and one of these virtues must be right reason.

[c] The investigation is begun by mentioning *action* and *truth*, because these are the ordinary employments or objects of the reasoning and scientific parts ; and to find how they are performed in the most perfect manner, is the same as to find the ἔργον : for the ἔργον is only the common employment performed well.   Therefore if intellect and desire (νοῦς καὶ ὄρεξις) influence every action, if we can discover what makes intellect and desire perfect, we shall have the action perfect ; and consequently we shall know the ἔργον of the reasoning part of the soul.

right, if the deliberate choice is good[f]. and the one [reason] must assent to, and the other [desire] pursue, the same things. This discursive power of the soul then, as well as this truth, are adapted for action.

2. But of that discursive power of the soul which is contemplative, and not practical, nor effective, the excellence and the fault are, truth[g] and falsehood, for this is the work of the whole discursive power. But of that power which is practical as well as discursive, truth, existing agreeably to right desire.

3. The principle therefore of action, whence motion proceeds, is deliberate choice, but not the causal principle[h]. But the principles of deliberate choice are desire, and that reason[i] which has some end in view : wherefore deliberate choice is not without intellect and the discursive power, nor is it without moral habit. For good conduct and the contrary of this in action, is not without the discursive power of the soul, and moral character. But it is not this discursive power that causes any motion, unless it is that which has some end in view and is practical. For this directs the producing part also. For every one that produces any thing does so on account of some particular thing : and that which is effected is not in itself the end, but has a reference to something, and belongs to something ; but not so that, which is the subject of action. For good conduct is the end

---

[f] i. e. before the deliberate choice can be good, the desire must be morally good, and reason must assent on true principles, which last is the most important.

[g] Truth therefore is at once the ordinary employment and the ἔργον of the scientific part : for in necessary truths there are no degrees of certainty, and nothing can make one truth more perfect than another.

[h] Two things may be called the principles of action : either the ulterior object, for sake of which we first think of the action : or that result of our deliberations, which tells us how we are to begin the action : the last is προαίρεσις.

[i] By desire and reason are here meant the same things which were called intellect and desire at the beginning of the chapter : and when they were said to influence action, it was, because they influence deliberate choice, which is the principle of action.

[of action], and desire aims at this.   Hence deliberate choice is intellect operating upon desire, or desire guided by intellect: and such a principle is man.

5. Nothing however already effected is an object of deliberate choice.   For instance, no one deliberately chooses to raze Troy.   For a person does not consult about the past, but about the future, and contingent.   For a thing that is done cannot be undone.   Wherefore Agatho has rightly said,

> Of one thing only God is not possess'd,
> That to undo, whatever has been done.

The work then of both the intellectual parts of the soul is truth.   The habits, therefore, according to which each of these parts declares the truth most correctly, are the virtues of both [k].

CHAP. III.

The intellectual virtues are divided into five, viz. intellect, science, wisdom, art, and prudence: science is shewn to be a demonstrative habit, and conversant with things necessarily and eternally subsisting.

1. COMMENCING therefore a deeper investigation of the subject, let us again speak concerning these [virtues].   Let those things then, by which the soul arrives at truth, in af-

---

[k] The substance of this intricate chapter seems to be this: the reasoning and scientific parts of the soul are always directed to action and truth respectively.   The motive principle of action is deliberate choice: and deliberate choice may be resolved into desire, (which chooses the end,) and reason, (which assents to the choice of means:) so that in order for the deliberate choice and the action to be good, reason must assent on true principles: therefore truth is the employment or ἔργον of the reasoning part; but it is truth harmonizing with good desires.   It requires no demonstration to shew that truth is the ἔργον of the scientific part.

firming or denying, be five[1] in number ; and these are, art, science, prudence, wisdom, intellect. For it is incidental to conception and opinion to be wrong.

2. What science is then, is manifest from this [which follows], if we must examine [the matter] accurately, and not follow similitudes. For we all have a conception of that which cannot subsist otherwise than it does ; but as to those things which may subsist otherwise, when they are out of our contemplation, it is hid from us whether they exist, or not[m]. The object therefore of science has a necessary existence ; therefore it is eternal. For those things which exist in themselves by necessity, are all eternal. But things eternal are increate, and incorruptible.

3. Moreover all science appears to be capable of being taught, and the object of science of being understood, by learning. Now all doctrine is derived from things previously known, as we have said in our analytics. For one part of it is obtained by induction, the other by syllogism. Induction is a principle, and belongs to universals ; but syllogism is composed of universals. Therefore there are certain principles of which syllogism is made up, and of which there is no syllogism, [i. e. which cannot be proved by syllogism.] Therefore there is an induction of them.

4. Science therefore is a demonstrative habit, and whatever else we have added to the definition of it in the analytics. For when a person believes in a manner that a thing is so, and when the principles are known to him, he has a

[1] For the soul seeks for truth in contingent matter for only two reasons ; either to perform some action, or to produce some work ; and the habit, which arrives at truth in the former is prudence, in the latter, art. In necessary matter the soul either contemplates principles, in which case the habit, which arrives at truth is intellect (νοῦς); or it contemplates the conclusion drawn from principles, where the habit is science. But this science can only be perfect, when the same habit has discovered the truth both of the principles and conclusions; and the habit which does this is wisdom.

[m] This is a good distinction between necessary and contingent matter : a contingency only exists while it is being contemplated; the subjects of necessary matter are eternal.

scientific knowledge of it. For if the principles are not better known to him than the conclusion, he will have science accidentally only. Concerning the distinctions of science therefore let it suffice to have spoken in the above manner.

CHAP. IV.

Concerning art; that it is a habit of the mind joined with true reason, productive, and conversant with things contingent.

1. OF that, however, which may subsist otherwise than it does, there is part which is the subject of production, and part which is the subject of action. But production and action are different: (and concerning these we trust to the exoteric discussions:) so that the practical habit which is joined with reason is different from the productive habit which is joined with reason. Neither are they contained, one by the other. For action is not production, nor production action.

2. But since building is a certain art, and the same as a productive habit in conjunction with reason; and since there is neither any art, which is not a productive habit in conjunction with reason, nor any such habit, which is not an art; art and productive habit in conjunction with true reason must be the same.

3. Every art, however, is conversant with generation, and producing the work of the art, and contemplating how some one of those things, which may exist, or not exist, and whose principle is in the producer, not in the thing produced, may be generated. For art belongs neither to those things which exist or are generated from necessity, nor yet to those which exist according to nature; for these contain the principle in themselves. Since, however, production and action are different, art must belong to production, and not to action.

4. Also chance and art are in a certain manner conversant with the same things, as Agatho also says,

Art loves fortune, as does fortune art.

Art therefore, as has been said, is a certain productive habit in conjunction with true reason. The absence of art, on the contrary, is a productive habit in conjunction with false reason, conversant with that which may subsist otherwise than it does.

CHAP. V.

Concerning prudence; that it is a habit of the mind in conjunction with true reason, practical of human good and evil, and conversant with things contingent.

1. WE shall gain a knowledge of prudence by considering whom we call prudent. Now it appears to be the part of a prudent man to be able to deliberate well upon those things which are good and expedient for him, not in part, as what things are conducive to health and strength; but what things are conducive to a good life universally. And a proof of this is, that we call men prudent in some particular thing, when, with a view to arrive at some particular end, they reason well in things of which there is no art. Wherefore he who is able to deliberate, is wholly prudent.

2. No one, however, deliberates upon those things which cannot be otherwise than they are, or which are impossible to him to perform. So that if science be attended with demonstration, and if there be no demonstration of those things whose principles may be otherwise than they are, (for all these [things] may subsist otherwise than they do,) and if there is no deliberation upon those things which exist from necessity, prudence can not be a science, nor an art: not a science, because the subject of

action may subsist otherwise than it does: and not an art, because the genus of action, and production, is different.

3. It remains therefore, that it be a true habit in conjunction with reason, practical about those things that are good and bad for man. For the end of production is something else [than production itself]; but the end of action is not always something else [than the action itself]. For acting well is itself an end of action. Hence we deem Pericles and others of the same class prudent men, because they can contemplate the things that are good for themselves, and for men in general; but such we deem the economical and political men to be.

4. Whence we give temperance its name σωφροσύνη, as preserving prudence. But it preserves such a conception of the mind as we have described; for the pleasant and the painful do not corrupt or pervert every conception of the mind[n]: for instance, [they do not corrupt or pervert the conception] that a triangle has or has not its angles equal to two right angles: but those only which are conversant with that which is the subject of action. For the principles of the subjects of action are that on account of which things that are the subjects of action are performed. But to him that has been corrupted by pleasure, or pain, the principle will not appear at all, nor will it appear to him that for the sake, and because of this, he ought to choose and perform every thing. For vice is destructive of the principle. Wherefore prudence must be a true habit joined with reason, practical about human goods.

5. Moreover, of art there is a virtue, but of prudence there is not[o]. And in art indeed, he that errs voluntarily is pre-

[n] The etymology of σωφροσύνη is σώζειν φρόνησιν. The property of temperance is to preserve the habit of deliberating well upon human good, and acting accordingly. The inference from these two statements is, that φρόνησις must be that habit.

[o] Having examined the two habits in contingent matter separately, we proceed to compare them, that we may discover which is the best: first, there are degrees of excellence (ἀρετή) in art, so that one art excels another, and some art must therefore be imperfect: but there are no de-

ferable to the contrary character: but in prudence, the
former is inferior to the latter, as well as in the virtues. It
is evident, therefore, that prudence is a certain virtue, and
not an art. But as the rational parts of the soul are two, it
must be the virtue of one, viz. the part conceptive of opinion.
For opinion and prudence are conversant with that which
may subsist otherwise than they do. Nor yet is it only a
habit joined with reason: and a proof of this is, that there
may be oblivion of such a habit, but of prudence there can
not.

CHAP. VI.

*Concerning intellect; that it is employed in the knowledge of
principles.*

1. SINCE, however, science is a conception of the mind,
engaged in universals, and in those things that exist from
necessity, and since there are principles of things demonstrable, and of every science; (for science is joined with
reason;) it will be neither science, nor art, nor prudence,
which discovers the principle of the subject of science. For
the subject of science is demonstrable; and the two others
(viz. art and prudence) are conversant with things that may
subsist otherwise than they do; neither therefore is it
wisdom; for the wise man must have demonstration in
certain things. If therefore those parts of the soul, by
which we declare the truth, and are never mistaken, in
things that may, or may not, subsist differently, are science,

grees in prudence; for a man is not called prudent, until he is able to
deliberate and act rightly; and if he could have deliberated or acted better, he was not a prudent man: secondly, when an artist errs voluntarily,
he is considered better *as an artist* than one who errs from ignorance;
though he may be considered worse *as a man:* but in prudence there can
be no such thing as voluntary error.

and prudence, and wisdom, and intellect[p], and if neither of
the three first has to do with the knowledge of principles;
I mean the three, prudence, wisdom, science; it remains that
intellect is that which discovers principles.

CHAP. VII.

*Concerning wisdom; that it is composed of science and intellect;
it is different from, and superior to, prudence, because its objects are divine and eternal, but those of prudence contingent.*

1. WISDOM in the arts, we attribute to those who are
most accurately skilled in the arts: for instance, we call
Phidias a wise sculptor, and Polyclitus a wise statuary: here,
therefore, signifying nothing else by wisdom than that it
is the excellence of art. But some men we deem wise universally, not partially; nor do we deem them any thing else
than wise, as Homer says in his Margites,

> The gods, nor miner him, nor yet a ploughman made,
> Nor wise in any other thing.

Wherefore it is manifest that wisdom be the most accurate
of the sciences. It is necessary then that the wise man
not only know those things which follow from the principles, but also arrive at truth about the principles[q].

2. Consequently wisdom will be composed of intellect and
science; and being, as it were, the head, it will be a science
of the most honourable things. For it would be absurd if

---

[p] Art is omitted, because the same reasons exclude it, which exclude
prudence; and it has already been shewn to be inferior to prudence.

[q] It is allowed that in art, the term wisdom and skill is applied to those,
who are most accurate in the **art**: therefore when we are talking of intellectual skill, or wisdom, we must make it the most accurate of the sciences: but knowledge or science cannot be entirely accurate or perfect,
unless the principles are known as certainly as the conclusions.

any one should think that the political science, or prudence,
is the best [science], unless man be the best of all things in
the world. If then one thing is salubrious and good to
man, and another to fishes, but what is white and straight is
always the same; all men will also say, that wisdom is always the same, but prudence is different at different times.
For they would say, that the being, who has a perfect view
of particulars pertaining to himself, is prudent, and to him
they would commit these particulars. Hence we say that
some brutes are prudent, viz. as many as seem to have a
power of forethought as far as regards their own life.

3. It is evident, however, that the political science and
wisdom cannot be the same. For if they denominate that
science, which is employed about things profitable to individuals, wisdom, there will be many kinds of wisdom. For
it is not one science that is employed about the good of all
animals, but a different one about that of each. Unless
there is also but one medical science that is employed about
all beings.

4. But whether men say that man is the best of all other
animals, matters not[1]; since there are other things much
more divine than man in their nature; for instance, those
visible objects of which the universe is composed. From
what has been said, therefore, it is clear that wisdom is
both a science and an intelligence of things most honourable
by nature. Hence men say, that Anaxagoras, and Thales,
and others of the same class, are wise, but not prudent,
when they see that they are ignorant of what is advantageous to themselves. And they allow that they understand
things that are extraordinary, and wonderful, and difficult,
and divine, but useless, because they seek not human goods;
but prudence is conversant with human goods, and such as
it is possible to deliberate about. For this, viz. to deliberate

---

[1] It was observed before, that prudence could not be better than wisdom,
because man is not the best of all things in the world: nor if it be insisted that man is better than all other animals could the superiority of
prudence be proved.

well, we say is especially the work of the prudent man. But no one deliberates about those things which cannot subsist otherwise than they do, nor about those things of which there is not some end, and this too, a practical good. He, however, deliberates well universally, who by reasoning aims at that practical thing which is best for man.

5. Neither indeed is prudence of universals alone, but it ought to be acquainted with particulars also; for it is of a practical nature: and action is conversant with particulars. Hence, some who have not scientific knowledge are more capable of action than some who have, and in other things the experienced [are more capable of action than mere theorists]. For although a person know that light flesh is easily digested, and productive of health, but is ignorant what meat is light, he will not produce health; but he will rather produce it, who knows that the flesh of birds is light, and productive of health. Prudence, however, is of a practical nature. Wherefore it is necessary that we should have the knowledge of both, [i. e. universals and particular,] or rather the latter: but here also there must be a kind of super-excellent prudence.

CHAP. VIII.

Another distinction is shewn in prudence, viz. that which consults the good of the individual, and that which consults the good of all the members of the state. The latter has already been mentioned as political science. The connection between these two is shewn.

1. Now the political science, and prudence, are the same habit, but their essence is not the same[a]; and of the science that is engaged about a state, the one part being as it were

---

[a] The same definition will apply to both, viz. a habit of deliberating well upon human good, and acting accordingly.

a master prudence, is called legislative; the other, being like something particular, has the common name of political science [t]: and this is practical, and deliberative. For a decree is practicable, as being the last thing. Hence men say that this class of prudent men alone manage the affairs of a state. For these alone act, as artificers do [u].

2. But that appears to be especially prudence, which is employed about one's self, and an individual; and therefore it has the common name, prudence. But of the former [species of prudence [x]], one is economy, another legislation, another the political science: and of this last, one part is deliberative, and another judicial. Therefore to be acquainted with one's own affairs will be a certain species of knowledge: but it admits of great difference. And he who knows his own affairs, and engages himself in them, appears to be a prudent man: but those who are engaged in political affairs, are men of much business. Wherefore Euripides also says,

> Where was my prudence, who from trouble free,
> And number'd with the martiall'd multitude,
> Might fortune with the wisest heads have shar'd?
> For Jupiter officious persons hates,
> And those who will be busy to excess.

For the former seek their own good, and think it necessary to do this; from this persuasion of theirs, therefore, it arises that they are prudent men. Though perhaps it is not possible for one to be acquainted with his own affairs, without economy and policy. And again, how a man ought to administer his own affairs, is a thing unknown, and requiring consideration.

[t] It was stated at the end of the last chapter that the prudence *of the individual* was divided into general and particular: so also political prudence is divided into two, legislative, and that which is peculiarly called political. And these two divisions correspond to the two former ones.

[u] Both those who legislate, and those who pass decrees, are said πολιτεύεσθαι, but the latter more especially: like a stone mason (who is a χειροτέχνης) may more properly be said to build a house than an architect.

[x] i. e. the political prudence.

3. A proof of what we have said is, that young men may become geometricians and mathematicians, and wise in things of this sort : but [no young man] appears to become prudent. And the reason is, because prudence is concerned with particulars, which become known by experience. But a young man is not experienced : for it is length of time that produces experience ; since a man should consider this also, viz. why a boy may become a mathematician, but not [become] wise, or skilled in physiology ? Is it because those [i. e. the objects or principles of mathematics] are abstracted from particulars ; but the principles of these [i. e. of physics] are known by experience? And youths do not believe the latter, but repeat them only. But with respect to those, [i. e. principles of mathematics,] it is evident what they are[y]. Moreover, error in deliberating, is either with respect to the universal or the particular. For [it is an error in the universal, for instance,] not to know that all heavy waters are bad ; and [in the particular], that a certain water is heavy.

4. That prudence, however, is not a science, is evident ; because it relates to the last thing, as has been said : for whatever is practicable is such ; it is therefore opposed to intellect. For intellect has to do with terms, upon which there is no reasoning, [or which cannot be obtained by syllogism.] But prudence belongs to the extreme, of which there is no science, but sense ; not the sense by which we know the properties of bodies, but such as that by which we perceive in mathematics, for instance, that the last thing is a triangle[z] ;

[y] For they are axioms or self-evident propositions.

[z] In every demonstration there are two things, which are known not by deductions of reason, but by a kind of intuitive faculty : first, the first principles or axioms, which are proved by induction : secondly, some figure, e. g. a triangle, must be given : and the perception of the triangle, which is an object of sense, is the last thing before the demonstration begins : the last thing therefore, τὸ ἔσχατον, is discovered by sense ; but the faculty which discovers the properties of the triangle is different from this. So in contingent matter also there are two extremes, which are not discovered by reasoning, but by induction and sense, νοῦς and αἴσθησις : and Aristotle chooses afterwards to call both these by the name of νοῦς, because their office is the same.

for it will stop there. But this prudence is rather sense; but of the other there is a different species.

CHAP. IX.

Good deliberation is considered.

1. To investigate, and to deliberate, are different. For to deliberate is to investigate something. But we must thoroughly comprehend good deliberation, what it is, whether it be a science, or opinion, or right conjecture, or some other genus. Now it is not a science, for men do not investigate what they know. But good consultation is a kind of deliberation; and he who deliberates, investigates and reasons. Nor yet is it right conjecture; for right conjecture is not joined with reason, and is something hasty. But men deliberate for a long time, and they say, that it is necessary, indeed, speedily to put into execution what has been deliberated upon, but to deliberate slowly. Moreover, sagacity and good deliberation are different. But sagacity is a kind of right conjecture. Neither indeed is any good deliberation, opinion. But since he who deliberates badly, errs, and he who deliberates well, deliberates rightly; it is evident that good deliberation is a kind of rectitude: but not of science, nor of opinion. (For of science indeed there is no rectitude, because there is no error. But truth is the rectitude of opinion. Besides, every thing of which there is an opinion, has been already determined, [but not so the object of good deliberation.] Moreover, good deliberation is not without reasoning; and therefore is inferior to the discursive power, for it is not yet a declaration; whereas opinion is not an investigation, but an actual declaration; but he that deliberates, whether he deliberates well or ill, investigates something, and reasons.) But good deliberation is a

rectitude of deliberation. Wherefore deliberation must first be investigated, both as to what it is, and what it is conversant with. But since rectitude is predicated in various ways, it is evident that not every rectitude is good deliberation. For the incontinent and depraved will obtain from reasoning what they have proposed to see. So that they will have deliberated rightly, but will have received a great evil. But to deliberate well seems to be something good ; for such a rectitude of deliberation as is calculated to obtain good, is good deliberation. But it is possible to obtain even this by false reasoning; and to obtain that which it is proper to effect, and yet not by proper means, but the middle term may be false. Wherefore that is not yet good deliberation, according to which a person obtains indeed what he ought, but not by the means he ought. Again, it is possible for one person to obtain after deliberating for a long time ; and for another to obtain it by a hasty deliberation. Wherefore neither is this yet good deliberation. But that is rectitude of deliberation which is according to utility, and calculated to obtain what is proper, and in the manner, and time, which is proper. Moreover it is possible to deliberate well generally, and with a view to a certain end. That which is generally so is that which succeeds in obtaining an end generally; but the particular rectitude is that which succeeds in obtaining some particular end. If therefore, to deliberate well belong to the prudent, good deliberation will be that rectitude which is according to utility, directed to a certain end, of which prudence has the true conception.

CHAP. X.

Of intelligence: that it is not any science, or opinion, wholly or partially; and that it is not the same with prudence, though conversant with the same things: the origin of its name.

1. INTELLIGENCE, however, and the want of intelligence, according to which we call men intelligent or unintelligent, are not wholly the same with science, or opinion; otherwise all men would be intelligent. Nor is it any one of the particular sciences, as medicine, for then it would be conversant with things productive of health; or geometry, for it would be conversant with magnitudes. For intelligence is neither conversant with those things which always exist and are immoveable, nor with those things which are generated in any way: but it is conversant with those things about which any one would doubt, and deliberate. Wherefore it is conversant with the same things as prudence; and yet intelligence and prudence are not the same thing. For prudence is imperative; for the end of it is, what it is necessary to do, or not to do. But intelligence is only judicial. For intelligence and right intelligence are the same thing; since intelligent men are also rightly intelligent. Intelligence however is neither the possessing nor the receiving of prudence; but like as learning is said to be, understanding, when it employs science, the same is the case in using opinion to judge of those things, about which prudence is conversant, when another person speaks, and to judge well. For the doing of a thing rightly, is the same with doing it well. And hence the name intelligence[a] is derived, according to which men are denominated rightly intelligent, viz. from understanding in learning, for we frequently say, to learn, instead of, to understand.

---

[a] The σύνετος and εὐξύνετος seem to be men of quick understandings: who though not possessing prudence themselves, are yet able to understand the motives and reasons of the prudent man, and to decide rightly at his suggestion. Σύνεσις might perhaps be translated apprehension, and εὐξυνεσία right apprehension.

CHAP. XI.

*Of judgment, intelligence or apprehension, prudence, and
intellect.*

1. But that which is called judgment, according to which
we say that men are judicious, and possess judgment, is the
right decision of the equitable man. A proof of which is,
that we say that the equitable man is especially apt to pardon, and that it is equitable to pardon in some cases. But
pardon is the right judgment of the equitable man ; and the
right judgment is that of the man who follows truth.

2. All these habits however naturally tend to the same
thing ; for referring judgment, intelligence, prudence, and
intellect to the same persons, we say that they possess judgment, and with it intellect, and that they are prudent, and
intelligent. For all these faculties belong to extremes [b] and
particulars. And the intelligent man, and he who has good
judgment, or is apt to pardon, is engaged in judging of those
things with which the prudent man is conversant. For
equitable things are common to all good men in their dealings with others. But all practicable things belong to particulars and extremes. For the prudent man ought to know
these. And intelligence and judgment are conversant with
things practicable ; and these are extremes.

3. Intellect is conversant with the extremes on both sides.
For it is intellect, and not reason, which perceives both the
first and the last terms ; that part of it which is engaged in
demonstrations is conversant with immutable and first principles ; but that which is engaged in practical things, is of
the extreme, and of the contingent, and of the particular
proposition ; for these are the principles of that on account of

---

[b] By τὰ ἔσχατα is meant the last step, which immediately precedes the
action. The first principles, which are discovered by induction, are also
called τὰ ἔσχατα, but generally when the word is used without any addition, it signifies that last extreme which immediately precedes the action.
They are both extremes, inasmuch as one is the beginning or foundation,
the other the end of the deliberation.

which any thing is done. For the universe is derived from particulars; therefore we ought to have a sensible perception of these; and this is intellect.

4. Wherefore, these appear to be natural. Whereas no one is wise by nature, but he has judgment, and intelligence, and intellect, [by nature.] A proof of which is, that we suppose these to accompany the progress of age; and that this or that particular age has intellect and judgment, considering nature as the cause of them. For which reason intellect is the principle and the end; for from these demonstrations are derived, and with these they are conversant. So that we ought to attend to the undemonstrated enunciations and opinions of the experienced and aged, or prudent, no less than to their demonstrations. For, because they have an eye from experience, they perceive the principles. What, therefore, wisdom and prudence are, and with what things each is conversant, and that each of them is a virtue of a different part of the soul, has been [sufficiently] shewn.

CHAP. XII.

The utility of wisdom and prudence is shewn.

1. But some one may start a question respecting these, in what they are useful. For wisdom contemplates nothing whereby man may be happy; for it does not belong to any thing which produces. But prudence possesses this quality; and yet to what end is there need of it, if prudence is that which is conversant with what things are just, and honourable, and good to man; and these are those things which it is the part of the good man to practise? Neither are we by the knowledge of these the more capable of practice, if the virtues are habits; as, neither [are we more capable of practice by the knowledge of] the things that are productive of health, and a good habit of body, as many as are spoken

of not as consisting in the power of action, but from habit ; for we are not the more capable of practice from possessing the medical or gymnastic art. But if we must grant that a man is prudent not on account of his possessing these, but for the sake of becoming good, prudence will not be at all useful to those who are already virtuous. Neither, again, will it be useful to those who do not possess any [virtuous habit,] for it will make no difference whether they possess prudence themselves, or obey others who possess it. And this would be sufficient for us in this case, as it is also in the case of health. For although we wish to be in good health, still we do not learn the medical art.

2.. In addition to this, it would seem absurd if, being inferior to wisdom, it should have greater authority than it. For that which produces, rules and commands in every thing. Of these therefore we must treat. For as yet, we have only advanced questions about them.

3. First, then, we say that inasmuch as they are virtues, of each part of the soul, they must be eligible in themselves ; even if neither of them produce any thing. Again, they do indeed produce something ; not, however, as the medical art produces health ; but as health produces happiness, so does wisdom[c]. For, being a part of universal virtue, it renders a man happy by the possession of it, and by energizing. Besides, the work is completed according to prudence and moral virtue. For this virtue makes the mark right, but prudence those things that lead to it. Such a virtue, however, does not belong to the fourth part of the soul, which is nutritive ; for this has not the power of acting or not acting any thing.

4. But with regard to [the objection], that we are not by means of prudence more capable of practising things noble and just, we must begin a little further back, taking this for a principle. For as we say that some persons who perform

---

[c] Wisdom does not produce happiness like cause and effect ; but in the same manner as a person cannot be happy without health, although health does not produce happiness, so he cannot be happy without wisdom.

just things, are not yet just, such as those who do the things enjoined by the laws, either against their will, or through ignorance, or on account of any other thing, and not for the sake of the things themselves, although they do what things it is fit they should, and as many as a good man ought; so, as it seems, it is necessary to perform every thing with a certain disposition, in order to be a good man. But I mean, through deliberate choice, for instance, and for the sake of the things done : now virtue causes the deliberate choice to be right, but [to discern] what things are naturally necessary to be performed for the sake of it, is not the part of virtue, but of another faculty.

5. Of these things, however, we must speak with attention, and greater perspicuity. There is, therefore, a certain faculty which men call cleverness. And this is such, that whatever things tend to [the attaining of] the end proposed, it is able to perform the same, and to obtain them. If, therefore, the end proposed be good, this [faculty] will be laudable; but if bad, it will be craftiness. Hence we say that prudent men are clever, and not crafty. Prudence, however, is not this faculty, nor yet is it without this faculty. But in this eye, as it were, of the mind, the habit is produced not without virtue, as has been said before, and is evident. For the syllogisms [d] of practical things contain the principle ; since the end is of this kind, and the best thing, whatever it may be. For let the end, for instance, be any thing. But this does not appear, but to the good man. For vice perverts, and causes us to form a false judgment with respect to practical principles. Wherefore it is evident that a man cannot be prudent, who is not good.

[d] Reasonings in practical affairs are always with a view to some end, which end is the principle of action ; but if by the good man only a good end is proposed, and if this cannot be attained without prudence being employed in reasoning, the habit, prudence, is not acquired without virtue.

CHAP. XIII.

Virtue is divided into natural and perfect: by which the appa-
rent contradiction is explained, that virtue cannot be obtained
without prudence, nor prudence without virtue.

1. AGAIN, therefore, we must consider virtue. For virtue
bears a relation, like prudence does to cleverness, being not
the same thing, but similar: for in the same manner is natural virtue with respect to virtue properly so called. For
every moral character appears to subsist in a certain manner
in all by nature; for we are disposed to be just, and temperate, and brave, and possess other good qualities, immediately from our birth. Still, however, we seek something
else, in speaking of that which is properly good, and think
that things of this kind subsist after another manner. For
the natural habits subsist in children and brutes; but without intellect they appear to be noxious. Nay, so much as
this may be evidently seen, viz. that, as it happens to a strong
body that is moved without sight to stumble grievously, because it does not possess sight, so it is in the case of natural
virtue: but if it receive intellect, it excels in action; and
the habit being uniform, will then be properly virtue. So
that, as in that part of the soul which is conceptive of opinion there are two forms, viz. cleverness and prudence; so
in the moral part also there are two, the one natural virtue,
and the other virtue properly so called. And of these, virtue
properly so called is not produced without prudence[e]. Wherefore men say that the virtues are prudences. And Socrates
considered the question partly with correctness, and partly
he erred. For inasmuch as he thought that all the virtues

---

[d] So also prudence is not formed without natural virtue: for unless
natural virtue makes a man frequently choose a good end at first, cleverness (that natural faculty, which makes choice of the means) will never
ripen into prudence: so that we may truly say without arguing in a circle
that prudence is not formed without [natural] virtue: and [perfect] virtue
is not formed without prudence.

were prudences, he erred ; but [in saying] that they are not without prudence, he said well, and this is a proof of it : for all now, when they define virtue, having said what it has a reference to, add that it is a habit according to right reason. And that is right [reason] which is according to prudence. All therefore seem to have a kind of natural notion that a habit of this kind which is according to prudence, is virtue. We must, however, make a little digression. For it is not that habit only which is *according to* right reason, but also that which is in conjunction with right reason, that is virtue. And prudence is right reason in these things. Socrates, therefore, thought that the virtues were reasons ; for [he said] they were all sciences : but we [say they are] in conjunction with reason. Therefore it is evident from what has been said, that it is impossible to become perfectly good without prudence ; nor for a man to be prudent without moral virtue. But in this manner also, that reasoning may be refuted, by which any one might argue that the virtues are separated from one another, because the same person is not naturally fitted for all [of them] : so that he will have obtained one already, but not another. For this may be the case in the natural virtues ; but it is not the case in those according to which a man is said to be simply good. For they will at once all subsist together with prudence, which is but one. It is evident, however, that although it were not practical, still there would be need of it, because it is a virtue of a part [of the soul], and because deliberate choice will not be right without prudence, nor without virtue. For the one is the end ; and the other causes us to perform those things which tend to the end. Nevertheless it has no rule over wisdom, nor over the better part of the soul. As neither has the medical art over health. For it does not employ it, [health,] but sees how it may be affected. It prescribes, therefore, for its sake, but not to it. Besides, it would be just as if one were to say that the political science rules the gods, because it gives injunctions concerning all the affairs of a state.

ARISTOTLE'S ETHICS.

BOOK VII.

CHAP. I.

The subject of this seventh book stated: and some popular opinions with respect to continence and incontinence.

1. AFTER what has been already said, we must make [a] another beginning, and state, that there are three species of things to be avoided in morals, vice, incontinence, brutality. The contraries of two of these are evident: for we call one virtue, and the other continence: but as an opposite to brutality, it would be most suitable to name a virtue above human nature, a species of heroical and divine virtue, as Homer has made Priam say concerning Hector, to express his excessive goodness,

> ———— nor does he seem
> The son of mortal man, but of a god.

So that if, as people say, gods are formed from men on account of excess of virtue, the habit, which is opposed to brutality, would evidently be something of that kind: for in the same manner as there is no vice or virtue in a beast, so also there is not in a god: but the one is something more dig-

---

[a] The construction in the Greek is somewhat singular, λεκτέον ... ποιησαμένους. There is a similar construction in book viii. c. 13. sect. 4. and in Polybius, l. xii. c. 9.

nified than virtue; and the other, a different genus of vice.
But since the existence of a divine man is a rare thing, (as
the Lacedemonians, when they admire any one exceedingly,
are accustomed to say, He is a divine man:) so also the
brutal character is rare amongst men, and is mostly found
amongst savages. But some instances arise from diseases
and bodily imperfections: and those, who exceed human
nature in consequence of vice, we call by this odious name.
But concerning such a disposition as this we must make some
mention hereafter: and we have spoken concerning vice
before.

2. But we must treat of incontinence and effeminacy, and
of continence and patience: for we must neither form our
idea of each of them as of the same habits with virtue and
vice, nor as being a different genus. But, as in other cases,
we must state popular opinions; and after first mentioning
the difficulties, then prove if we can all the opinions that
have been entertained on the subject of these passions; but
if not that, the greatest number and the most important:
for if the difficulties are solved, and the opinions are left un-
contradicted, the subject would be explained sufficiently.

3. It is a common opinion then, first, that continence and
patience are amongst the number of things good and praiseworthy; but incontinence and effeminacy, amongst things
bad and reprehensible. Secondly, That the continent man is
the same with the man, who abides by his determination;
and the incontinent, with the man, who departs from his determination. Thirdly, And the incontinent man, knowing
that the things are bad, does them through passion; but the
continent man, knowing that the desires are bad, does not
follow them in obedience to reason. Fourthly, And they
think that the temperate man is continent and patient: but
as to the latter, some think that every one of them is temperate; others think not: and they call the intemperate
man incontinent, and the incontinent intemperate, indis-
criminately; but others say that they are different. Fifthly,
And as to the prudent man, sometimes they say it is impossible for him to be incontinent; at other times, that some

men both prudent and clever are incontinent. Sixthly,
Again, they are said to be incontinent of anger and honour
and gain. These are the opinions, that have been given.

--~~~~~~~--

CHAP. II.

*The different opinions stated in the last chapter are briefly con-
sidered here.*

1. A PERSON might doubt, how any one forming a right
conception is incontinent. Some say, that if he has certain
knowledge, it is impossible: for it is strange, as Socrates
thought, if knowledge exists in the man, that any thing else
should prevail, and draw him about like a slave. Socrates
indeed opposed the argument altogether, as if there was no
such thing as incontinence: for that no one forming a right
conception acted contrary to what is best, but only through
ignorance. Now this system is at variance with what we see
evidently; and we must enquire concerning this passion, if
it proceeds from ignorance, what kind of ignorance it is; for
that the incontinent man, before he is actually in the passion, does not think that it is right, is evident.

2. There are some who grant part of this, but not the
rest: for that nothing is superior to knowledge, they allow:
but that no one acts contrary to what appears best, they do
not allow: and for this reason they say, that the incontinent
man is overcome by pleasures, not having knowledge, but
opinion. But still if it is opinion, and not knowledge, nor a
strong conception, which opposes, but a weak one, as in
persons who are doubting, the not remaining firm to these
against strong desires is pardonable: but vice is not pardonable, nor any thing else which is reprehensible [b]. [If then

---

[b] And the first of those six opinions in the last chapter was that incontinence is reprehensible.

it is not a *weak* opinion], it must be prudence which opposes;
for this is the strongest.   But that is absurd; for then the
same man will at once be prudent and incontinent: but no
one would say that it is the character of the prudent man
willingly to do the most vicious things.   Besides this, it has
been shewn before, that the prudent man in particular is
distinguished in action : for he has to do with the last extremes, and possesses the other virtues.

3. Again, if the continent man consists in having strong
and bad desires; the temperate man will not be continent,
nor the continent temperate: for excess does not belong to
the temperate man, nor the possession of bad desires.   But
nevertheless the continent man must have them; for if the
desires were good, the habit, which forbids him to follow
them, is bad : so that every species of continence would not
be good ; and if they are weak and not bad, there is nothing
noble [in conquering them] : nor if they are bad and weak,
is there any thing great.

4. Again, if continence makes a man adhere to every opinion, it is bad; as, for instance, if it makes him adhere to
a false one: and if incontinence makes him depart from
every opinion, some species of incontinence will be good ; as
the Neoptolemus of Sophocles in the Philoctetes ; for he is
praiseworthy for not adhering to the persuasions of Ulysses,
because he felt pain in telling a lie.   Secondly ; Again, the
sophistical reasoning, called *Mentiens,* causes a difficulty[c] :
for because they wish to make the other party allow something contrary to his opinion, in order that they may appear
clever when they succeed, the syllogism, which is formed,
becomes a difficulty : for the intellect is at a stand, when it

[c] The whole of this section relates to the second of the six opinions in
the last chapter; and different absurdities are shewn to result from the
hypothesis, that the incontinent man is the same with him who departs
from his opinion.   The second absurdity is this: a sophist, by getting me
to allow his premises, makes me allow his conclusion, which common
sense tells me is false, but which I cannot refute : by allowing it therefore I have departed from my opinion, and consequently according to the
above hypothesis, I am incontinent : which is absurd.

does not wish to stop there, because the conclusion does not please; but it cannot advance, because it cannot solve the argument. Thirdly; And by one mode of reasoning it happens that folly in conjunction with incontinence becomes virtue; for it acts contrary to its conceptions on account of incontinence; but its conception was, that good was evil, and that he ought not to practise it: so that he will practise what is good and not what is evil [d]. Fourthly; Again, he who practises and pursues what is pleasant from being persuaded that it is right, and after deliberate choice, would appear to be better than the man [e] who does so not from deliberation, but from incontinence; for he is more easily cured, because he may be persuaded back again; whereas the incontinent man comes under the proverbial expression,

When water chokes, why need we drink it more [f]?

For if he had [g] been persuaded, that what he does is right, he might have been persuaded back again, and have desisted: but now although he is persuaded that it is not right, nevertheless he acts contrary to that conviction.

5. Again, if incontinence and continence are exhibited in every thing, who is the man who is simply called incontinent? for no man possesses every species of incontinence; but we say, that there are some simply so.

6. The difficulties are some such as these: and of these

d This is still upon the same hypothesis. Being foolish, (i. e. not having φρόνησις,) he will mistake good for evil: being incontinent, he will (according to that hypothesis) depart from his opinion, and act contrary to it: consequently he will unintentionally act virtuously.

e i. e. the intemperate man.

f When reason leads a man astray, or at least does not prevent him, what use is there in reasoning with him?

g I follow Lambinus in leaving out the negative: the argument is, that as the incontinent man reasons rightly up to the very commencement of the action, but then departs from his opinion and from reason, it is hopeless to reason with him; whereas the intemperate man, as he is only mistaken in his reasoning, might, if the thing was set properly before him, be brought to act well. The fallacy is solved in c. 8.

we must remove some, and leave others; for the solving of a difficulty is a discovery.

<hr/>

CHAP. III.

The third question is considered, whether the incontinent act contrary to the knowledge of their duty.

1. FIRST then we must consider, whether men are incontinent, knowing what is right, or no; and in what manner knowing. Secondly; Next, what we must call the subject matter of the continent and incontinent; I mean, whether it is every pleasure and pain, or some definite ones. Thirdly, and whether the continent and patient man are the same, or different. So also as many other subjects as are connected with this speculation. The beginning of the consideration is, whether the continent and incontinent differ in the subject, or in the manner: I mean, whether the incontinent man is incontinent merely from being employed in this particular thing; or whether it is not that, but it is in the manner; or whether it is not that, but it results from both. Next, whether incontinence and continence are displayed in every thing, or no: for he that is simply called incontinent, is not so in every thing, but in the same things with which the intemperate is concerned: nor is he so from merely having to do with these things, (for then it would be the same as intemperance,) but from having to do with them in a particular manner: for the one [the intemperate] is led on by deliberate choice, thinking that he should always pursue what is pleasant at the moment: the other does not think so, but still pursues it.

2. Now whether it be a true opinion, but not knowledge, in opposition to which men are incontinent, makes no difference as to the argument: for some of those who are in doubt, do not feel any doubt, but think that they know for

certain. If then those, who form opinions, in consequence of a weak assent to them act contrary to their conception more than those who have knowledge, knowledge will in no respect differ from opinion : for some trust to what they think, no less than others do to what they know : Heraclitus is an instance of this.

3. But since we speak of a man having knowledge in two ways ; (for he that possesses, but does not use his knowledge, as well as he that uses it, is said to have knowledge ;) there will be a difference between his doing what he ought not to do, when he possesses but does not use it, and when he possesses and uses it.

4. Again, since there are two kinds of propositions, [universal and particular,] nothing hinders a man from acting contrary to knowledge, when he *possesses* both ; that is, when he uses the universal but not the particular[h] : for particulars regulate action. There is a difference also in the universal ; for it partly relates to the person, and partly to the thing. As, for instance, a person knows that dry meats are good for every man ; and that *this* is a man, or that such and such a thing is dry ; but whether this is such and such a thing, either he does not possess the knowledge, or does not use it. In this manner there will be a vast difference : so that in one way there seems to be no absurdity, but in the other way it would be wonderful.

5. Again, it is possible for men to possess knowledge in a different manner from those that have been mentioned : for we see the habit differing, in consequence of a man possessing, but not using knowledge ; so that in a manner he has it and has it not ; such as the person who is asleep, or mad, or drunk. Now those who are under the influence of passions are affected in the same way : for anger, and sensual desires, and some such things as those, evidently even alter the body ; and in some they even create madness. It is

---

[h] Thus a man may *possess* the knowledge, that all intemperance is bad : and that drinking a particular quantity of wine is intemperance : but when he comes to act, he forgets, and does not use the latter.

evident therefore that we must say that the incontinent are
in a similar situation to these. But the fact of their using
expressions which must have proceeded from knowledge, is
no proof to the contrary; for those who are under these
passions, recite demonstrations and verses of Empedocles;
and those who are learning for the first time, connect sentences together, but do not yet understand them; for they
must grow up with them; and this requires time. So that
we must suppose the incontinent use these expressions in
the same manner as actors.

6. Again, one might take a view of the cause physically
in this manner. There is one opinion upon universals, and
another upon those particulars, which sense has the direction
of: and when one is formed from the two united, the soul
must necessarily assent to the conclusion, and if it is a practical matter must immediately act upon it: for instance, if
it is right to taste every thing sweet, and *this*, as being some
particular thing, is sweet, then the person, who has the
power and is not prevented, when he puts these two together, must necessarily act. When therefore one universal
opinion exists in the man, which forbids him to taste; and
another [universal one], that every thing sweet is pleasant,
and this particular thing is sweet; and the last universal
acts, and desire happens to be present; the first universal
tells him to avoid this particular thing, but desire leads him
on; for it is able to move each of the parts. So that he
happens in a manner to act incontinently from reason[i] and
from opinion: not that these two are opposed to each other
naturally, but accidentally: for it is the desire and not the

---

[i] For it is an act of reason to put the last universal and the particular
opinion together, and to draw an inference from them. The argument
is this: the man possesses two universal opinions; one, that it is wrong
to indulge in sweet things: the other, that all sweet things are pleasant:
he has also a particular opinion, viz. that *this* (whatever it may be) is
pleasant: now if this particular opinion was united to the first universal,
he would not taste it: if to the second, he would: and when desire exists
in him also, that together with the second universal overpowers the first,
and he tastes it: so that desire is really the cause.

opinion, which is opposed to right reason. So that for this reason brutes are not incontinent, because they have no universal conceptions, but only an instinct of particulars and memory. But how the [temporary] ignorance ceases, and the incontinent man again becomes possessed of knowledge, the case is the same with a man drunk or asleep, and is not peculiar to this passion; which case we must hear explained by physiologists. But since the last [i. e. the particular] proposition is an opinion formed by the sensitive part, and decides the actions, the man, who is under the passion, either does not possess this, or possesses it in such a way, that the possessing[k] it is not to have knowledge, but merely to repeat [what proceeds from knowledge], like the drunken man repeats the verses of Empedocles. And because the last extreme [i. e. the particular opinion] is not universal, and does not appear to convey knowledge so much as the universal, that which Socrates enquired into seems to be the fact: for the passion does not take place when that, which appears properly to be knowledge, is present; nor is this dragged about by the passion; but it is, when that opinion which is formed by sense is present. Concerning the question therefore of acting incontinently with knowledge, or without, and how it is possible to do so with knowledge, let this suffice.

CHAP. IV.

The sixth question is considered, viz. what is the subject matter of incontinence.

1. WE must next consider, whether any one is absolutely incontinent, or all are so in particular things; and if the former, what is the subject matter. Now that the continent and patient, the incontinent and effeminate appear so in

---

[k] I follow Lambinus in reading τὸ ἔχειν.

pleasures and pains, is evident. But since some of those things which create pleasure are necessary, and others, though chosen for their own sakes, yet admit of excess, bodily pleasures are necessary: I mean by such, the pleasures of food, and sensual pleasures, and such bodily pleasures, as we have stated to be the subject of intemperance and temperance: others are not necessary, but chosen for their own sakes; I mean, for instance, victory, honour, wealth, and such like good and pleasant things. Now those, who exceed in these contrary to the right reason, which is in them, we do not simply call incontinent, but we add, incontinent in money, in gain, in honour, or anger: but not simply incontinent, as if they were different, and called so only from resemblance; as the victor at the Olympic games was called man; for to him the common appellation differred a little from his own, but yet it was different[1]. A proof of what I have said is this: incontinence is censured, not only as an error, but also as a species of vice, either simply so, or partially: but nobody, who runs into the other failings, is so censured. But of those who indulge in bodily enjoyments, in which we have said that the temperate and intemperate are distinguished, he, that pursues the excesses of pleasures, and avoids excesses of pain, as hunger and thirst, heat and cold, and every thing connected with touch and taste, not from deliberately choosing, but contrary to his deliberate choice and his judgment, is called incontinent, not with the addition, that it is in this particular thing, such as anger, but simply so. A proof of it is this: people are called effeminate in these matters, but in none of those others: and for this reason we rank the incontinent and intemperate, the continent and temperate, under the same head, but not any of the others, because the former are in a manner concerned with the same pleasures and pains. They are indeed concerned with the same things, but not in the same manner; but the one deliberately choose them, the others do not.

[1] This passage is translated literally, without professing to understand the meaning of it.

Wherefore we should call the man, who pursues excesses and avoids moderate pains, not from desire, or, if at all, a faint desire, more intemperate than him, who does the same from vehement desire; for what would the former have done, if he had felt also youthful desire, and excessive pain in the want of necessary things?

2. But since some desires and pleasures come under the genus of things honourable and good; for of things, which are pleasant, some are eligible by nature, some are the contrary of those, and others between both, (as we distinguished them before,) for instance money, and gain, and victory, and honour: in all such things and those between both, men are not blamed for feeling, or desiring, or loving them, but for doing this in a certain manner, and carrying them to excess. Wherefore as many as are overcome by, or pursue, what is by nature honourable and good contrary to reason, such as those who are very anxious and more so than they ought for honour, or for their children or parents, [these are censured:] for these come under the head of goods, and those, who are anxious about them, are praised; but still there is a kind of excess even in them, if any one, like Niobe, strove even against the gods, or, like Satyrus surnamed Philopater, in his duty to his father, for he was thought to be excessively foolish. There is therefore no depravity in those matters, for the reason given, that each of them comes under those things, which are by nature chosen for their own sakes; but their own excesses are bad and to be avoided. So also there is no incontinence in them; for incontinence is not only a thing to be avoided, but is reckoned also amongst things censurable. But from the similarity of the affection, they add the particular incontinence, and use the term to each; in the same manner as they call a man a bad physician and a bad actor, whom they would not simply call bad. As therefore in these instances they would not simply call them so, because each of them is not really a vice, but from its proportionate resemblance; so also in the other case we must evidently suppose that only to be incontinence and continence, which has the same subject matter with temperance

and intemperance. But in the case of anger, we use the
term from resemblance : wherefore we call the man incontinent, adding, in anger, as in honour and gain.

CHAP. V.

Upon brutality.

1. BUT since some things are pleasant by nature, (and of
these, some are so universally, others to different kinds of
animals and men :) others are pleasant not from nature, but
some from bodily imperfections, some from custom, and
others from depravity of disposition, in each of these we may
see corresponding habits. I mean brutal habits : for instance, that woman, who, they say, ripped up women with
child, and devoured the children ; or such things, as they say
some savages about Pontus delight in, some with raw meat,
some with human flesh, and others to lend their children to
each other for a feast : or what is said of Phalaris. These
are brutal habits. Others are produced in some people from
disease and madness, like the man, who slaughtered and ate
his mother, and another ate his fellow-servant's liver. Others
come from disease or from custom, as the pulling of hair and
biting of nails, and farther the eating coals and earth : to
which may be added the love of males : for these things
happen to some by nature and to others from custom ; for
instance, to those who have been accustomed to them from
childhood. With whomsoever nature is the cause, no one
would call them incontinent ; as they would not call women
so, from the natural distinction of sex ; the case is the same
with those, who are habitually diseased. Now to be subject
to any of these is out of the limits of vice, as also is brutality.
But when subject to them, to conquer them or to be conquered by them is not absolutely [continence or] incontinence,
but in resemblance only ; in the same manner as we must

say of the passionate man, that he has this part of the affection [m], but not that he is entirely incontinent : for with respect to every excessive vice, and folly, and cowardice, and intemperance, and rage ; some of them are brutal, and some from disease ; for the man, who is by nature such, as that he fears every thing, even if a mouse makes a noise, is subject to a brutish cowardice ; and another man was afraid of a cat from disease. And of fools, those who are irrational by nature, and live only by sense, are brutish, as some tribes of distant barbarians ; but those, who are so from disease, for instance, epilepsy or madness, are constitutionally diseased. But it is possible only to be subject to some of these occasionally, and not to be conquered by them : I mean, for instance, if Phalaris had restrained himself, when he felt a desire to eat his child, or for unnatural pleasures. It is possible also not only to be subject to, but to be conquered by, them. As therefore in the case of depravity, that which is natural to man, is simply called depravity : and another kind, with the addition, that it is brutish or constitutional, but not simply so : in the same manner evidently incontinence is partly brutish, and partly constitutional ; but simply, only that, which is akin to human intemperance. Therefore that incontinence and continence only exist in the same things with intemperance and temperance, and that in other things there is another species of incontinence, called so metaphorically and not absolutely, is evident.

[m] I have endeavoured to translate this passage without altering the text : but perhaps Lambinus's emendation is requisite : πάθος with the article τὸ prefixed is used all throughout this book for the particular way in which the incontinent man is affected : i. e. it is used to signify incontinence.

CHAP. VI.

A comparison between incontinence in anger, and incontinence in desire.

1 LET us now consider the circumstance, that incontinence in anger is less disgraceful than incontinence in desires. For anger seems to listen in a manner to reason, but to listen imperfectly; as hasty servants, who, before they have heard the whole message, run away, and then make a mistake in executing it : and dogs, before they have considered whether it is a friend, if he only makes a noise, bark : thus anger, from a natural warmth and quickness, having listened, but not heard the order, rushes to vengeance. For reason or imagination has signified, that the slight is an insult; but anger, as if it had drawn the inference that it ought to quarrel with such a person, is immediately exasperated. But desire, if reason or sense only say that the thing is pleasant, rushes to the enjoyment of it. So that anger follows reason in a manner, but desire does not[n]: it is therefore more disgraceful; for he that is incontinent in anger, is in a manner overcome by reason; but the other by desire, and not by reason.

2. Again, it is more pardonable to follow natural appetites, since it is also more pardonable to follow such desires as are common to all, and as far as they are common. But anger is more natural, and excessive anger is more natural than desires carried to excess and unnecessary ones; like the man who defended himself for beating his father, because, said he, my father beat his father, and he again beat his; and this also (pointing to his child) will beat me, when he be-

---

[n] This may seem to contradict the last sentence; for there is a kind of inference drawn in the case of desire, as well as anger. But mere instinct is sufficient in the former case; whereas in anger, reason does not only point out that the slight is an insult, but that the insult must be revenged; which are not the operations of instinct.

comes a man; for it is natural to our family[o]. And he that was dragged by his son, bid him stop at the door, for that he himself had dragged his father so far.

3. Again, those who are more insidious, are more unjust. Now the passionate man is not insidious, nor is anger, but open; whereas desire is so, as they say of Venus,

———Deceit-contriving Venus.

And Homer says,

———the Cestus, [wherein dwelt]
Deceit, which tricks the senses of the wise.

So that if this incontinence is more unjust, it is also more disgraceful than incontinence in anger, and is absolute incontinence, and in a manner vice.

4. Again, no one insults feeling pain; but every one, who acts from anger, acts feeling pain; whereas he that insults, does it with pleasure. If then those things are more unjust with which it is most just to be angry, then incontinence in desire is more unjust; for there is no insolence in anger[p]. Consequently that incontinence in desires is more disgraceful than that in anger, and that continence and incontinence are concerned with bodily desires and pleasures, is evident.

5. But we must understand their different forms: for, as has been said at first, some are human and natural, both in kind and in degree; some are brutal; and others come from bodily defects and diseases: but temperance and intemperance are only concerned with the first of those. Wherefore we never call beasts temperate or intemperate, except metaphorically, or if any kind of animals differ in some respect entirely from another kind in wantonness and mischievousness, and in being voracious: for they have no deliberate choice, nor reason, but depart from nature, like human beings that are mad.

6. But brutishness is a less evil than vice, though more

[o] This story seems to be brought as an instance of unnecessary and excessive desires.

[p] Because, as we learn from Rhet. b. ii. c. 2. anger is felt in consequence of insult.

formidable : for the best principle has not been destroyed, as in the human being, but they never possess it. It is the same therefore as to compare an inanimate with an animate substance, to see which is worse; for viciousness is always more harmless in that which is without principle ; but intellect is the principle. It is therefore almost the same to compare injustice [the abstract] with an unjust man [the concrete]: for it is possible that either may be the worse : for a vicious man can do infinitely more evils than a beast [q].

CHAP. VII.

A comparison between incontinence and intemperance, and continence and patience. Two different forms of continence are described.

1. But with respect to the pleasures and pains connected with touch and taste, and desires, and aversions, (to which intemperance and temperance have already been defined to belong,) it is possible to have them in such a manner, as to be overcome even by those which the generality overcome ; and it is possible to conquer even those to which the generality give way. Of these, he that is concerned with pleasure, is either incontinent or continent ; he that is concerned with pain is either effeminate, or patient. But the habits of the generality are in a medium, although they incline most to the bad.

2. But since some pleasures are necessary, while others are not so, and necessary up to a certain point, but their excesses and deficiencies are not necessary ; so is it also with

---

[q] And yet, as was said above, the beast is more formidable, as it has no intellect. The case seems to be this: were we to see a lion and a vicious man together, we should fear the lion more than the man ; and yet were they both absent, we should fear the man most, because he is able to plot against us. Or to take another case, if we see an assassin with a dagger, it is really the dagger that we fear, but it is the assassin who is able to do so much harm.

desires and pains : he that pursues those pleasures which are in excess, or pursues them to excess, or with deliberate choice, and for their own sakes, and not for any ulterior result, is intemperate : for such a man must necessarily be out of the way of repentance; so that he is incurable. He that is deficient, is the opposite of the above; he that is in the mean, is temperate. It is the same with the man who flies from bodily pains, not from being overpowered, but from deliberate choice. But of those who do the same without deliberate choice, one is led on by pleasure ; another from avoiding the pain which comes from desire : so that they differ from each other. But every one would think a man was worse, if he did any thing disgraceful, having no desires, or at least a slight one, than if he had very strong desires ; and if he struck another without being angry, than if he had been angry : for what would he have done, had he been under the influence of passion? wherefore the intemperate is worse than the incontinent.

3. Of those then that have been mentioned, one is rather a species of effeminacy, the other is incontinent. The continent is opposed to the incontinent, and the patient to the effeminate; for patience consists in resisting, continence in conquering : but to resist and to conquer are different, in the same manner as not being defeated differs from gaining a victory. Wherefore also continence is preferable to patience. But the man that fails in resisting those things which the generality strive against and prevail, he is effeminate and delicate; (for delicacy is a species of effeminacy;) who drags [r] his cloak after him, that he may not be annoyed with the pain of carrying it : and imitating the invalid, he does not think himself unhappy, when he is very like an unhappy man.

4. The case is the same with continence and incontinence;

---

[r] I follow Lambinus and several manuscripts in omitting εὐχ. I conceive the meaning to be the same in Juvenal, Sat. i. v. 27. Tyrias humero revocante lacernas. Where Schrevelius has this note : Adeo enim fractus erat mollitie, ut *penulam in humero propter pondus non retinuerit, sed deorsum vergere passus sit*, ita ut humerus ipsum crebro revocaret.

for it is not strange, if a person is overcome by violent and excessive pleasures or pains ; but it is even pardonable, if he struggled against them, (as the Philoctetes of Theodectes, when he had been bitten by the viper, or the Cercyon of Carcinus[s] in the Alope : and like those who endeavour to stifle their laughter, burst out, as happened to Xenophantus :) but it is strange, if any one is conquered by and cannot resist those which the generality are able to resist, not from their generic nature, or from disease, as effeminacy is in the kings of Persia generically ; and as the female differs from the male. He that is greatly given to mirth, is thought to be intemperate : but he is effeminate ; for mirth is a relaxation, if it is a cessation : and amongst those who carry relaxation to excess, comes the man who is given to mirth.

5. One species of incontinence is precipitancy, another is weakness : for the latter having deliberated, do not abide by their determinations, owing to their passions : but the former, from not having deliberated at all, are led on by passion. For some, (like those, who when they have tickled themselves[t] beforehand, do not feel the tickling of others,) having notice of it previously, and foreseeing it, and rousing themselves and their reason beforehand, are not overpowered by the passion, whether it be pleasant or painful. Those who are quick, and those who are melancholy, are generally subject to the precipitate incontinence : for the former from haste, and the latter from excess of feeling, do not wait for reason, because they are in the habit of following their fancy.

[s] In the note to Wilkinson's edition it is written Καρχῖνος, whereas it should be Κάρχινος, for the penultima is short. Aristoph. Nub. 1261. Vesp. 1501, 1505. Pax. 782, 864.

[t] One manuscript reads προγαργαλισθέντις, which would be better : but I should prefer προγαργαλισάμινοι.

CHAP. VIII.

*In what the vicious or intemperate and the incontinent differ
from, and in what they resemble, each other.*

1. THE intemperate man, as has been said, is not in the
habit of repenting; for he adheres to his deliberate choice;
but the incontinent man, under every form of incontinence,
is in the habit of repenting. Wherefore the fact is not according to the difficulty stated above[n] : but the former is
incurable, and the latter curable : for depravity resembles
dropsy and consumption in diseases, and incontinence resembles epilepsy; for the former is a constant, the latter not
a constant failing. And on the whole the genus of incontinence and vice is different ; for vice acts imperceptibly.;
but incontinence does not act imperceptibly.

2. But of these themselves, those that are forced from
their opinion, are better than those who have reason, but
do not adhere to it; for these last are overpowered by a
weaker passion, and are not without premeditation, as the
others are : for the incontinent resembles those who are intoxicated quickly, and with a little wine, and less than the
generality.

3. Consequently that incontinence is not vice, is evident :
but perhaps it is to a certain degree : for the one is contrary,
the other according to deliberate choice. Not but that they
are similar in their effects : like the saying of Demodocus
about the Milesians ; for the Milesians are not fools, but
they do such things as fools would : and the incontinent are
not unjust, but they act unjustly. But since the character
of the one is such, that he follows those bodily pleasures,
which are in excess and contrary to right reason, not from
being persuaded that he should do so; but the other is persuaded to it, because his character is such, as inclines him to
pursue them ; for this reason the former is easily persuaded
right, but the latter is not. For as to virtue and depravity,

[u] At the end of the fourth section of the second chapter.

one destroys and the other preserves the principle: but in practical questions, the *object* is the principle[x], as the hypotheses are in mathematical questions. In the latter case reason does not teach the principles, nor in practical questions, but virtue either natural or moral teaches the habit of thinking rightly upon the principle. Such a character therefore is temperate, and the contrary is intemperate. But there is a character, which from passion is forced out of right reason, whom passion so far conquers, as that he does not act according to right reason; but it does not conquer him so far, as that he is of such a character as to be persuaded that he ought to follow such pleasures without any restraint. This is the incontinent man; better than the intemperate, and not wholly vicious; for the best, i. e. the principle, is preserved. But another character is opposite to this, he that adheres to reason, and is not forced out of it, at least not from passion. It is evident then from all this, that one habit is good, the other bad.

CHAP. IX.

The second question is discussed; and the difference shewn between continence and obstinacy.

1. Is he then continent, who adheres to any reason and to any deliberate choice whatever, or he, who adheres to the right? and is he incontinent, who does not adhere to any deliberate choice and to any reason whatever, or he who does not adhere to true reason and right deliberate choice, in the manner that we doubted before? or is it accidentally he, that adheres to any whatever, but in real fact the one ad-

---

[x] It has already been seen, particularly in the 6th book, c. 2. that there are two principles of action, the causal and the motive principle, the latter of which is the *προαίρεσις*: but it is the former which is destroyed by intemperance and preserved by temperance.

heres and the other does not adhere to true reason and right deliberate choice^y? For if any one chooses or pursues this particular thing for the sake of that, he really pursues and chooses that; but accidentally the former; and speaking generally we mean that which he really pursues. So that it is possible that the one adheres to, and the other departs from, any opinion whatever; but absolutely, the true one.

2. But there are some, who adhere to their opinion; and there are some, whom they call obstinate, such as those who are difficult to be persuaded, and not easy to be turned from their persuasions, who have some resemblance to the continent, like the prodigal has to the liberal, and the rash to the courageous; but they are different in many respects. For the one is not led by passion and desire to change, and that is the continent; for the continent man will be easily persuaded under certain circumstances; but the other, not even by reason; since many of them take up desires, and are led by pleasures. The self-willed, and the uneducated, and clowns, are obstinate; the self-willed; from pleasure and pain: for they take delight in getting the better, if they are not forced to give up their opinion; and they feel pain, if their decisions, like public decrees, are not ratified. So that they resemble the incontinent more than the continent.

3. But there are some, who do not adhere to their opinions, not from incontinence, like Neoptolemus in the Philoctetes of Sophocles; and yet it was on account of pleasure that he did not adhere, but it was a noble pleasure; for to speak truth was to him noble, and he had been persuaded by Ulysses to speak falsely: for not every one that does any thing from pleasure is intemperate, or vicious, or incontinent, but he who does it for a vicious pleasure.

4. But since there is such a character, as takes less delight than he ought in bodily pleasures, and does not adhere to reason, the character between that and the incontinent is the

<hr>

y He that adheres to any opinion, adheres to it because he thinks it is founded upon right reason; therefore he really, καθ' αὑτό, adheres to right reason; and his adherence to the other is only accidental.

continent: for the incontinent, in consequence of some excess, does not adhere to reason; and the other, in consequence of some deficiency; but the continent adheres to it, and does not change from either cause. But if continence is good, both the opposite habits must be bad, as they appear to be: but because the one appears in few persons and seldom, in the same manner as temperance seems to be only opposed to intemperance, so does continence to incontinence.

5. But since many expressions are used from resemblances, the continence of the temperate man has followed from their resemblance: for the continent man is inclined to do nothing contrary to reason for the sake of bodily pleasures, and so is the temperate; but the former possesses, the latter does not possess bad desires: and the character of the latter is not to be pleased contrary to reason, but of the former, to feel pleasure, though not to be led by it. The case is the same with the incontinent and intemperate; they are different, but both follow bodily pleasures: the one thinking that it is right, the other not thinking so.

CHAP. X.

The fifth question, whether the prudent man can be incontinent.
A comparison between incontinence and vice.

1. IT is impossible for the same man to be at once prudent and incontinent: for when a man is prudent, he has been shewn to be at the same time morally good. Again, a man is not prudent from merely knowing, but from being also able to act; but the incontinent is not able to act. But nothing hinders the clever man from being incontinent; whence some men now and then seem to be prudent, and yet incontinent, because cleverness differs from prudence in

the manner that has been mentioned above[z], and resembles it with respect to reason, but differs with respect to deliberate choice.

2. Nor yet is the incontinent like one, who has knowledge and uses it, but like one asleep or drunk: and he acts willingly; for he in a manner knows both what he does and why; but he is not wicked; for his deliberate choice is good; so that he is half-wicked, and not unjust, for he is not designing. For one of them is not apt to adhere to his deliberations; and the melancholy does not deliberate at all. Hence the incontinent man resembles a city, which passes all suitable decrees, and has good laws, but uses none of them, like the jest of Anaxandrides,

> The state decrees, which careth nought for laws:

but the wicked man resembles a city, which uses laws, but uses bad ones.

3. Incontinence and continence are displayed in that which surpasses the habit of the generality; for the one adheres more, and the other less, than the ability of the generality. But the incontinence of the melancholy is more curable than that of those, who do deliberate, but do not adhere to their deliberations; and those who are incontinent from custom, than those who are so by nature; for it is easier to change custom than nature. For the same reason also it is difficult to change custom, because it resembles nature, as Euenus says,

> Practice, my friend, is lasting: which becomes
> A second nature in the end to man.

What then continence is, and what incontinence, and patience, and effeminacy, and what relation these habits bear to one another, has been explained.

[z] Book vi. c. 12. sect. 5.

———————————

The four chapters which follow, being generally considered as spurious, and as the same subject is treated of at the beginning of the 10th book, I have not translated them.

ARISTOTLE'S ETHICS.

BOOK VIII.

———

CHAP. I.

Friendship is necessary to all conditions and ages : it is natural, the bond of society, and noble. Different opinions as to the formation of it.

1. IT would follow next after this to treat of friendship; for it is a species of virtue, or united to virtue. Secondly; It is also most necessary for life; for without friends no one would choose to live, even if he had all other goods. For to the rich, and to those in office and authority, there seems particularly to be a need of friends: for what profit is there in such good fortune, if the power of conferring benefits is taken away, which is shewn in the greatest degree and in the most praiseworthy manner towards friends? or how could it be kept up and preserved without friends? for by how much the greater it is, so much the more likely is it to fall. And in poverty and other misfortunes they think that friends are the only refuge. Thirdly; It is also necessary to the young to preserve them from error, and to the old to attend upon them, and supply that which is deficient in their

actions from weakness[a] : and to those in the vigour of life to further their noble deeds,

> Two going together, &c. &c. &c.

For they are more able to conceive and to execute.

2. It seems also naturally to be felt by the thing producing towards the thing produced; and not only amongst men, but also in birds, and in most animals, and in those of the same tribe towards one another, and most of all amongst men: where we praise the friendly. One may see also in travelling, how intimate and friendly every man is to another.

3. Friendship also seems to keep states together, and legislators to pay more attention to it than to justice; for unanimity seems to be something resembling friendship; and they are most desirous of this, and banish sedition as being the greatest enemy. And when men are friends, there is no need of justice; but although they are just, they still want friendship. And of all the feelings of justice, the principal seems to be the feeling of friendship.

4. It is not only necessary, but also honourable; for we praise those, who love their friends; and the having many friends seems to be one species of things honourable.

5. But there are not a few disputes concerning it; for some consider it a kind of similarity, and that those, who are similar, are friends : whence they say, "Like to like," "Jackdaw to jackdaw," and such like proverbs : others on the contrary say that all such are like *potters* to one another. And concerning these matters they carry their enquiries higher and more physically : Euripides says,

> The earth parch'd up with dryness loves the rain;
> The clouds, when charg'd with rain, from their high seats
> Love to descend to earth.

Heraclitus also thought that contrariety is advantageous,

---

[a] I have omitted βοηθείας, for which there seems no necessity, and which hardly admits of any construction, as it stands now.

and that there is the most beautiful harmony from things different, and that every thing is generated in strife. Empedocles and others thought contrary to this; that like is fond of like.

6. Now the physical questions must be passed over; for they do not belong to our present consideration. But as many as belong to man, and refer to his morals and his passions, these let us consider: such as, first, whether friendship exists in all, or whether it is impossible for the depraved to be friends: secondly, whether there is only one species of friendship, or more: for those, who think there is only one, because it admits of being greater or less, do not trust to a sufficient proof; for things differing in species also admit of being greater or less; and we have spoken about this before.

CHAP. II.

The three objects of friendship, and the perfect definition of it.

1. PERHAPS some certainty would appear about these matters, if the object of friendship were known; for it seems that it is not every thing that is loved, but only that, which is an object of friendship; and this is, what is good, pleasant, or useful. But that might be reckoned useful, by means of which there is produced some good or pleasure: so that the good and the pleasant would alone be objects of friendship, considered as ends.

2. Whether then do men love the good, or what is good to them? for these sometimes are different. The case is the same with the pleasant. But each seems to love that, which is good to himself; and really and truly the good is an object of friendship, but to each individual, that which is so to each. But each loves not what *is* good to himself, but what *appears* so: and this will make no difference: for the object of friendship must be that, which appears to be one.

2. But since there are three things, for which men love, in a fondness for inanimate things the term friendship cannot be used: for there is no return of fondness, nor any wishing of good to the other. For it is perhaps ridiculous to wish good to wine; but if a man should do so, he wishes it to be preserved, that he himself may have it. But we say that men should wish good to a friend for the sake of that friend; and those, who wish it in the above manner, we call well-disposed, unless there is also the same feeling from the other party: for good-will where both parties feel it is friendship; or must we add that this mutual good-will must not be unknown to both parties? for many feel good-will towards those, who they have never seen, but who they suppose are good or useful to them. But if any one of the others feels this towards him, these certainly appear well disposed to one another; but how can one call them friends, when they do not know how they are disposed to them? They ought therefore to have good-will towards each other, and wish them what is good, not unknown to each other, and for one of the motives mentioned above.

CHAP. III.

The three species of friendship are explained, and the persons who feel each. Why friendship for the good is best.

1. But these motives differ in species from one another; therefore the affections do so likewise, and the friendships. For there are three species of friendship, equal in number to the motives of friendship; since in each there is a mutual fondness, and that not unknown to both parties. But those who love one another, wish goods to one another according to that motive for which they love. Now those who love one another for the useful, do not love them for their own sakes, but inasmuch as there results some good to themselves

from one another. So also with those who love for pleasure: for they do not love the facetious from their being of
a certain character, but because they are pleasant to them :
and therefore those who love for the useful, love for the
sake of what is good to themselves : and those who love for
pleasure, love for the sake of what is pleasant to themselves ;
and not for the consideration that the person loved is in
existence, but that he is useful or pleasant. These friendships therefore depend upon accident ; for the person loved,
whoever he may be, is not loved in respect to his existence,
but inasmuch as they furnish something either good or
pleasant. Consequently such friendships are easily dissolved,
if the parties do not continue in similar circumstances ; for
if they are no longer pleasant, or useful, they cease to love :
but the useful does not continue, but becomes different at
different times. Therefore when that is done away, for
sake of which they became friends, the friendship also is
dissolved, which clearly shews that the friendship was for
those motives.

2. Such friendship seems mostly to exist amongst old
men ; (for men at such an age do not pursue the pleasant,
but the useful ;) and as many of those in the vigour of life
and in youth, as pursue the useful. But such people do not
altogether associate with one another, for sometimes they are
not pleasant. Nor indeed do they want the addition of such
society, unless they are useful to each other ; for they are
pleasant so far as they entertain hopes of good. Amongst
those also they rank the friendship of hospitality. But the
friendship of young men seems to be for the sake of pleasure ; for they live according to passion, and mostly pursue
what is pleasant to themselves and immediate. But as their
age changes, what is pleasant also becomes different ; wherefore they quickly become friends and quickly cease ; for
their friendship changes together with what is pleasant : and
of such pleasure as this the change is quick. Young men
also are given to love ; for the principal part of love is from
passion and for pleasure. Wherefore they feel a friendship, and quickly cease to feel it, changing many times in

the same day. But these wish to pass their time together, and to associate; for their feelings of friendship are thus formed.

3. But the friendship of the good, and of those who resemble each other in virtue, is perfect: for these equally wish good to one another, inasmuch as they are good; but their goodness is inherent in themselves; and those, who wish good to their friends for the friends' sake, are friends in the greatest degree; for they have this feeling for sake of the friends themselves, and not from accident. Their friendship therefore continues, as long as they are good; and virtue is lasting. And each is good abstractedly, and to his friend; for the good are both abstractedly good and useful to one another. In the same manner also they are pleasant: for the good are pleasant both abstractedly and to one another: for to each their own peculiar actions, and those which agree with their character, are pleasant: but the actions of the good do agree with their character, or resemble it. Such friendship as this is naturally lasting: for it contains in it every thing, which friends ought to have. For every friendship is for the sake of good or pleasure, either abstractedly or to the person loving, and from a certain resemblance. But in this friendship, all that has been mentioned exists in the parties themselves; for in this there is a similarity, and all the other requisites, and that which is abstractedly good, is also abstractedly pleasant: but these are principally the motives of friendship; and therefore the feeling friendship, and friendship itself, exists principally in these, and is the best. But it is natural for such to be rare; for there are few such characters as these. Moreover it requires time and long acquaintance: for, according to the proverb, it is impossible for men to know one another, before they have eaten salt together: nor can they admit each other, nor become friends, before each appears to each worthy of friendship, and obtains his confidence. But those, who hastily perform offices of friendship to one another, are willing to be friends, but are not really so, unless they are also worthy of friendship, and know this to be the case.

Therefore a wish for friendship is formed quickly, but not friendship. This species of friendship therefore both with respect to time and every thing else is perfect, and is formed upon the basis of all these requisites, and is the same from each to each; which ought to be the case between friends.

CHAP. IV.

Equality is the bond of friendship. What kind of men each friendship suits.

1. But friendship for the agreeable has a resemblance to that; for the good are agreeable to one another. So also that for the useful: for the good are useful to one another. But in these also the friendships continue most, when there is an equal return from each other, for instance, of pleasure. And not only thus, but an equal return from the same thing, for instance, from the facetious to the facetious, and not as from the lover to the person loved: for these do not feel pleasure in the same things, but the one in loving the other, and the other in receiving attention from the lover. But when the personal beauty ceases, sometimes the friendship ceases also: for the face is no longer agreeable to the one, and the other does not receive attention. Many however continue friends, if from long acquaintance they love the character, being of the same character. But those, who in love affairs do not return the agreeable but the useful, are friends in a less degree, and continue less. But those, who are friends for the useful, separate together with the useful; for they were not friends to one another, but to that which was profitable. Consequently for the sake of pleasure and the useful it is possible for the bad to be friends with one another, and the good with the bad, and a man that is neither good nor bad with either; but for the sake of the parties themselves, evidently only the good can be friends; for the

bad feel no pleasure in the persons themselves, unless there is some advantage. And the friendship of the good is alone free from complaints; for it is not easy to trust any one concerning that, which has been proved by ourselves from a long space of time : and between such persons there is confidence, and an anxiety never to offend, and every thing else, which is expected in real friendship. But in the other friendships nothing hinders such things from occurring. Consequently since men call those friends who are so for the useful, as cities are; (for alliances seem to be formed between cities for the sake of advantage :) and those who love one another for pleasure, as children do; perhaps we also must say that such men are friends, but that there are many species of friendship; and first and principally that of the good, inasmuch as they are good; and the others from their resemblance; for inasmuch as there is something good or like it, so far they are friends; for the agreeable is a kind of good to those who love the agreeable. But these two do not generally unite, nor do the same people become friends for the useful and the agreeable; for two things which depend upon chance are not often united. Friendship therefore being divided into these species, the bad will be friends for pleasure or utility, being similar in that respect; but the good will be friends for the friends' sake; for they will be so inasmuch as they are good. These therefore are really and truly friends; the others accidentally, and from their resemblance to the former.

CHAP. V.

The difference between the habit and exercise of friendship. Of the friendship of the aged, and the good.

1. BUT as in the case of virtue, some men are called good from the habit, others from the exercise of it, so is it also in

friendship : for some take pleasure in each other, and mutually confer benefits, by living together ; but those who are indolent, or locally separated, do not act, but are so circumstanced, that they could act in a friendly manner: for difference of place does not absolutely destroy friendship, but the exercise of it. But if the absence is long, it seems also to produce a cessation of friendship : whence it has been said,

Privation of conversation has dissolved many friendships.

2. But the aged and the morose do not appear to be fit for friendship ; for the feeling of pleasure is weak in them ; and no one can pass his time with a person that is disagreeable, or not pleasant: for nature is particularly shewn in avoiding what is disagreeable, and desiring what is pleasant. But those who merely approve of one another without living together, seem rather well-inclined, than friends ; for nothing is so strong a mark of friendship, as to live together : for the needy long for assistance ; and the happy wish to pass their time together ; since it least of all becomes them to be solitary. But it is impossible for men to associate, if they are not agreeable, and do not take pleasure in the same things ; which seems to be the case with the friendship merely between companions.

3. That between the good therefore is friendship in the greatest degree, as has been said frequently: for that which is in itself good or pleasant, seems to be an object of friendship and of choice, and to each individual, that which is so to him; but the good man is an object of friendship and choice to the good for both these reasons. Fondness is like a passion, and friendship like a habit; for fondness is felt no less towards inanimate things : but men return friendship with deliberate choice, and deliberate choice proceeds from habit. They also wish goods for those they love, for their sakes, not from passion, but from habit : and when they love a friend, they love that which is good to themselves ; for the good man, when he becomes a friend, becomes a good to him whose friend he is. Each therefore loves that

which is a good to himself, and makes a return that is equal both in wish and in form; for equality is said to be friendship. These requisites therefore exist mostly in the friendship of the good.

CHAP. VI.

The old are rather well-inclined than friends. In perfect friendship we can only be friends with a few. Comparison between the agreeable and the useful. Of the friendship of the great.

1. But in the morose and the aged there is less friendship, in proportion to their being more difficult to be pleased, and their taking less pleasure in society; for those seem to belong to friendship, and to produce it in the greatest degree. Wherefore young men soon become friends, but old ones do not; for they never become friends of those in whom they do not take pleasure; nor the morose in the same manner. But such men as these are well-inclined to one another; for they wish what is good, and meet each other's wants; but they are not generally friends, because they do not pass their time together, nor take pleasure in each other; which things seem particularly to belong to friendship.

2. To be friends with many, is a thing impossible in the perfect friendship; the same as it is to be in love with many at once; for love is something exceeding; and that which exceeds is naturally felt towards one object. And for the same man greatly to please many at once is not easy[b], and perhaps it is good that it should not be so. They must also become acquainted with one another, and be similar in character, which is very difficult. But for the useful and for the agreeable it is possible to please many; for many are of

---

[b] Lambinus translates this passage differently. My only doubt is as to the latter clause, εὐδ᾽ ἀγαθὸν εἶναι. There is no doubt but that ἀρέσκειν may govern an accusative.

that character, and the services required are performed in a short time.

3. But of these, that which is for sake of the agreeable is most like friendship, when the same things are produced by both, and they take pleasure in one another, or in the same things; of which description are the friendships of the young; for there is more liberality in them. But that which is for the useful, suits mercenary characters.

4. The happy do not want useful but agreeable friends, for they wish to have some persons to live with; and they bear any thing painful for a short time only; nor could any one bear it constantly, not even good itself, if it were painful to him; hence they seek for agreeable friends. Perhaps also they must seek for good friends, who are so by character, and also to them; for thus they will have whatever friends ought to have. Those who are in authority seem to use different kinds of friends; for some are useful to them, and others agreeable. But the same men are not generally both: for they do not seek for friends who are agreeable from their virtue, nor useful for honourable exploits; but they wish the former to be facetious, when they desire the agreeable, and the latter to be clever in executing commands: and these qualities do not generally meet in the same person. And yet we have said that the good man is at once agreeable and useful; but such a character does not become the friend of a man high in power, unless the latter is exceeded by the other in virtue; otherwise the person who is inferior in power, does not make a proportionate return: but such men are not frequently found [c].

5. All the friendships therefore which have been mentioned, consist in equality: for the same things proceed from both parties, and they wish the same to each other; or else they exchange one thing for another, such as pleasure for profit. But that these are friendships in a less degree and

---

[c] There is some obscurity here. The sense seems to be, that men, who have very much power, generally speaking have not very much virtue also.

continue less, has been mentioned; they seem also from their being like and yet unlike the same thing, to be and yet not to be friendships. For from their resemblance to that which is formed for virtue's sake, they appear friendships; since one contains the agreeable and the other the useful, and both of these exist in the former also. But from that being free from complaints and lasting, whereas these quickly fall off, and differ in many other respects, they appear not to be friendships from their dissimilitude to the other.

CHAP. VII.

Of friendship between parties, which are unequal.

1. THERE is another species of friendship, where one of the parties is superior; as that of a father for his son, and generally an older for a younger person, and a husband for his wife, and every one in power for the person under him. But these differ from one another: for it is not the same from parents to children, as from governors to the governed; nor even from a father to his son, as from a son to his father, nor from a husband to his wife, as from a wife to her husband: for the perfection and the office of each of these is different; therefore the motives of their friendship are different. Consequently their affections and their friendships themselves are different: hence the same offices are not paid from each to the other, nor ought they to require them. But when children pay to their parents what is due to those who begat them, and parents to their sons what is due to children, the friendship of such as these is lasting and sincere. But in all those friendships, where one party is superior, the fondness also ought to be proportionate; as that the better person should be loved in a greater degree than he loves, so also the more useful person, and every other in the same

way. For when the fondness is proportional, then there is in a manner an equality ; which seems to be a property of friendship.

2. But equality does not seem to be the same in justice as in friendship ; for equality in proportion to merit holds the first place in justice, and equality as to quantity is the second ; but in friendship, that which relates to quantity is first, and that which relates to merit is secondary. This is evident, if there is a great distance between the parties in virtue, or vice, or prosperity, or any thing else : for they are then no longer friends, and they even do not expect it. It is most evident in the case of the gods ; for they possess all goods to the greatest excess : it is also evident in the case of kings ; for they who are very inferior do not presume to be friends with them ; nor do the worthless presume to be so with the best or wisest men.

3. Between such parties as these there is no strict limitation, how far they may be friends ; for although we take away much from one party, still the friendship continues ; but when one is very far removed from the other, as from a god, it continues no longer. Whence also there is a doubt whether friends wish their friends the greatest goods, for instance, that they should become gods ; for then they would no longer be their friends ; and therefore they would not be goods to them ; for friends are goods. But [d] if it has been rightly said, that a friend wishes his friend good for his sake, the friendship ought to continue, whatever the other party may become. He will therefore [e] wish him to have the greatest goods, as a man ; though perhaps not every good ; for each wishes goods for himself most of all.

CHAP. VIII.

*Friendship consists more in loving than being loved.   Concerning
the duration of friendship.*

1. MOST men from desire of honour seem to like to be
loved rather than to love : wherefore the generality are fond
of flattery ; for the flatterer is a friend who is inferior to the
other, or pretends to be so, and to love rather than to be
loved : and to be loved seems to resemble the being honoured,
which most men are desirous of.   They do not however seem
to choose honour for its own sake, but contingently ; for the
generality delight in being honoured by those in power on
account of hope; for they think that they shall obtain from
them whatever they want.   Thus they delight in honour,
as an earnest of receiving favours.   But those who are desirous of honour from men of equity and judgment, are
anxious to confirm their own opinion of themselves : thus
they take delight in the idea that they are good, trusting to
the judgment of those who say so.   But they feel delight in
being loved merely for the sake of being loved ; wherefore
to be loved might seem to be better than to be honoured, and
that friendship chosen for its own sake consisted in this; but
it really seems to consist in loving rather than being loved.
A proof of this is, that mothers take delight in loving ; for
some give their children to be nursed, and knowing that they
are their children love them, though they do not seek to be
loved in return, if the feeling cannot be mutual ; but it seems
sufficient to them if they see them doing well : and they love
their children, although the latter from ignorance cannot
repay to their mother what is due.   But since friendship
consists more in loving, and those who love their friends
are praised, to love seems to be the perfection of friends.

2. So that the parties between whom this takes place pro-
portionately are lasting friends, and the friendship of such is
lasting.   But in this manner those who are unequal, may
also be the greatest friends ; for they may be brought to an

equality. But equality and similarity is friendship, and particularly the similarity of the virtuous: for as they continue the same to themselves, they also continue the same to each other, and neither want any thing bad, nor contribute to the procuring it, but if we may so, they even prevent it: for it is characteristic of the good, neither to commit faults themselves, nor to suffer their friends to contribute to it. But the wicked have no stability; for they do not remain consistent even with themselves; but they become friends for a short time, taking delight in each other's wickedness. The useful and the agreeable continue friends longer than these; for they continue as long as they furnish pleasure and profit to one another.

3. But of those who are in opposite situations, there seems to be most friendship for the useful; for instance, a poor man with a rich one, an uneducated with a learned man; for whatever a needy person wants, being desirous of that, he makes other presents in return. Under this head one might bring in the lover and the person loved; the handsome and the ugly. Whence also lovers sometimes appear ridiculous, when they expect to be loved as much as they love: when they are equally objects of love, they may perhaps expect it; but when they possess nothing of the kind, it is ridiculous. But perhaps opposite never desires opposite for itself, but contingently; and the aim is directed to the mean; for that is a good: for instance, what is dry desires not to become moist, but to arrive at the mean; so also what is warm, and every thing else in the same way. Let us have done with this, however, for it is foreign to our purpose.

CHAP. IX.

All friendship, as well as justice, is in community: and every community is subordinate to the general community.

1. FRIENDSHIP and justice appear, as was said at first, to be about the same things, and between the same persons; for in

every community there seems to be some justice and some friendship. Thus they call fellow-sailors and fellow-soldiers friends, and so likewise those in any other community. But as far as they have any thing in common, so far is friendship; for justice is also thus far. And the proverb, that the property of friends is common, is right; for friendship consists in community: and to brothers and companions all things are common; but to others, certain definite things, to some more, to other less, for some friendships are stronger and some weaker. There is also a difference in justice; for it is not the same between parents and children, as between brothers and one another; nor between companions as between citizens, and so on in every other friendship. Injustice is therefore different between each of these, and is aggravated by being done to greater friends; for instance, it is more shameful to rob a companion of money than a fellow-citizen, and not to assist a brother than a stranger, and to strike one's father than any one else. But justice naturally increases together with friendship, as they are between the same parties, and of equal extent.

2. But all [f] communities seem like parts of the political community; for men travel together for some advantage, and furnishing some of the necessaries of life. Political community seems also originally to have been formed and still to continue for sake of advantage; for legislators aim at this, and say that what is expedient to the community is just. Now the other communities desire advantage in some particular thing; as sailors that which is peculiar to sailing, either for the gaining of money, or something of that kind; soldiers that which belongs to war, desirous either of money, or victory, or the taking of a city; so also people of the same tribe and borough seek each their own advantage. Some communities seem to have been formed for the sake of pleasures, such as merry-makings and clubs; for these were formed for the sake of sacrifice and sociability: for [g] the

---

[f] Read πᾶσαι.

[g] There is evidently some corruption here, and some transposition seems necessary: I have followed one much less violent than that of Muretus.

ancient sacrifices and general meetings seem to have been held after the gathering of harvest; the first-fruits, for instance; for the people had most leisure at that time, when they were offering sacrifices and paying honours to the gods in those meetings, and providing themselves an agreeable relaxation. But all these seem to be subordinate to political community; for this desires not present advantage, but what is so for the whole of life. All communities therefore seem to be parts of the political community; and similar friendships will follow similar communities.

CHAP. X.

Of different forms of government, monarchy, aristocracy, timocracy; and the corruptions of them, tyranny, oligarchy, and democracy. A counterpart of each of these is found in private families.

1. THERE are three forms of civil government, and as many deflections, which are as it were corruptions of them. The governments are, a kingdom, an aristocracy, and a third from the influence of property, which it seems proper to call a timocracy: but the generality are accustomed to apply the term government or commonwealth exclusively to this last.

2. The deflection from kingly power is tyranny; for both are monarchies: but there is the greatest difference between them; for the tyrant looks to his own benefit, the king to that of his subjects; for he is not a king who is not independent, and who does not abound in all goods; but such a person as this wants nothing else; and consequently he would not be considering what is beneficial to himself, but to his subjects; for he that does not act so, must be a kind of king chosen by lot. But tyranny is opposite to this; for a tyrant pursues his own peculiar good. And it appears more

evidently in this respect, that it is the worst form of all; for that is worst, which is opposite to the best. But the deflection from kingly power is to tyranny; for tyranny is a viciousness of monarchy, and a vicious king becomes a tyrant.

3. The deflection from aristocracy is to oligarchy, through the ill conduct of those in power, who distribute the offices of the state without a consideration of merit, give all or most goods to themselves, and the offices of state constantly to the same people, paying most consideration to wealth: consequently a few and vicious people are in power instead of the best.

4. The deflection from timocracy is to democracy; for they border upon one another, since a timocracy is also generally in the hands of the multitude, and all who are raised by their estates are equal. But democracy is the least depraved; for this form of government is only a small deflection. Such then are the most frequent changes of governments; for thus they depart the least and in the most natural manner from their proper form.

5. One may find resemblances, and as it were examples of these even in private families: for the community of a father and his sons wears the form of kingly power: for the father takes care of the children. Hence also Homer calls Jupiter Father; for the kingly power is generally a paternal authority. But in Persia the authority of a father is tyrannical; for they use their sons like slaves. The authority of a master over his slaves is also tyrannical: for in that the benefit of the master is consulted. This therefore appears right, but that of the Persians is wrong; for the power of those who are in different circumstances ought to be different. Secondly, The community of a man and his wife seems to be aristocratical: for the husband governs because it is his due, and in those things which a husband ought; and whatever is suitable for the wife, he gives up to her. When the husband lords it over every thing, it departs into an oligarchy; for he does this beyond what is his due, and not in consideration of his superiority. But sometimes women,

when they are heiresses, have the authority. Thus the power is not according to merit, but according to wealth and influence, as in oligarchies. Thirdly, The community of brothers is like a timocracy; for they are equal, except as far as they differ in age. Wherefore if there is a great disparity in their ages, the friendship is no longer that of brothers. A democracy takes place mostly in families, where there is no master, for then all are equal; and wherever the ruler is weak, and each has his own power.

CHAP. XI.

In each form of government there is a peculiar friendship.

1. IN each of these forms of government there seems to be a friendship, to the same extent that there is justice. That between a king and his subjects consists in conferring superior benefits; for he does good to his subjects, if he is good and takes care of them, that they may be happy, like a shepherd takes care of his sheep; whence also Homer calls Agamemnon "the shepherd of his people." Such also is paternal friendship: but it exceeds the former in the magnitude of its benefits; for the father is the cause of the son's existence, which is thought to be the greatest thing, and of food and of education. The same also may be said of ancestors; for a father is by nature the ruler of his sons, and ancestors of their descendants, and a king of his subjects. But these friendships consist in one party being superior; whence also parents receive honour: therefore also justice is not the same between the two parties, but according to proportion; for thus also must the friendship be.

2. Between man and wife there is the same friendship as in an aristocracy: for the greater good is given according to merit and to the better person, and to each that which is suitable. Justice between them is also in the same way.

3. The friendship of brothers is like the friendship of com-

panions; for they are equal and of the same age; and such persons generally learn the same things, and have the same moral character. The friendship of a timocracy is therefore like this; for citizens think themselves equal and good: consequently the government is held by turns, and equally. Such also is the friendship.

4. But in the deflections, as justice has little influence, so also has friendship, and least of all in the worst. For in a tyranny there is no friendship, or very little; for between those parties, where the ruler and the ruled have nothing in common, there is no friendship: for there is no justice: but the same as between a workman and his instrument, the soul and the body, a master and his slave; for all these are benefited by the employers. But there is no friendship nor justice felt towards inanimate things, neither is there towards an horse or an ox, nor towards a slave, considered as a slave; for there is nothing in common; since a slave is an animated instrument, and an instrument is an inanimate slave. Considered as a slave therefore, there is no friendship towards him, but only as he is a man: for there seems to be some sort of justice between every person and every one, who is able to participate in a law and a contract; some sort of friendship therefore accompanies every state of man. Hence friendship and justice extend but a little way in tyranny; those in democracies extend farthest; for there are many things in common to those, who are equal.

CHAP. XII.

How and why different relations love one another.

1. Every friendship therefore is in community, as has been said already: but one might separate that of relations and companions: those between citizens, and tribesmen, and fellow-sailors, and such like, more resemble those in commu-

nity; for they seem as it were to follow a kind of agreement. Amongst these also one might rank the friendship of hospitality. That also between relations seems to have many forms, and all to depend upon the paternal friendship.

2. Parents love their children, as being something of their own : children love their parents, as being themselves something from them. But parents know what comes from themselves, better than the offspring knows that it does come from them: and the original cause is more intimately connected with the thing produced, than the thing produced is with that which produced it: for that which proceeds from a thing, belongs to the thing from which it proceeded, as a tooth, or hair, or any thing whatsoever, belongs to the possessor of it: but the original cause does not belong to any of those, or in a less degree. In length of time also [the love of parents exceeds that of children]: for the former love them as soon as ever they are born; but the latter love their parents in process of time, when they have acquired intellect or sense: from this also it is evident why mothers feel the greater love. Parents then love their children as themselves; for that which proceeds from them, becomes by the separation like another self; but children love their parents, as being sprung from them.

3. Brothers love one another from being sprung from the same parents; for the identity with the latter produces an identity between each other. Whence the expressions of the same blood, the same root, and such like. They are therefore in a manner the same even in things distinct. Being educated together, and being of the same age, greatly contributes to friendship; for " coeval pleases coeval:" and those of the same character are companions. Whence also the friendship of brothers is like that of companions. Cousins and other relations owe their connection to these; for it is from their being sprung from the same stock : some are more near, others more distant, from the parent stock being nearer or farther off.

4. The friendship, which children feel towards parents, and men towards gods, is as it were towards something good

and superior; for they have conferred the greatest benefits; since they are the cause of existence, of food, and education to their offspring. Such a friendship as this contains the agreeable and the useful, more than that between strangers, inasmuch as their mode of living is more in common. They are contained also in the friendship between brothers, as they are in that between companions: and more so between the good, and in general between similar people, inasmuch as they are more connected, and love one another immediately from their birth; and inasmuch as they are more similar in character, who come from the same stock, and who are fed together, and educated similarly; and the trial, which is made by time, is here the longest and most certain. The duties of friendship are proportional in all other relationships.

5. Between man and wife friendship seems to exist by nature; for man is by nature a coupling rather than a political animal, inasmuch as a family is earlier and more necessary than a state, and procreation is more common to animals. To other animals therefore community proceeds thus far only; but men associate not only for the sake of procreation, but for the necessaries of life; for the offices of man and wife are distinct from the very first, and different. They therefore assist one another, making a common stock of their private property. For this reason also the useful and the agreeable seems to exist in this friendship: it may also be formed for virtue's sake, if they are good; for there is a virtue of each, and they may take delight in this. But children seem to be the bond; wherefore those who have no children, sooner separate; for children are a common good to both, and that which is common, binds together. But the enquiry how a man is to live with his wife, and, in short, a friend with his friend, seems in no respect different from the enquiry, how justice exists between them: for it does not seem the same between a friend and a friend, a stranger, a companion, and a fellow-traveller.

CHAP. XIII.

*In what kind of friendship complaints arise. Two kinds of
friendship for the useful, moral, and conventual. The receiver
is to decide the value of the return.*

1. THERE being then three kinds of friendship, as was
said at first, and in each of them some being friends on an
equality, and others with a superiority on one side; (for those
who are equally good become friends, and the better with
the worse; so also do the agreeable, and so also for the
useful forming an equality by mutual benefits, although they
differ:) those who are equal ought [to be friends] on an
equality, by making their love and every thing else equal;
and the unequal should be friends, by making a proportionate return to the superiority of the other party.

2. Accusations and complaints arise in the friendship for
the useful, and in that only, or mostly so, which might be
expected; for those who are friends for virtue's sake, are
anxious to benefit each other; for such is the property of virtue and friendship: and when they are contending for this,
there are no complaints or quarrels; for no one dislikes one
who loves and benefits him; but if he is polite, he returns
the kindness. And he who surpasses the other, since he obtains what he wanted, cannot complain of his friend; for
each was aiming at something good. Nor do they often
arise in friendships formed for pleasure; for both parties obtain at once what they want, if they take pleasure in living
together: and he would appear ridiculous, who complained
of another not giving him pleasure, when it is in his power
not to live with him. But the friendship for the useful is
liable to complaints; for since they make use of one another
for their own benefit, they are constantly requiring something more, and think that they have less than their due,
and complain that they do not receive as much as they
ought, although they deserve it: and those who confer benefits cannot assist them as much as the receivers require.

3. But it seems that like as justice is twofold; (for part is unwritten, and part enacted by law ;) so also of the friendship for the useful, part is moral, and part conventual. Now complaints arise chiefly when they. do not make a return in the same kind of friendship which they formed at first: but conventual friendship is formed upon settled terms, one kind of it altogether mercenary, from hand to hand ; another kind more liberal, as it allows time, but it is still settled by agreement, what is to be returned for what : in this the debt is evident, and does not admit of dispute, but it allows a friendly delay in the payment ; whence among some people, there are no trials for these kind of agreements, but they think that those who made any contract upon the faith of the other party, should be satisfied with that. Moral friendship is not upon settled terms, but each party makes a present, or does any thing else to the other, as to a friend. But he expects to receive what is equal, or more, as if he had not given, but lent ; and if he is not repaid in the manner in which he contracted the friendship, he will complain. This happens, because all or the greatest number wish what is honourable ; but upon deliberation they choose what is profitable : now it is honourable to confer benefits, not with the intention of receiving again : but it is profitable to receive benefits.

4. He therefore that has the means, must return the value of what he has received, and that voluntarily : for we must not make a man our friend against his will, as in that case he would have erred at the beginning, and received a kindness from one, from whom he ought not ; for he would not have received it from a friend, nor from one who conferred it for the sake of friendship : he must therefore repay it, as much as if he had received the benefit upon settled terms ; and he would allow, that if he had the means he would repay it ; and if he can not, the giver would not even expect it. So that if he is able, he must repay it : but he should consider at first by whom he is benefited, and upon what grounds, that he may keep to these, or not.

5. But it admits of dispute, whether we ought to measure

the return by the benefit done to the receiver, and make it according to that, or by the kindness of the conferrer. For the receivers say that they have received such things from their benefactors, as were trifling to them, and which they might have received from others, diminishing the favour: the others on the contrary say, that they were the greatest favours they had, and which they could not have received from any others, and that they were conferred in time of danger, or such like exigencies. Is not therefore the benefit of the receiver the measure in friendship for the useful? for he is the person in want, and the other assists him, as if he was to receive an equivalent: the assistance therefore is as great as the benefit which the other receives: and consequently he must repay as much as he has found it to be worth, or more; for that is more honourable. But in friendship for virtue's sake there are no complaints; and the deliberate choice of the conferrer seems to be the measure; for the distinguishing part of virtue and moral conduct lies in deliberate choice.

CHAP. XIV.

Of friendship between unequal and dissimilar parties.

1. Differences also arise in friendships, where one party is superior; for each expects to receive more: and when this takes place, the friendship is dissolved: for the better character thinks that it is his due to have more, because more is given to the good man; so also does he, who renders the greater assistance; for they say, that an useless person should not have equal, since it will be a burthensome service, and not friendship, if the profits of the friendship shall not be in proportion to the offices done. For they think, that as in

pecuniary partnerships those who contribute more, receive more, so also it ought to be in friendship. But the needy and the worse character argue differently; for they say, that it is the duty of a good friend to assist the needy; for what advantage is there, they say, in being the friend of a good or powerful man, if they are to receive nothing from it?

2. Each party seems to claim what is right, and it seems that each ought to give to each a greater share out of the friendship, but not of the same thing: but to the wealthy, a greater share of honour, to the needy, a greater share of gain; for honour is the reward of virtue and kindness, and gain is an assistance to indigence. This seems to be the same also in states; for he, who furnishes no good to the community, is not honoured; for public property is given to the public benefactor, and honour is public property. For we cannot receive money and honour at once from the public stock; for no one puts up with a less share of every thing. Consequently to him who puts up with less money, they give honour; and to him who likes presents, money; for proportion equallizes and preserves friendship, as has been said.

3. On this footing then the unequal must associate; and he, who has received benefit from the money or virtue of the other, must make a return of honour, repaying whatever he is able; for friendship requires what is possible, not what is proportionate: for this is not possible in every thing, for instance, in honour paid to the gods and to parents: for no one can ever make a proportionate return; but he, who attends upon them to the extent of his ability, is considered good. Whence also it would appear unlawful for a son to abandon his father, but lawful for a father to abandon his son: for he that is in debt, ought to pay; but there is nothing which the son can do equivalent to the benefits received; so that he is always in debt; and those who have debts owing them, have power to release the debtor; consequently the father has. At the same time perhaps it would seem that no one would separate himself, unless the other

party was excessively depraved; for besides natural friend-ship, it is not likely that man would reject assistance; but to assist him, when he is depraved, is to be avoided, or not eagerly sought after. For most men wish to receive bene-fits, and avoid conferring them, as unprofitable. Enough then has been said upon these matters.

ARISTOTLE'S ETHICS.

BOOK IX.

CHAP. I.

How friendships between unequal parties are preserved, and when broken. Who is to fix the return.

1. IN all the dissimilar friendships, proportion equalizes and preserves the friendship, as has been stated; like as in political community, the shoemaker receives a proportionate return for his shoes, and the weaver, and every one else. In these instances a common measure is provided, money: every thing therefore is referred to this, and is measured by it. But in amatory friendship, the lover sometimes complains, that although he loves exceedingly, he is not loved in turn, when perhaps he possesses nothing to excite love: and frequently the person loved complains, that the other having promised every thing at first, now performs nothing. Such cases as this occur, when the one loves the other for pleasure's sake, and he loves the lover for the useful, and these things are found not to exist in both. For as the friendship was formed on these motives, a separation takes place, when they do not obtain that, for which they loved; for it was not the persons, that they loved, but something belonging to them, which happens not to be lasting; wherefore the friendships are the same also. But a friendship founded upon

character, as it is felt for its own sake, continues, as has been stated.

2. Differences also arise, when they receive something else, and not what they were desirous of; for it is the same as having nothing, when they do not have what they desired. Like the man, who made promises to the harper, and by how much the better he performed, so much the more he promised; and when in the morning he claimed these promises, he said that he had repaid him pleasure for pleasure. Now if each party had wished this, it would have been sufficient; but if the one wishes entertainment, the other gain, and the one receives his wish, the other not, the exchange cannot be fair. For each attends to that which he happens to want, and for sake of that gives what he does give.

3. But whose office is it to fix the value? the person's who first gives? or is it not rather his who first receives? for the person who gives, seems to allow the other to decide: which they say is what Protagoras did; for when he gave any lessons, he ordered the learner to fix how much he thought the knowledge was worth, and so much he received. In some such transactions, "The promised reward, &c." is sufficient.

4. But those who receive the money beforehand, and then perform none of their promises, because they were so excessively great, are with justice complained of; for they do not execute their agreements. The Sophists perhaps are forced to do this, because no one can give money in return for knowledge. These therefore, when they do not perform that for which they received pay, are justly complained of. But when there is no agreement made about the service performed, it has been stated that those, who give for sake of the persons themselves cannot complain: for friendship for sake of virtue is of this kind.

5. The return must be made according to the intention; for it is this which characterizes friendship and virtue. It seems also that those who have philosophy communicated to them, must act thus; for the value of it is not measured

by money, and no equivalent price can be paid. But perhaps, as towards the gods and parents, that which is in our power is sufficient. But when the present is not made in that manner, but in hopes of something, perhaps it is best that a return should be made, which seems to both parties to be proportionate. But if this cannot be, it would seem not only necessary that he who first receives should settle it, but also just : for as great as was the benefit which he received, or at what cost he would have purchased the pleasure, so much will the other receive in return, and have an equivalent. For in sales this seems to be done : and in some places there are laws forbidding trials to be held upon voluntary contracts : as if it was right, when we have trusted any one, to settle with him, according to the intimacy : for they think that it is more just for him to decide to whom the matter was entrusted, than him who entrusted it to him ; for people do not in general put the same value upon things which they have received, as they did when they were wishing to receive them ; for what belongs to us, and what we give away, seems to each of us to be very valuable. But nevertheless the return is made at such a rate as the receivers would fix : though perhaps he ought not to value it at so much as it seems worth, when he has received it, but according to what he valued it at before he received it.

CHAP. II.

Of the relative duties of friends and relations.

1. Such questions as these cause a difficulty; for instance, whether we ought to give every thing to our father, and obey him in every thing? or whether when sick we should obey a physician, and choose a military man to be a general? In the same manner must we serve a friend rather than a good man? And must we rather return a favour to a benefactor,

than give to a companion, supposing that we cannot do both ? To define all these things accurately is not easy ; for they contain many and various differences in being great or small, honourable or necessary.

2. But that we must not bestow every thing upon the same person, needs no proof : and generally we must rather return kindnesses, than give them to companions, in the same manner as we must rather return a debt to a creditor, than give to a companion. But perhaps this is not always so : for instance, must a person who has been ransomed from robbers, do the same in return to him who ransomed him, whoever he may be, or should he repay a man who has not been taken prisoner, but who demands a debt from him ? or should he ransom his father rather than the other ? for it would seem that he ought to ransom his father even before himself. As we stated therefore, in general the debt should be repaid : but if the present [which he wishes to make] exceeds [the payment of the debt] in being honourable, or necessary, he should incline to the latter. For sometimes there is no equality in returning the prior favour of another, when the other conferred it, knowing that the person was good : but the latter has to return it to one whom he thinks is wicked. For sometimes a man must not lend in return to him who lent to him ; for the other, thinking that he should receive back, lent to one who was good ; but the latter does not hope to receive back from a wicked man. If then the circumstances are really such, the claim is not equal ; or if they are not so really, but they think that they are, it would not be thought that they act strangely.

3. Therefore as we have frequently stated, treatises upon passions and actions admit of strict definition correspondently to the subject matter. Now that we must not give the same to every body, nor every thing to our father, in the same manner that we do not sacrifice every thing to Jupiter, needs no proof. But since different things are due to parents, and brothers, and companions, and benefactors, we must give to each their own, and what suits them. In fact, men seem to act thus ; for they invite relations to marriages ;

since the family is common to them, and consequently family affairs. And for the same reason they think that it is most suitable for relations to meet at funerals. But it would seem that they ought to assist their parents most of all in nourishing them, being as it were in debt; and that it is more honourable to assist the authors of their existence in that respect than themselves. They should also give honour to their parents, as to the gods; but not every honour: for they do not give the same to father and mother: nor again the honour of the wise man, or the general, but the honour of a father, and so also of a mother. They should also give to every old man the honour becoming his age, by rising up, and making him sit down, and such-like offices. To companions and brothers they should give full liberty of speech, and a partnership in every thing. To their relations and tribesmen, and fellow-citizens, and every one else, they should always endeavour to give what belongs to them, and to compare the claims of each with respect to relationship, or virtue, or acquaintance. Now between relations the decision is easy; but between different people it is more difficult; we should not however for that reason desist, but as far as it is possible, so should we distinguish between them.

CHAP. III.

When it is lawful to dissolve friendship.

1. THERE is a difficulty in the question, whether we should dissolve friendship or no with those who do not continue the same? or is it, that with those who became friends for the useful or the agreeable, when they no longer possess those, there is nothing strange in breaking with them? for they were friends only for those qualities, upon the failure of which it is natural to feel friendship no more.

2. But a person might complain, if another loving him really for the useful or the agreeable, pretended that it was

on account of his character: for, as we stated at first, most differences in friendships arise, when the parties are not friends according to their real sentiments. When therefore a person is deceived, and fancied that he was loved for his character, when the other did not at all act, as if it was so, he should blame himself. But when he is deceived by the profession of the other, he is justified in complaining of the deceiver, and even more so than with those who counterfeit money, inasmuch as the crime is committed upon a more valuable subject.

3. But if he admits him to his friendship, as being a good man, and then he becomes wicked, or if he even seems to be so, must he still love him? or is this impossible, since not every thing is an object of love, but only the good? We are not then to love a wicked man, nor is it right: for we should not be lovers of wickedness, nor assimilate ourselves to the bad: and it has been stated, that like is friendly to like.

4. Must we then immediately separate? or not with all, but only those who are incurable from their wickedness? and should we not rather assist those who admit of improvement in their character than in their property, inasmuch as it is better, and belongs more peculiarly to friendship? But still the person who separates, would not be thought to do any thing extraordinary; for it was not that man, or such an one as he, that he was in friendship with: when therefore he is unable to recover the person so alienated from him, he withdraws. But if the one continues the same, while the other becomes better, and greatly improves in virtue, must he still consider the other as his friend? or is that not possible? This is most evident when the difference becomes great, as in friendships contracted from childhood: for if one continues a child in intellect, and the other becomes one of the most perfect men, how can they be friends, when they no longer take pleasure in the same things, nor feel joy and pain together? for these feelings will not exist in them towards each other. But without these it has been stated that they are no friends; for it is impossible that they can live together: and we have treated of all this already.

5. Must he then feel no otherwise towards him, than if he had never been his friend? or ought he to remember the past intimacy, and like as we think that a man should do favours to friends rather than to strangers, so ought he to bestow something upon those who were his friends, for sake of the past friendship, when the separation does not take place from excessive wickedness?

CHAP. IV.

All the feelings of friendship are the same as those of the good man towards himself.

1. The feelings of friendship towards friends, and all the definitions of friendship, seem to flow from the feelings of a man towards himself; for they define a friend to be, first, he who wishes and does what is good, or seems to be so, for the other's sake: or, secondly, he who wishes his friend to exist and to live for his own sake, which is the feeling of mothers towards their children, and of those friends who have had a slight quarrel[h]. Thirdly, Others define him to be, he who passes his time with, or chooses the same things as, or, fourthly, who has the same pleasures and pains with, his friend: this latter also is found mostly in mothers. By some one of these all men define friendship.

2. But each of these feelings exist in the good man towards himself; and in others, in proportion as they fancy themselves to be good; for virtue and the virtuous man seem, as has been stated, to be a standard to each; since he agrees with himself, and desires the same things with all his soul. Hence he wishes for himself what is good, or what

[h] For as they cannot expect any favours for themselves, on account of the quarrel, all good wishes must be disinterested.

appears so, and practises it; for it is characteristic of the
good man to labour for what is good, and for his own sake;
for it is for sake of his intellectual part, which is thought to
constitute the existence of every one. Secondly, He also
wishes himself to live and be preserved, and particularly that
part by which he thinks: for existence is a good to the virtuous man: and each one wishes good to himself; and no
one, were he to become another person, would wish that
which he was before[1], to possess every thing: for the Deity
now possesses the *summum bonum*; but whatever he is, he
is always[k]. The intellect also must be thought to be the
essence of every one, or for the most part. Thirdly, Such a
man also wishes to live with himself; for he does this
agreeably to himself; since the recollection of the past is
pleasant, and the hopes of the future are promising; but
such recollections and hopes are agreeable. Moreover he has
abundant subjects for contemplation in his mind. Fourthly,
He also participates in his own pleasures and pains to the
greatest degree; for the same thing is constantly painful or
pleasant, and not now one thing and now another; for he
is never subject to repentance, if we may say so.

3. Consequently from the good man having all these feelings towards himself, and feeling towards his friend as he
does towards himself; (for his friend is another self;) friendship also seems to consist in some one of these feelings, and
they to be friends in whom they reside. But whether there
is or is not friendship towards one's self, let that question be
dismissed for the present. But friendship must be thought

[1] Lambinus translates ἐκεῖνο τὸ γενόμενον, id, in quod commutatus sit,
which I cannot reconcile with the Greek, or the context. The argument
appears to me to be this: every man wishes the greatest good for himself;
and were he to change his identity, he would still wish for himself in his
new character the greatest good; and consequently he would no longer
wish the greatest good for that which he once wished might possess
it.

[k] I suspect the text to be corrupt here: as it stands at present, it is
perhaps meant to be an argument for the immutability of God, from the
possession of the *summum bonum* being always one of his attributes.

to exist there, where there are two or more of the above-mentioned definitions; and excessive friendship to be like that
of a man towards himself. These feelings however seem to
exist in many, although they are bad men. Do they then
partake of them so far as they are agreeable to themselves,
and fancy themselves to be good? since they do not exist,
nor even appear to exist, in any who are excessively bad and
atrocious : indeed they scarcely exist in the bad.

4. For the bad are at variance with themselves; and they
desire one thing, but wish another, like the incontinent; for
instead of what seems to them to be good, they choose the
agreeable, which is detrimental. Others again from cowardice and idleness abstain from doing what they think best
for themselves. Secondly, Some indeed, who have done many
atrocious things and are detested for their wickedness, fly
from life and destroy themselves. Thirdly, The wicked also
seek for persons, with whom they may pass their time, and
fly from themselves; for they call to mind many unpleasant
acts, and expect others of the same kind, when they are by
themselves; but when they are with others, they forget them.
And since they possess nothing amiable, they have no
friendly feeling towards themselves. Fourthly, Consequently
such men do not partake of their own pleasures and pains ;
for their soul is divided, and one part from depravity feels
pain, because it is restrained from something, while the
other part feels pleasure ; and one draws him this way, another that, as if they were pulling him asunder. But if it is
impossible to feel pain and pleasure at the same time, yet
after a little while he feels pain at having been pleased, and
wishes that these things had not been agreeable to him : for
bad men are full of repentance. The bad man therefore
seems not to have a friendly disposition, even to himself,
because he possesses nothing amiable. If then such a con-
dition as this is excessively miserable, he should anxiously
fly from wickedness and strive to be good ; for by this a
man may have friendly feelings towards himself, and become the friend of others.

CHAP. V.

Of the difference between good-will and friendship.

1. Good-will resembles friendship, and yet it is not friendship; for good-will is felt towards people we do not know, and without being expressed; but friendship is not: all which has been said before. Nor yet is it fondness; for good-will has no earnestness, nor desire: but both of these attend upon fondness. And fondness is formed after acquaintance; but good-will may be sudden; as it is when felt for wrestlers; for they wish them well, and partake in their wishes, but they would not assist them at all; for, as we have stated, they feel good-will suddenly, and their love is superficial.

2. It seems then to be the beginning of friendship: in the same manner as the pleasure, which comes from sight, is the beginning of love: for no one feels love, unless he has first found pleasure in the form: but he that takes pleasure in the form is not necessarily in love, except he longs for the person when absent, and desires his presence. In the same manner then it is impossible to be friends without having felt good-will. But well-wishers are not necessarily friends; for they only wish good to those, for whom they have good-will; but they would not assist them at all, nor take any trouble about them. Wherefore one might call it metaphorically inactive friendship; and say, that when it has continued some time, and arrived at familiarity, it becomes friendship, but not that for the useful or the agreeable: for good-will does not arise from those motives. For he that has received a benefit, returns good-will for what he has received, therein acting justly: but he that wishes any one to be prosperous, having some hope of plenty through his means, appears to be well disposed not to the other person, but rather to himself: in the same manner as he is not a friend, if he pays attention to him for sake of some profit. On the whole, good-will is formed on account of virtue, or

some goodness, when any one appears honourable, or manly, or something of that kind to any one: as we have stated it to be in the case of wrestlers.

CHAP. VI.

Of the difference between unanimity and friendship.

'1. UNANIMITY also seems to belong to friendship, wherefore it is not the same as agreement in opinion; for that may exist between people who are strangers to each other. Neither do we say, that they who think the same upon any subject whatever, have unanimity; for instance, those who think the same about the heavenly bodies; for unanimity upon these matters does not belong to friendship. But we say, that states have unanimity, when they think the same upon questions of expediency, and deliberately make the same choice, and execute public decrees. It seems then that men have unanimity upon practical matters, and out of them, upon those which are important, and which may exist in both parties, or in all; for instance, states are unanimous, when all agree that the magistrates should be elected, or that an alliance should be made with Sparta, or that Pittacus should be in administration, when he wished it also himself. But when each party wishes for himself, as the two brothers in the Phœnissæ, they quarrel; for this is not unanimity, that each party should conceive the same thing, whatever it may be, but that their conceptions should meet in the same person: for instance, when both the people and the better part agree for an aristocracy; for thus all obtain what they desire. Unanimity then seems to be political friendship, as indeed it is said to be; for it is upon matters of expediency, and those which have a reference to life.

2. But such unanimity exists between the good; for these

have unanimity both with themselves and each other, being engaged, as we may say, upon the same subjects: for the counsels of such men as these continue firm, and have no flux and reflux, like the Euripus: and they wish what is just and expedient; which also they desire in common. But it is impossible for bad men to have unanimity, except in a small degree; as it is impossible for them to be friends, since they are desirous of more than their share in what is profitable, but in labours and public services they take less. But when each party wishes the same things for himself, he examines into and prevents his neighbour; for if they are not on the watch, the state is destroyed. It happens therefore that they split into factions, as they use force to one another, and are not willing themselves to do what is just.

CHAP. VII.

Those, who confer kindnesses feel more love than those who receive them: the common and the true explanation of this.

1. BENEFACTORS seem to love those whom they have benefited, more than those who have received favours love the conferrers; and as if this were contrary to reason, an enquiry is made into it. Now the opinion of the generality is, that the one party are debtors, and the other creditors: consequently in the same manner as in the case of debts, the debtors wish their creditors not to live, but those who have lent take care actually of the health of their debtors; so also they think that those who have conferred favours, wish the receivers of them to live, as being about to receive them back again, while the other party has no anxiety to repay them. Now Epicharmus perhaps would say that they hold this language, because they take their views from the bad part of mankind: but it seems like a true picture of man;

for the generality are forgetful, and are more desirous of receiving than conferring benefits.

2. But the reason should appear to be more natural, and not like this, which is taken from lenders; for there is no fondness towards the other party in them, but a wish for their preservation, for the sake of receiving a return. But those who have conferred favours, are fond of and love the receivers of them, even if they neither are, nor ever will be, useful to them : which also is the case with workmen; for every one loves his own work, more than he could be loved by the work, were it to become animate. This perhaps happens most to poets; for they love their own poems exceedingly, doating upon them like children. Such then seems to be the case of benefactors; for that, which has received a kindness, is a work of theirs : consequently they love this more than the work loves the producer of it. The reason of this is, that existence is an object of choice and love to all; but we have our existence in action; for we have it in the act of living and doing. The work then may in a manner be considered the producer of it in actions : hence he loves the work, because he loves his existence. But this is taken from nature; for the work shews in action that which exists in power.

3. At the same time also the result of the action is honourable to the benefactor, so that he takes pleasure in the person in whom that appears : but to the receiver there is nothing honourable in the conferrer; but if any thing, advantage : and this is less agreeable or less an object of love. The actual performance of a thing when present is agreeable, and so is the hope of it when future, and the recollection of it when past: but the actual performance of it is most agreeable, and most an object of love. To the conferrer therefore the work continues; for that which is honourable, is lasting : but to the receiver, the useful soon passes away. The recollection also of honourable things is pleasant; but of useful things, not generally so, or in a less degree. The expectation seems to be the contrary of this. Fondness also is like something active; but the being loved is like something passive: upon

those therefore who are conspicuous in the active part, love and all the feelings of friendship attend. Again, all feel greater love for what they have acquired with labour; as those, who have acquired their money, love it more than those who have inherited it. Now to receive favours seems to be without labour; but to confer them is laborious. For this reason also mothers are more fond of their children; for the bringing them forth is more painful, and they feel more convinced that they are their own. The same also would seem peculiarly to belong to those, who have conferred favours.

CHAP. VIII.

Whether a man should love himself most: mistakes have arisen from not distinguishing between proper and improper self-love. Why a good man must love himself most.

1. But there is a difficulty, whether a man should love himself most, or another: for we are apt to censure those, who like themselves best; and as if it were disgraceful, we call them selfish. The bad man also seems to do every thing for his own sake; and the more so, in proportion to his wickedness. They therefore complain of him, as if he did nothing foreign from his own interest: but the good man acts from honourable motives, and by how much the better he is, so much the more does he act from honourable motives, and for his friend's sake; but he passes over his own interest.

2. But facts are at variance with these remarks, and that not unreasonably: for it is a common saying, that a man should love his greatest friend best; but he is the greatest friend, who wishes the other person good for that person's sake, and even if nobody knows it: but this and every other feeling, by which a friend is defined, exists in a man most of all towards himself; for we have stated, that from himself

proceed all the feelings of friendship, which he has for others. All proverbs agree in this : such as, " one soul :" and " the " property of friends is common :" and " friendship is " equality :" and " the knee is nearer than the calf :" for all these feelings exist mostly towards himself ; for he is the greatest friend to himself ; and therefore he must love himself most.

3. But the question is reasonably asked, which of these two must we follow, since both seem worthy of credit ? Perhaps then we should divide and distinguish such conclusions as these, and shew how far and in what respect each are true. If then we can understand in what sense each use the word self-love, perhaps the thing would be plain. Those therefore who bring it into disrepute, call them selfish, who give to themselves a greater share of money, or honour, or bodily pleasures ; for the generality are desirous of these, and extremely anxious about them, as if they were the best things ; whence also they are subjects of contention. Those therefore who are covetous of these things, gratify their desires, and in short their passions, and the irrational part of the soul. But the generality are of this kind : whence also the appellation has arisen from the generality, which are bad. Consequently reproach is justly cast upon those who are selfish in this sense. But that the generality are accustomed to call those selfish, who give such things as these to themselves, requires no proof. For if any one is constantly anxious that he himself more than any other person should do what is just, or temperate, or any thing else connected with virtue, and in short is always for gaining something honourable for himself, no one would call such a man selfish, nor blame him. And yet such a character as this would seem to be particularly selfish ; for he gives to himself what is most honourable and the greatest goods, and gratifies the governing part of himself, and obeys that in every thing. And like as that part, which has most authority, seems particularly to constitute the state, and in every other body the same, so is it also in man : and therefore he, who loves this part and gratifies it, is particularly selfish.

So also a man is called continent or incontinent, according as the intellect has authority or not, as if this constituted each individual. And men think that what they do most in obedience to reason, they do themselves and voluntarily. That this therefore mostly constitutes each individual, requires no proof, and that the good man particularly loves this. Wherefore he must be particularly selfish, in a different manner from the person who is reproached for it, and differing in as great a degree, as living in obedience to reason differs from living in obedience to passion, and desiring the honourable differs from desiring what seems to be advantageous.

4. Now all approve of and praise those who are particularly anxious about performing honourable actions : and if all contended for what is honourable, and strove to perform the most honourable acts, there would be to every one generally what is right and proper, and to each individually the greatest goods ; at least if virtue is such as we have described it. So that the good man must necessarily be selfish ; for he will be delighted in performing honourable acts himself, and will give what is profitable to others. But there is no necessity for the wicked man to be so ; for he injures both himself and his neighbours, by following evil passions. To the wicked man therefore, what he ought to do, and what he does, are at variance ; but what the good man ought to do, that he does ; for every intellect chooses what is best for itself ; and the good man obeys his intellect. It is true also of the good man, that he performs many acts for his friends and his country, even if he is required to die for them : for he will give up money and honours, and in short all goods, which others contend for, securing to himself that which is honourable. For he would prefer being pleased for a short time excessively, than for a long time slightly ; and to live one year honourably, than many years in the ordinary manner ; and to perform one honourable and great act, rather than many small ones. To those who die for their country, this perhaps actually happens. Thus they choose something greatly honourable for themselves, and they would

give up money on conditions that their friends should receive more of it : for the friend receives money, and he himself what is honourable ; but he gives the greater good to himself. The same rule holds with respect to honours and offices ; for he gives up all these to his friend ; since this is honourable to himself and praiseworthy. With reason then he has the reputation of being a good man, choosing what is honourable in preference to every thing else. It is possible also that he may give up the performance of these actions to his friend, and that it may be more honourable for him to be the cause of action to his friend, than to act himself. In all praiseworthy things therefore, the good man seems to give to himself the greater share of what is honourable. In this sense therefore it is right to love one's self, as has been stated ; but in the manner that the generality do, it is not right.

CHAP. IX.

In what manner and for what reason the happy man wants friends.

1. BUT there is also a question about the happy man, whether he wants friends or no ; for it is commonly said that those, who are prosperous and independent, do not require friends ; since they have all goods already, and therefore that being independent, they require nothing additional; but that a friend, being another person, provides what the man is unable to provide of himself. Whence comes the saying,

> When fortune favours us, why need we friends ?

And yet it seems an absurdity to attribute all goods to the happy man, but not to give him friends, which seem to be the greatest of all external goods. And if it is more the part of a friend to confer than to receive favours, and to do good is characteristic of a good man and of virtue, and it is

more honourable to benefit friends than strangers, the good
man must require some persons to receive his favours.
Whence it has even been asked, whether there is greater
need of friends in adversity or prosperity : as the man in adversity wants some persons to benefit him, and those in prosperity want some persons whom they may benefit. And it is
perhaps absurd to make the happy man a solitary being ; for
no one would choose to possess all goods by himself; since
man is a political animal, and formed by nature to associate :
this therefore is the case with the happy man ; for he possesses whatever is by nature a good. But it is evident that
it is better to pass our time with friends and good men, than
with strangers and ordinary persons. The happy man therefore wants friends.

2. What then is the argument of the first-mentioned people, and how far do they speak truth ? is it not that the generality consider those only to be friends, who are useful?
The happy man will have no need of such friends as these,
since he is in possession of all goods ; nor consequently those
who are friends for sake of the agreeable, or only in a small
degree ; for his life being agreeable, does not require any
adventitious pleasure. But since he does not require such
friends as these, he has been thought not to require friends
at all. But this perhaps is not true ; for it was stated at the
beginning that happiness is a kind of energy : and an energy
is evidently produced, not merely possessed, like any property. And if happiness consists in living and energizing,
and the energy of the good man is good and pleasant in itself,
as was stated at the beginning ; and if that which peculiarly
belongs to us is amongst the number of pleasant things, and
we can observe others better than ourselves, and their actions
better than our own, then the actions of good men, when
they are their friends, are pleasant to the good; for both
possess what is naturally pleasant : and consequently the
happy man will want such friends as these, if his principle is
to observe actions which are good, and peculiarly his own.
But such are the actions of the good man, when he is his
friend.

3. But it is thought that the happy man ought to live pleasantly. Now to a solitary person life is irksome : for it is not easy to energize constantly by one's self, but with and towards others it is easy. The energizing therefore will be more constant, when it is pleasant in itself ; which ought to be the case with the happy man ; for the good man, inasmuch as he is good, takes delight in actions proceeding from virtue, and feels pain at those which proceed from vice : just as the musician is delighted with beautiful songs, but feels pain at bad ones. And there may be a kind of practice for virtue from living with good men, as Theognis has remarked.

4. But if we examine the question more on natural principles, it appears that the good friend is by nature an object of choice to the good man ; for it has been stated, that what is good by nature, is in itself good and pleasant to the good man. But life is defined to consist, in animals, in the faculty of sensation, and in men, of sensation or intelligence ; and the faculty is referred to the energy ; and the principal part consists in the energy. Life then seems peculiarly the exercise of sensation or intellect ; and life seems to be one of those things which are good and pleasant of themselves ; for it is something definite ; and that which is definite partakes of the nature of the *summum bonum* ; and that which is a good by nature, is a good also to the good man : whence it seems to be pleasant to all. But we must not take a depraved and corrupt life, nor one involved in sorrows ; for such a life as this is undefined, as are the circumstances of it ; which will be more evident in what is to follow upon the subject of pain. But if life is a good, it is also pleasant ; which seems to be the case from all desiring it, and particularly the good and happy : for to them life is most eligible, and their mode of life is most happy. But he that sees, feels that he sees, and he that hears, feels that he hears, and he that walks, that he walks ; and in every thing else in the same manner there is something which feels that we are acting : we must also feel that we are feeling, and understand that we are understanding. But this very fact of our feeling

or understanding, is to say, that we are existing; for existence was defined to be the act of feeling, or understanding. But to feel that one is alive, is amongst those things which are pleasant in themselves; for life is a good by nature: and to perceive that there is a good inherent in one's self is pleasant. But life is eligible, and particularly to the good, because existence is to them good and pleasant; for when they feel sensible of that which is in itself a good, they are pleased. But the good man feels towards his friend, as he does towards himself; for the friend is another self; in the same manner therefore as to exist one's self is eligible to every one, so also is it for one's friend to exist, or nearly so. But existence was said to be eligible, on account of the perception of that which is a good; and such a perception is pleasant in itself. We ought therefore at the same time to be sensible of the existence of our friend; and this must take place in associating with him, and sharing his words and thoughts; for this would seem to be the meaning of the word society, when applied to men, and not as in the case of cattle, the merely feeding in the same place. If then existence is in itself eligible to the happy man, being by nature something good and pleasant, and if the existence of a friend is nearly the same, then a friend must also be amongst objects which are eligible. But that which is eligible to a man, he ought to possess; or else he is deficient in that respect: he therefore that is to be happy will want good friends[1].

[1] The argument of this fourth section may be briefly stated thus: that which is by nature good and pleasant in itself, is so to the good man: life is by nature good and pleasant in itself: therefore it is so to the good man. But life consists in the exercise of perception or intellect: and consequently to perceive his own existence must be good and pleasant to the good man: but he feels towards his friend, as he does towards himself: therefore to perceive his friend's existence is good and pleasant to him; but if it is a good, the happy man ought to possess it; therefore the happy man must have friends.

CHAP. X.

Upon the number of friends which it is possible or desirable to have.

1. Must he then make as many persons his friends as possible? or as it seems to have been appositely said in allusion to hospitality,

> May I neither have many nor few to entertain,

so also will it apply in the case of friendship, that he should neither be without friends, nor yet carry the number of his friends to excess. The saying would seem to apply altogether to those who are friends for the useful: for it is laborious to return favours to a great many, and life is not sufficient for them to do it. Consequently more than what are sufficient for each particular kind of life, are superfluous, and an impediment to living honourably; and therefore there is no need of them. And a few friends are sufficient out of those who are friends for pleasure's sake; like sauce in meats. But with respect to the good, should we have as great a number as possible? or is there some limit to number in friendship, as there is in a city? for neither can there be a city composed of ten people, nor is it any longer a city when composed of an hundred thousand: but the quantity is not perhaps some particular number, but all between certain fixed limits.

2. With friends therefore there is also some definite number; and perhaps the greatest number with whom one can associate; for this appeared to be the greatest sign of friendship. But that it is not possible for the same person to associate and continue in friendship with many, requires no proof. Besides these, other persons must also be friends to each other, if all intend to pass their time with each other; and this is difficult in a great number. It is also difficult to share exactly the same pleasures and pains with many people; for it is likely to happen at the same time, that a man may be rejoicing with one friend and grieving with another. Perhaps then it is well not to seek

to have as many friends as possible, but so many as are sufficient for society; for it would seem impossible to be a
friend to many in a great degree. Whence it is impossible
to be in love with many; for this is generally a kind of excess of friendship: and this is directed to one object; and
therefore excess in it can only be felt towards a few. So it
seems to be in real fact: for in friendship between companions, many do not become friends; but those which are
most celebrated, are between two only. Those who have
many friends, and are familiar with every body, are by no
one thought to be friends, except in a political sense; and
they call them obsequious. In a political sense then a man
may be a friend to many even without being obsequious,
but really as a good man : but for sake of virtue and the
persons themselves, it is impossible to be a friend to many;
it is a great thing indeed to find a few such.

CHAP. XI.

*Upon the duties and advantages of friends in prosperity and
adversity.*

1. Is there greater need of friends in prosperity or in adversity? for they are sought for in both : since the unfortunate want assistance, and the fortunate want companions
and persons whom they may benefit; for they wish to do
good.

2. It is more necessary to have them in adversity; whence
in this case there is need of useful friends: but it is more
noble in prosperity ; whence also they seek for good friends;
since it is more desirable to benefit them, and to live with
them.

3. Besides this presence of friends is agreeable both in
prosperity and adversity ; for those who are in pain feel
lightened, when their friends grieve with them. Whence

one might ask the question, whether they as it were share the burthen; or perhaps it is not that, but their presence being agreeable, and the idea of condolence, make the pain less. Whether then they feel lightened from this or any other cause, we may omit to consider; but what we stated seems to be the fact.

4. But the presence of them seems in a manner to cause a mixed feeling; for the fact of seeing friends is pleasant, and particularly to one in misfortune, and it becomes a kind of assistance to hinder pain : since a friend is consolatory both in look and in words, if he manages well; for he knows the character of the other, and what things give him plea-sure and pain. But to perceive his friend feeling pain at his own misfortunes is painful; for every one avoids being the cause of pain to his friends. Wherefore those who are of a manly disposition, guard against letting their friends share their pain; and unless a person is himself excessively devoid of pain, he cannot endure that his friends should feel pain [on his account]: nor does he at all call in fellow-mourners, because he is not given to mourning himself. But women and womanish men delight in having people to mourn with them, and love them as friends and partners in affliction. But in every case we ought of course to imitate the best.

5. The presence of friends in prosperity produces an agreeable mode of passing the time, and the consciousness that the friends are feeling pleasure at our good. Wherefore it would seem that we ought to invite friends to our pros-perity eagerly; for it is an honourable thing to be benevolent : but to adversity, with reluctance; for we ought to impart our misfortunes as little as possible : whence is the saying,

I am enough to mourn.

A person should call them in mostly, when they may render him great assistance, with a little trouble.

6. He should go perhaps on the contrary to those who are in misfortune, without being called in and eagerly. For it becomes a friend to confer benefits, and particularly upon

those who are in need and did not ask it; for in both cases it is more honourable and pleasant: but to those who are in prosperity, if it is to cooperate with them, he should go willingly; for this is the use of a friend: but if it is to enjoy their abundance, he should go reluctantly; for it is not honourable to be anxious to receive assistance. But perhaps he must guard against appearing ungracious in his refusal: for this is sometimes the case. The presence of friends then is necessary in all circumstances.

CHAP. XII.

Society is the great bond of friendship.

1. Is it not then, that like as sight is most desirable to lovers, and they choose that sense more than the others, as if love existed and arose mostly in that, so also society is most desirable to friends? for friendship is community. And like as he feels towards himself, so does he towards his friend; and with respect to himself, the perception of his existence is desirable; it is the same therefore with respect to his friend. But the exercise of their friendship consists in society; so that it is with reason that they are desirous of it.

2. And whatsoever existence is to either party, or on whatever account they choose life, in that they wish to pass their time with their friends. Wherefore some drink together, some play together, others exercise and hunt together, or learn philosophy together; each passing their time in that occupation, which they love most of all things in life; for when they wish to associate with their friends, they perform and share with them those things, by which they think that their society is kept together.

3. Therefore the friendship of bad men is depraved: for they participate in what is bad, being unsettled; and they

become depraved, from assimilating themselves to each other; but that of good men is good, being mutually increased by acquaintance. Besides, men appear to become better by exercising friendship, and correcting one another: for they copy from each other whatever they are pleased with: whence is said,

Learn what is good from the good.

Concerning friendship therefore let thus much be said. It would now follow that we treat of pleasure.

ARISTOTLE'S ETHICS.

BOOK X.

CHAP. I.

The reasons why it is necessary to treat of pleasure.

1. IT follows next perhaps to discuss the subject of pleasure; for it seems above every thing else to be intimately connected with our formation. Hence they educate young men, steering them by pleasure and pain. It seems also to be of the greatest consequence towards the attainment of moral virtue, that they should take delight in what they ought, and hate what they ought; for these feelings continue through the whole of life, carrying with them great weight and influence towards virtue and a happy life; for men deliberately choose what is pleasant, and fly from what is painful.

2. But it would seem that we ought by no means to pass over such feelings as these; especially as they give rise to much difference of opinion. For some say that pleasure is the *summum bonum*; others, on the contrary, that it is utterly bad; some of these last perhaps persuaded that it really is so; but others thinking that it is better for human life to declare pleasure to be among bad things, even if it is not so, because the majority of mankind incline towards it, and are slaves to their pleasures; and therefore that it is right to lead

them to the contrary, by which means they would arrive at the middle course.

3. But perhaps this is not good language to hold; for arguments about matters of suffering and acting are less persuasive than facts. When therefore arguments are at variance with what is evident to the senses, they are despised, and destroy the truth also; for if he who censures pleasure, is ever seen to be desiring it, he appears to have a leaning towards it, as if all pleasure were of the same nature; for to draw nice distinctions is not the character of the multitude.

4. True arguments therefore seem not only to be very useful for obtaining knowledge, but also with a view to life; for when they agree with facts, they are believed. Hence men exhort those who understand them, to live according to them. Enough then of such matters; and let us go over what has been said upon the subject of pleasure.

CHAP. II.

The arguments by which Eudoxus maintained pleasure to be the summum bonum.

1. EUDOXUS thought that pleasure was the *summum bonum*, because he saw all things, both rational and irrational seeking it; and in every thing that which is an object of choice is good, and that which is most so is the greatest good : but he considered that for every thing to have an inclination towards the same object proved that object to be the best for all; because each finds that which is good for himself as he does food; consequently that which is good to all, and which all aim at, he thought was the *summum bonum*. And his words were believed, more from the excellence of his character, than from themselves; for he had the reputation

of being singularly temperate : it therefore seemed that he did not hold this language as being a friend to pleasure, but that the case really was so.

2. But he considered it to be not less evident from the contrary of pleasure; for pain is in itself an object of aversion to all, and its contrary is in the same manner an object of choice : and that is in the highest degree an object of choice, which we choose not on account of any thing else : but pleasure is confessedly of this nature; for no one asks why he is pleased, as if pleasure was eligible on its own account, and if added to any good whatsoever, makes it more eligible; for instance, if added to the act of justice or temperance: and therefore good is increased by this [pleasure]. This argument certainly seems to prove it to be amongst goods, but [m] not more so than any thing else; for every thing is more eligible when in conjunction with another good, than when left alone. By a similar argument indeed Plato destroys the idea of pleasure being the *summum bonum* ; because a pleasant life is more eligible when joined with prudence than without; but if the union of the two is better, pleasure simply is not the *summum bonum* ; for the *summum bonum* must be eligible, though nothing be added to it : and it is evident that nothing else can be the *summum bonum* [n], which becomes more eligible when joined to any of those things which are eligible on their own account.

3. What idea then of the *summum bonum* is of such a nature that we also entertain it ? for such is the object of our enquiry. Those who insist that that is not a good which all aim at, perhaps talk nonsense; for we affirm, that what appears to all, must really exist. And he who tries to overthrow this proof is not at all more worthy of being followed; for if it had been said that unintelligent beings only sought

---

[m] I would read ἀλλ' for καί.

[n] This does not contradict what he said in book i. c. 7. that happiness became greater, if added to even the smallest good: for although it may thus be increased in quantity, it cannot (as is the expression here) become more eligible from being joined to any good *which is chosen for its own sake ;* because happiness implies the possession of all such goods.

pleasure, there might be something in the objection; but if beings possessing prudence also seek it, how can they be said to argue sensibly? and perhaps even in the inferior beings there is some natural good principle, superior to their general character, which aims at that good which is peculiarly adapted to them.

4. Neither does what they say about the contrary appear to be said well: for they say that although pain be an evil, it does not follow that pleasure is a good; for evil is opposed to evil [o], and both are opposed to that which is neither good nor evil; in which they do not speak amiss, but it does not happen to be true in the case before us: for if both were evils, both must be objects of aversion, or if neither of them were, then neither would be, or they would be so correspondently: but men are seen to avoid the one as an evil and to choose the other as a good: they are therefore opposed in the manner which was stated.

CHAP. III.

Other objections against pleasure being a good are obviated; and it is proved that there must be different species of pleasure.

1. Nor yet if pleasure is not amongst qualities, is it therefore not amongst goods; for the energies of virtue are not qualities, nor is happiness. But it is said that good may be defined, but pleasure is undefinable [P], because it admits of being more or less. Now if they form this opinion from the

---

[o] As we have seen in the two extremes of excess and deficiency.

[P] To say that a thing is undefinable or is not a quality is the same; a quality being only a logical term to express any thing which admits of definition: for every definition consists of a genus and difference; and as the genus is said to be predicated in *quid*, and the difference in *quale*, any thing which admits of definition may be said to be predicated in *qualequid*, in Greek ποῖόν τι, and therefore the thing itself is called ποιότης, a quality.

exercise of pleasure, the same thing will apply to justice and the other moral virtues, (from following which it is allowed that men evidently become of a certain quality in a greater or less degree,) and to virtue generally ; for some men are just and courageous in a greater degree : it is possible also to perform the acts of justice and temperance in a greater or less degree. But if they apply their assertion to pleasure abstractedly, I imagine they do not mention the cause, if some pleasures are unmixed and some mixed[q]. But what objection is there, that like as health, which is defined, admits of being greater or less, pleasure should be in the same state ? for there is not the same formation in all men, nor in the same person is it always one, but although relaxed, yet it continues up to a certain point[r], and differs in being greater or less. It is possible then that the case of pleasure may be the same.

2. Laying down the *summum bonum* to be perfect, and motions and creations to be imperfect, they attempt to prove pleasure to be a motion and a creation[s]. But it seems that their argument is not correct, and that it is not a motion ; for quickness and slowness appears to belong to every motion ; and if not absolutely, as in the motion of the world, yet relatively. But neither of these exist in pleasure ; for it is possible to become pleased quickly, as it is to become angry ; but not to feel pleasure quickly, not even relatively ; but only to walk, or to grow, and all such things. It is possible therefore to change[t] into a state of pleasure quickly

[q] For although the mixed pleasures may be undefinable, the pure and unmixed will admit of definition, which distinction the opponents of pleasure ought to have stated, when they argued against its being a good on the ground of its not being definable.

[r] Two people will be said to be in health, although one is certainly more perfectly so than the other ; and it is impossible to fix the limits where a good state of health ends and a bad state begins ; and yet health itself is definable.

[s] i. e. that pleasure itself is not the feeling produced in the mind, but that which generates and produces that feeling ; or that it is the moving from a state of pain, or absence of pleasure, into pleasure.

[t] And this is what the objectors conceived pleasure to consist in.

or slowly; but to exercise the feeling of pleasure quickly is not possible : (which is expressed by the Greek term ἥδεσθαι.)

3. How also can it be a creation [or something creative]? for it appears that any thing is not generated from any thing; but from whatever it is generated, into that it is dissolved ; and that which pleasure generated, pain [u] de-, stroys.   But they say that pain is a want of something which nature requires, and that pleasure is the supplying of that want.   But these are bodily feelings : consequently if pleasure is the supplying of that which nature requires, that thing must feel the pleasure, in which the supplement takes place; that is, the body must feel it.   But this does not seem to be the case ; therefore pleasure is not the supplying of a want ; but when the supplement has taken place, then a man may feel pleasure; in the same manner that when he has been cut, he feels pain [x].   But this opinion seems to have had its origin from the pains and pleasures connected with food : for when men are in want and have previously felt pain, they feel pleasure at having the want supplied. But this does not happen in all pleasures : for the pleasures of mathematics are without pain ; and of the pleasures of the senses, those which come by smelling and hearing and seeing; many recollections also and hopes.   To what then will these give birth ? for there are no wants of any thing, which may be supplied.

4. In answer to those who bring forward reprehensible pleasures, one might say, that these are not pleasant ; for we are not to think that because they are pleasant to evil-disposed persons, they are also pleasant in themselves, except to these particular persons ; in the same manner as we are not to think those things wholesome, or sweet, or bitter,

---

[u] If pleasure merely consisted in generating a certain feeling in the mind, that feeling would be resolved again into pleasure ; but it continues there till it is expelled by pain.

[x] It is not pain which cuts a man, but after he has been cut, he feels pain : so it is not pleasure which supplies the want, but when it is supplied pleasure is felt.

which are so to the sick : nor again those to be white, which appear so to persons with diseased eyes. Or should one answer thus, that pleasures are eligible, but not from these sources; as wealth is eligible, but not to one who gets it by treachery ; so is health, but not to one who gets it by eating all kinds of things. Or is it not rather that pleasures differ in species? for those which proceed from honourable sources are different from those which come from disgraceful ones; and it is impossible to have the pleasure of the just man without being just, or that of the musician, without being musical ; and so in other cases.

5. But the circumstance of the friend being different from the flatterer seems to prove either that pleasure is not a good, or that pleasures are different in species; for the former seems to associate for good, the latter for pleasure ; and the one is reproached, but men praise the other ; as if they associated for different motives. Secondly, And no one would choose to live, having the intellect of a child throughout his life, taking pleasure in those things which please children, even to the greatest degree; nor to take delight in doing any disgraceful thing, not even if he was never to feel pain for it. Besides, we should take pains about many things, even if they brought no pleasure, as seeing, remembering, knowing, possessing virtue. But whether pleasures follow these things of necessity or no, makes no difference ; for we should choose them, even if pleasure did not arise from them.

6. Consequently that pleasure is not the *summum bonum*, nor every pleasure eligible, seems to be evident : and that some are eligible for their own sakes, differing either in species, or the source from whence they come. Let this then be sufficient as to the opinions which have been entertained upon the subject of pleasure and pain.

CHAP. IV.

*It is proved more at large that pleasure is not a motion, but
that it makes the energy complete.*

1. But what is the genus or species of pleasure would
become more evident if we resume the subject from the beginning. For vision seems to be perfect at any period of
time; for it is not in want of any thing, which by coming
afterwards will make its species perfect. But pleasure resembles this; for it is something entire: and there is no
particular time at which one might feel pleasure, the species
of which would be perfected if it lasted a longer time.
Wherefore it is not a motion; for every motion consists in
time, and is directed to some end; for instance, the motion
of building is perfect, when it produces what it is aiming
at; it is therefore perfect either when the whole time is out,
or at this or that particular time. But in the separate parts
of time all the motions are imperfect, and different in species
from the whole motion, and from one another: for the
putting together of the stones is different from measuring the
perpendicularity of the column, and these are different from
the completion of the temple. And the motion of the temple is perfect: because it wants nothing towards the end
proposed; but the motion of the foundation and the triglyph
is imperfect: for each belongs only to a part. Consequently
they differ in species; and it is not possible at any particular
time to take a motion which is perfect in its species; but if
it is ever perfect, it must be in the whole time. It is the
same in walking, and every other motion. For if loco-motion is the moving from one part of space to another, the
specific differences of loco-motion must also be so also, as
flying, walking, leaping, and such like. But not only thus,
but even in walking itself; for the *whence* and the *whither*
are not the same in the stadium, and in part of the stadium,
or in one part of it and the other. Nor is it the same thing
to pass this line or that; for a person does not only pass a
line, but a line in one particular part of space; and this is

in a different part of space from that. We have treated minutely of motion in another place. It seems however not to be perfect in every part of time, but that the greater number are imperfect and different in species, if the *whence* and the *whither* form the species. But the species of pleasure is perfect at any time whatsoever. It is evident therefore that pleasure and motion must be different from each other, and that pleasure belongs to things entire and perfect. This also would appear from the fact of its being impossible to move except in time, but we may feel pleasure without reference to time; for that which is felt at this particular moment is something entire. But from all this it is evident, that men do not correctly say that pleasure is a motion or creation; for these terms are not applied to every thing, but to those which are devisable and not entire: for there is no generation of vision, nor of a point, nor of a unit: nor is any thing the motion or generation of these things, nor consequently of pleasure; for it is something entire.

2. But since every sense acts upon the object of sense, and that acts perfectly which is well-disposed towards the best of all the objects which fall under it: (for a perfect act seems particularly to be of this nature; and whether we say that the sense acts, or that in which the sense is, makes no difference; but in every thing the act is best of that which is well-disposed towards the best of all the objects which fall under it:) this must be the most perfect and the most pleasant: for pleasure attends upon every sense, as it does also upon every act of intellect and contemplation: but the most perfect is the most pleasant, and the most perfect is that of the thing which is well-disposed towards the best of all the objects which fall under it. Pleasure therefore makes the act perfect[y]: but pleasure does not make it perfect in the same

---

[y] The argument seems to be this: every act is attended by an operation either of intellect or sensation: but every such operation is attended with pleasure, and the most perfect operation of sensation and intellect must be attended with the most perfect pleasure; consequently no act whatsoever can be perfect and complete, unless there is a perfect and complete pleasure attending it: i. e. pleasure makes the act perfect.

manner that the object and the sense do if they are good; as health and the physician are not in the same manner causes of a person being healthy.

3. But that there is a pleasure in every act of sense is evident: for we say that acts of vision and hearing are pleasant: and it is also evident that this is most so, when the sense is the best, and acts upon the best object. But if the object of sense and the thing which feels the sense are of this nature, there will always be pleasure as long as there is an active and a passive. But pleasure makes the energy complete, not as the inherent habit, but as some end added to it, as personal grace to those in the prime of life. As long therefore as the object of sensation or intellect be such as it ought, as also the faculty which judges or contemplates, there will be pleasure in the energy: for when the patient and the agent are similar and correspond to one another, the same effect is naturally produced.

4. Why then is no one continually pleased? is it that he becomes fatigued? for no human things have the power of energizing continually. Pleasure therefore cannot[z], for it follows the energy. But some things cause delight when they are new, and for the same reason they do not cause it in the same degree afterwards: for at first the mind is inclined towards them, and energizes earnestly in them, like as in the case of sight those who fix their eyes; but afterwards the energy is not of the same kind, but relaxed. Wherefore also the pleasure becomes obscured.

5. But one might imagine that all men seek pleasure, because all are desirous of life; and life is a species of energy; and every one energizes upon and in those things which he loves most; as the musician, in hearing, upon music; the studious man, in his intellect, upon theorems; and so with the rest. But pleasure makes the energy perfect, and therefore it makes life perfect, which men desire. It is with reason therefore that they are also desirous of pleasure; for it makes life, which is an object of choice, perfect to every

---

[z] I have ventured to read δύναται for γίνεται.

one. But let the question whether we choose life for the sake of pleasure, or pleasure for the sake of life, be omitted for the present, for these seem to be intimately connected, and not to admit of separation; for without an energy pleasure is not produced, and pleasure makes every energy perfect.

CHAP. V.

Different energies require different energies to make them perfect: and to know what pleasure is the best, we must look to the best man.

1. WHENCE also they seem to differ in species; for we think that things which are different in species are made perfect by different things; for such seems to be the case with natural things and works of art, as animals and trees, and painting and statues, and a house and furniture. So also we think that energies which differ in species are made perfect by things which differ in species.

2. But the energies of the intellect differ from the energies of sensation, and each of these differ from one another in species: consequently the pleasures which perfect them differ. This would also appear from each pleasure being intimately connected with the energy which it perfects; for the appropriate pleasure contributes to increase the energy; for persons who act with pleasure judge of every thing and perform it accurately in a greater degree; as those become geometricians who take pleasure in geometry, and they perceive every thing more distinctly. So also those who are fond of music, or fond of building, and every one else make a progress in their peculiar employment, taking pleasure in it. Pleasures therefore contribute to increase the energy; but what contributes to increase must be closely connected: and things which are closely connected with objects differing

in species, must themselves be different in species. Again, this would appear still more from the fact that pleasures arising from other things are impediments to energies ; for those who love music cannot attend to conversation if they hear any one playing, because they take more pleasure in music than in their present energy. The pleasure therefore which attends music destroys the energy that was employed in conversation. This is the same in every other case, when a man is employed upon two things at once : for the pleasanter energy drives out the other ; and if there is a great difference as to the pleasure, so much the more, so that he cannot energize at all upon the other. Wherefore when we take excessive delight in any thing, we generally do not do any thing else; and we do something else, when we are but moderately pleased with the other thing, as persons who eat sweetmeats in the theatre, do it most when the actors are bad. But since the appropriate pleasure makes the energies accurate, and more lasting, and better, but the pleasures arising from any thing else spoil them, it is evident that they are very distinct. For pleasures arising from something else have nearly the same effect with pains from the thing itself ; for pains in the thing itself destroy the energies ; for instance, painting or reasoning is unpleasant and painful to any one, the one does not paint, and the other does not reason, the energy being painful. The contrary effect therefore is produced in energies from pleasures and pains which peculiarly belong to them : but those peculiarly belong to the energy which follow it of itself. It has been mentioned also that pleasures from other objects produce nearly the same effect with pain ; for they destroy the energy, but not in the same way.

3. But since energies differ in being good or bad, and some are to be chosen, some to be avoided and others neither, the pleasures also are in the same way ; for there is a pleasure peculiarly belonging to every energy. That therefore which belongs to the good energy is just, and that which belongs to the bad energy is vicious ; for the desires of honourable things are praiseworthy, of disgraceful ones,

reprehensible. But the pleasures, which are in energies, more peculiarly belong to them than the desires; for the latter are different according to time and disposition; but the former follow close upon the energies, and are so inseparable from them, that it admits of dispute, whether the energy is the same with the pleasure. It appears however that pleasure is not an operation of intellect or sensation; for it is absurd; but because they are not separated, they appear the same to some people. As therefore the energies are different, so are the pleasures. But sight differs from touch in purity, and hearing and smelling from taste: the pleasures therefore differ in the same way; and the pleasures of intellect differ from these, and each from one another. But there seems to be a pleasure peculiarly belonging to every animal, as there is a peculiar work; for it is that which belongs to the energy. And if we examine each particularly, this would appear to be the case; for the pleasure of a horse, of a dog, and of a man is different; as Heraclitus says, that an ass would prefer rubbish to gold; for food is pleasanter than gold to asses. The pleasures therefore of things differing in species are different; but it is reasonable that the pleasures of the same things should have no difference.

4. But they have no small difference with respect to men: for the same things give pain to some and pleasure to others; and to some they are painful and hateful, to others pleasant and delightful. The same is also the case in sweet things; for the same things do not seem sweet to a man in a fever and a man in health; nor does the same thing seem warm to an invalid and a man in a good state of body; the same is also the case with every thing else. But in all these cases that which appears to the most excellent[a] of the kind

---

[a] Lambinus translates τῷ σπουδαίῳ, viro bono, virtuteque prædito. In which I conceive that he is wrong, or at least that he only gives one part of the meaning of the term. In the examples quoted in the preceding sentence, the ὑγιαίνων is σπουδαῖος compared with the πυρέττων, and the εὐεκτικός compared with the ἀσθενής.

seems to be the true appearance. If this remark is true, (as it appears to be,) and excellence, and the good man, so far as he is good, are the standard of every thing; those must be pleasures which appear so to him, and those things pleasant in which he delights. But if the things which are disagreeable to him seem pleasant to any one, it is no wonder; for there are many things which corrupt and injure men; but such things are not pleasant, except to those men and others who are so disposed. With respect to those which are acknowledged to be disgraceful, it is evident that we must not call them pleasures except to the corrupted. But of those pleasures which seem to be good, what particular one or what kind must we say is the pleasure of man? or is this discoverable from the energies? for pleasures follow them. Whether then there be one or more energies of the perfect and happy man, the pleasures which perfect them must properly be called the pleasures of man; and the rest must be so in a secondary and promiscuous manner, like the energies.

CHAP. VI.

Happiness is an energy according to virtue.

1. As we have treated of the virtues, of friendships, and of pleasures, it remains that we should discuss the subject of happiness in the outline, since we have laid this down to be the end of human actions. Wherefore if we recapitulate what has been said before, the argument would be more concise.

2. But we have said [b] that it is not a habit; for if it were, it might exist in a man who slept throughout his life, leading the life of a vegetable, and unfortunate in the greatest de-

---

b Vide b. i. c. 7.

gree. If then this does not please us, but we must rather bring it under a kind of energy, as was said before; and of energies, some are necessary and chosen for the sake of something else, others are chosen for their own sakes; it is evident that we must consider happiness to be one of those which are chosen for their own sakes, and not one of those which are chosen for sake of something else: for happiness is in want of nothing, but is self-sufficient.

3. Now those energies are chosen for their own sakes, from which nothing additional is sought for beyond the energy. But actions done according to virtue seem to be such; (for the performance of noble and excellent acts is amongst things chosen for their own sakes:) and of amusements, those which are pleasant: for men do not choose these for sake of any thing else; for they are rather injured by them than benefited, since they neglect their persons and property. But many of those who are called happy fly to such pastimes as these: wherefore those who have a good turn for such pastimes as these are in favour with kings; for they make themselves agreeable in those things which the others desire; and such are the men that they require. These things therefore seem to belong to happiness, because those who are in power pass their leisure in them. But such men are perhaps no proof; for virtue does not consist in having power, nor does intellect, from which two things good energies proceed; nor if these men, who have never tasted real and liberal pleasure, fly to bodily pleasures, must we therefore think that these pleasures are more eligible; for children think that those things which are esteemed by them are the best. It is reasonable therefore to suppose, that as different things appear honourable to children and to men, so also they do to the bad and the good. Wherefore, as we have said very often, those things are honourable and pleasant which are so to the good man. But to every man that energy is most eligible which accords with his peculiar habit; and therefore to the good man, that which accords with virtue. Consequently happiness does not consist in amusement; for it is absurd that the end should be amusement, and that

men should toil and suffer inconvenience all their life for the
sake of amusement : for we choose every thing, as we might
say, for the sake of sómething else, except happiness; for
that is the end. But'to be serious, and to labour for the sake
of amusement, appears foolish and very childish.   But to
play that we may be serious, as Anacharsis said, seems to be
right ; for amusement resembles recreation.   Recreation
therefore is not the end, for it is had recourse to for sake of
the energy.

4. But the happy life seems to be according to virtue ; and
this is serious, not in amusement.   We say also that serious
things are better than those which are ridiculous and full of
amusement ; and that the energy of the better part and of
the better man is more serious ; and the energy of the better
man is superior, and therefore more connected with happiness.   Besides any person whatsoever and a slave may enjoy
bodily pleasures no less than the best man; but no one
allows a slave to partake of happiness unless he does also of
[a virtuous] life : for happiness does not consist in such modes
of passing life, but in energies directed by virtue, as has been
stated already.

CHAP. VII.

Happiness consists in the energies of the intellectual virtues;
which energies are shewn by induction to contain all the re-
quisites for happiness more than the moral energies.

1. BUT if happiness is an energy according to virtue, it is
reasonable to suppose that it is according to the best virtue ;
and this must be that of the best part.   Whether then this
best part be intellect, or any thing else, which seems naturally to have the rule and government, and to possess ideas
upon noble and divine subjects ; or whether it is itself divine,
or the most divine of any thing within us ; the energy of

this part according to its peculiar virtue must be perfect happiness : and that this energy is contemplative has been stated [c].

2. This also would seem to agree with what was said before, and with the truth : for this is the best energy; since the intellect is the best thing within us, and of subjects of knowledge, those are best with which the intellect is concerned.

3. It is also most constant; for we are able to energize more constantly than to do any thing else.

4. We think also that pleasure ought to be united to happiness : but of all the energies according to virtue, that according to wisdom [d] is confessedly the most pleasant : at least wisdom seems to contain wonderful pleasures both in point of purity and continuance : and it is reasonable that life should be pleasanter to those who have knowledge, than to those who only seek it.

5. Also that which is called independence must exist most in contemplative happiness; for both the wise man, and the just, and all other men require the necessaries of life ; but supposing them to be sufficiently supplied with such goods, the just man requires persons towards whom and between whom he shall act justly ; so also the temperate man, and the courageous, and every other morally virtuous man. But the wise man, even if by himself, is able to contemplate; and the more so, in proportion as he is wise ; perhaps he will energize better, if he has coadjutors ; but still he is most independent.

6. This would seem also to be the only energy which is

---

[c] We have now arrived by a different process at the same definition of happiness which was given in the first book, c. 7. viz. An energy of the soul, according to the best virtue ; but as we are now able to explain what is the best virtue, we may substitute the one word Θιωρία, contemplation, for the whole of the definition.

[d] Wisdom was shewn in the 6th book to be the best of the intellectual virtues : contemplation therefore (which is an energy) is the exercise of wisdom, (which is an habit :) and wisdom was shewn (in the 6th book, c. 7.) to contain knowledge.

loved for its own sake; for nothing is produced from it besides contemplation; but from the active energies, we gain
more or less besides the performance of the action.

7. Happiness seems also to consist in leisure [e]; for we are
actively engaged, that we may have leisure; and we go to
war that we may be at peace. Now the energies of the
active virtues seem to consist in political or military affairs;
but actions in these appear to have no leisure. Certainly
military actions are altogether without it : for no one chooses
war for the sake of war, nor even to make preparations for
war; for a man would seem to be altogether sanguinary, if
he made his friends enemies in order that there might be
battles and murders. The energy of the political character
is also without leisure; besides the actual administration of
the state, being engaged in gaining power and honour, or
happiness for himself and his citizens, which is evidently different from the political science that we are in search of [f].

8. If then of all actions according to the virtues, the civil
and the military excel in beauty and greatness; and these
are not in leisure and aim at some end, and are not chosen
for their own sakes; but the energy of the intellect seems to
excel in intensity, as it is contemplative, and to aim at no
end beyond itself, and to have a pleasure peculiarly belong-

[e] i. e. in being disengaged from active energies, that we may have
time for contemplation.

[f] There appears to be some corruption of the text in this place. I have
ventured to read δῆλον ὡς ἑτέραν οὖσαν τῆς πολιτικῆς, ἥν καὶ ζητοῦμεν, so as not
to repeat the words ἑτέραν οὖσαν twice. But still there is some confusion :
for although there are certainly two kinds of πολιτική, one which is engaged
in the administration of the state, and another in providing for the happiness of the people; yet this last cannot be said to be different from the
πολιτική, " which we are in search of," because it is that and not the execu-
tive πολιτική, which we have been considering all throughout the book.
Besides the construction seems to require ἑτέραν οὖσαν to agree with εὐδαι-
μονίαν rather than with πολιτική. I would therefore either substitute
εὐδαιμονίας for πολιτικῆς, or follow Eustratius in reading θεωρητικῆς. The
sense will then be evident: for undoubtedly the happiness which the
πολιτικὸς seeks for his citizens is not contemplative happiness, but happiness in the popular sense of the word.

ing to it; and if this increases the energy; and if self-sufficiency, and leisure, and freedom from decay, (as far as any thing human can be free,) and every thing which is attributed to the happy man, seem to exist in this energy; then this must be perfect happiness of man, when it receives the end of life complete; for nothing is incomplete of those things which are classed under happiness.

9. But such a life [it will be objected] would be too good for man; for he will lead such a life as this, not inasmuch as he is man, but inasmuch as there is something divine in him. But so far as this divine part excels the whole compound, so much does its energy excel the energy of the rest of virtue. If then the intellect be divine when compared with man, also the life which is in obedience to that will be divine when compared with human life. But a man ought not to entertain human thoughts, as some would advise, because he is human, nor mortal thoughts because he is mortal; but as far as it is possible he should abstract himself from mortality, and do every thing with a view to living in obedience to the best of all things within him; for if this is small in size, yet in power and value it very far exceeds all. Besides each of us would seem to exist in this part, if it is the ruling and the better part. It would be absurd therefore, if a man were to choose not his own life, but the life of something else[g]. And what was said before will apply now; for that which is peculiarly suited to each by nature, is best and most pleasant to every one; and therefore to man the life according to intellect is most pleasant, if this is particularly man. That life therefore is the most happy.

[g] As intellect is the proprium of man, intellect may be said to be man; and therefore a life according to intellect is the proper life for men; and a life according to any of the other parts which make up the compound, man, would be the life of that compound, and not of man.

CHAP. VIII.

Intellectual happiness is shewn by several arguments to be superior to moral happiness: and this notion is confirmed by the opinions of other philosophers.

1. BUT that life which is according to the rest of virtue is happy in a secondary manner; for the energies according to that virtue are human; for we perform what is just, and courageous, and every thing else belonging to the moral virtues, in our intercourse with each other, and in our wants, observing what is suitable for each in every kind of action and passion. But all these appear to be human. Some of them even seem to result from the body, and moral virtue seems in many respects to be intimately connected with the passions. Prudence[h] also is united to moral virtue, and this to prudence; if the principles of prudence are acquired by the moral virtues, and the perfection of the moral virtues by prudence. But these are connected with the passions, and must relate to the whole compound of man; and the virtues of the compound are human; and therefore the life according to them and the happiness are human. But the happiness of the intellect is separate; for let thus much be said about it, since extreme accuracy is beyond the subject proposed.

2. It would also seem to require external aid in a small degree, or in a less degree than moral happiness. For let it be granted that both are in need of necessary things: (although the man engaged in civil science is employed more about the body and things connected with that:) for in this there is but little difference, but with respect to the energies there will be a great difference; for the liberal man will want money, in order to perform liberal acts; and the just man will want means to make returns; the courageous man also will want power, if he is to perform any thing connected

---

[h] Prudence is the connecting link between the intellectual and moral virtues; it being itself intellectual, and serving as a guide in moral action.

with virtue; and the temperate man will want an opportunity [to shew his temperance.] For otherwise how will he or any other character be known. For wishes are uncertain, and even the unjust pretend that they wish to act justly [i]: and there is a question [k], whether the principle or the actions themselves have the greater influence over virtue, since it consists in both: it is evident therefore that the perfection [of virtue] must reside in both; but with a view to actions, it is in want of many things; and by how much greater and nobler the actions are, so many the more will it want. But the contemplative man requires no such things, at least to perform his energy; but as we might say they are even impediments to his contemplation. But in his capacity of man and of associating with many, he will choose to perform acts of moral virtue. He will therefore require such things in order to fulfil his human character.

3. But that perfect happiness is a kind of contemplative energy might be shewn also from hence; that we suppose the gods to be preeminently blessed and happy. But what moral acts can we attribute to them? shall they be just acts? or will they not appear ridiculous making bargains, and restoring deposits, or any such things as these? But shall we give them courageous acts, that they may undergo formidable things and meet danger, because it is honourable? or liberal acts? but to whom will they give? and it is absurd if they are to have money, or any thing of that sort. But if they are temperate, what would follow? is not the praise absurd, because they have not bad desires? And if we went through every case of moral action, they would seem small, and unworthy of gods. But yet all suppose that they live, and therefore energize; for they do not sleep, like Endymion. To him therefore who lives, but is abstracted from moral action, and still more so from production, what is left besides contemplation? So that the energy of the Deity, as it exceeds in blessedness, must be contemplative:

[i] A slight transposition of the sentences has been made here.

[k] Vide book iii. c. 2. sect. 1.

and therefore of human energies that which is nearest allied to this, must be the happiest.

4. A proof of it also is, that other animals do not partake of happiness, which are deprived altogether of such an energy. For to the gods, their whole life is happy; and to men, as far as there is some resemblance to such an energy: but no other animal is happy, because they in no way partake of contemplation. As far therefore as contemplation extends, so far does happiness; and in whom there is more contemplation, in them there is more happiness, not from accident, but in consequence of the contemplation; for this is honourable of itself. So that happiness must be a kind of contemplation.

5. But the happy man will want external prosperity, as far as he is man; for nature is not sufficient of itself to contemplate; but the body must be in health, and food and other necessaries must be present. We must not however imagine that the person who is to be happy, because it is impossible for him to be so without external goods, will therefore want many and great goods; for independence does not consist in excess, nor does decision, nor action[1]. But it is possible for men to perform noble things without being lords of earth and sea; for a man may be able to act according to virtue with moderate means. We may see an evident proof of this: for private individuals seem to perform good acts no less than men in power, but even more so. And it is sufficient that so many [goods] are present, [as enable him to energize without interruption:] for the life of that man will be happy, who energizes according to virtue.

6. Solon also perhaps gave a good description of happy men, when he said that in his opinion they were those who were moderately supplied with external goods, who had done the most noble deeds, and lived temperately; for it is

---

[1] A person is not independent then only when he possesses every thing to excess: nor do we decide in favour of a thing, because it is in excess: nor does the perfection of a moral act consist in its being done to excess.

possible that men who have moderate possessions should do what they ought. It seems also that Anaxagoras conceived the happy man to be neither the rich nor the powerful, when he said, that he should not be surprised if he appeared in an absurd light to the multitude ; for these judge by externals, having a perception only of such things[m]. The opinions of wise men also seem to agree with what has been said ; such facts therefore carry with them some credit. But truth in practical matters is decided from facts and from life ; for the important part of them depends upon these : and we ought to try all that has been said, by applying it to facts and to life ; and if our arguments agree with facts, we may receive them ; but if they are at variance, we must consider them as mere words.

7. Also he that energizes according to intellect, and pays attention to that, and has it in the best state, is likely to be most beloved by the gods : for if any regard is paid to human things by the gods, as there seems to be, it must be reasonable that they would take pleasure in what is the best and nearest allied to themselves ; but this must be intellect ; and that they would be kind in return to those who love and honour this most, as to persons who take care of what is dear to them, and who act rightly and nobly. But that all these things exist most in the wise man requires no proof ; he is therefore most beloved by the gods. It is probable also that the same person is most happy. So that in this way also the wise man must be most happy.

[m] If the multitude thought Anaxagoras absurd, because they judged from external things ; it is plain that Anaxagoras differed from them, and did not judge from external things, and so far agreed with Aristotle in his opinion of happiness.

CHAP. IX.

As no moral precepts are attended to unless the hearer has been
previously disposed to virtue, the subject of education is con-
sidered. If children could be educated by the laws, as in
Sparta, it would be better; but as that is not the case, every
one who has the care of education, should study legislation as
much as he can. But as the science of legislation has not been
taught like other sciences, or has been taught erroneously, the
author himself promises to write a treatise upon politics.

1. IF then we have treated sufficiently of these matters,
and the virtues, and also of friendship and pleasure, must
we think that our original plan is completed? or is the end
in practical matters, according to common saying, not the
contemplating and knowing every thing, but rather the
practising them? and therefore it is not sufficient to have
knowledge of virtue, but we must endeavour to possess and
employ it; or if we become good in any other way.

2. Now if precepts were sufficient of themselves to make
men good, justly " would they have received many and great
" rewards," as Theognis says, and we should be obliged to
provide ourselves with them. But the case is, that they seem
to have power to urge on and to excite young men of liberal
minds, and to make a character that is generous and truly
fond of what is noble easily led by virtue; but that they
have no power to excite the multitude to what is virtuous
and noble. For it is not the nature of such men to obey a
sense of shame, but fear; nor to abstain from vicious things
because it is disgraceful, but on account of the punishments;
for they live according to passion, and pursue their peculiar
pleasures, and any thing which will create them; they fly
also from the contrary pains: but of what is honourable and
truly pleasant, they have no idea, as they never tasted them.
What reasoning then can bring back such characters as
these? for it is not possible, or at least not easy, to change
what has been for a long time impressed upon the cha-

racter; but it is perhaps a great thing, if when every thing is present by which we are thought to become good, we can arrive at virtue.

3. But it is thought that men become good either by nature, or practice, or teaching. Now it is evident that what comes from nature does not belong to ourselves, but exists by some divine cause in those who are truly fortunate. But reasoning and teaching perhaps does not avail in every case, but the mind of the hearer must be previously formed by practice to feel pleasure and aversion properly, like the soil which nourishes the seed. For he that lives in obedience to passion, would not listen to reasoning which turns him from it, nor would he understand it. And how is it possible to bring back by persuasion such a man as this? On the whole, it appears that passion does not submit to reasoning, but to force. There must therefore previously exist a character in some way connected with virtue, loving what is noble, and abhorring what is disgraceful.

4. But for a person to meet with a good guidance towards virtue from his childhood is difficult, unless he is brought up under such laws: for to live temperately and patiently is not pleasant to the generality, particularly when young. Wherefore education and institutions ought to be regulated by laws; for they will not be disagreeable when they are familiar. But perhaps it is not sufficient that they should meet with good education and attention when young; but since when they are arrived at manhood they ought also to make them their study, and practise them, we should require laws also for this purpose: in short, we should want them for the whole life; for the generality are obedient to necessity rather than to reason, and to punishments rather than to any noble principle. Wherefore some think that in legislating we ought to exhort to virtue, and to urge them on upon a principle of honour, since those who are good in their practice will obey when they are led: but to appoint chastisements and punishments for those who are disobedient and untoward, and utterly to expel the incurable; because he that is good and lives after a principle of honour will

obey reason; but the bad man aims at pleasure, and is corrected by pain like a beast. Wherefore it is a common saying, that there ought to be such pains as are most opposed to the pleasures which are loved.

5. If then, as has been said, he that is to be a good man must be educated well, and habituated to it, and thus continue to live in good institutions, and never practise what is bad, either involuntarily or voluntarily; and if this is to be done by their living in obedience to some intelligent principle, and some right regulation, which has strength: now the authority of a father hath no strength, nor compulsory force; nor, in short, the authority of any one man, unless he is a king, or something of that sort; but the law possesses a compulsory power, being reason proceeding from a certain prudence and intelligence. Besides, men hate those individuals who oppose their appetites, even if they do it rightly: but the law is not offensive when it prescribes what is good.

6. But in the city of Lacedæmon alone, with a few others, the legislator seems to have paid attention to education and institutions; but in most states such matters have been neglected, and each lives as he pleases, like the Cyclops,

Making laws for his children and wife.

It would be best therefore that attention to these matters should be public, and on right principles, and that it should have power to effect this: but since it has been neglected as a public measure, it would seem to be incumbent upon every individual to contribute to the virtue of their children and friends, or at least to intend to do it. But from what has been said, it would seem that he would have most power to do this if he made himself acquainted with legislation: for public institutions for education are evidently made by the laws; and those are good which are made by good laws. But whether these laws be written or unwritten would seem to make no difference; nor whether they are those by which one or many persons are to be educated, as it does not in music, in the gymnastic, and other lessons. For in the same way that legal enactments, together with moral dispositions, have authority in states, so also the words of a father, together with moral dispositions, have authority in private families; and still greater on account of the relationship, and the benefits conferred: for the parties previously love each other, and are naturally docile.

7. But yet the education of separate individuals differs from public systems of education, as is the case in medicine: for generally abstinence and rest are good for a man in a fever; but to a particular individual perhaps they are not; and the teacher of boxing perhaps does not teach the same style of fighting to all. And it would seem that he might practise greater accuracy in individual cases, if the education was private; for then each is more likely to meet with what suits him. But a physician, or a gymnastic, or any other master, would take the best care of the individual, if he knew the universal, viz. what is good for all men, or for all of a certain class: for the sciences are said to belong, and really do belong, to what is general. Nevertheless there is nothing to hinder a person from taking good care of an individual, even if he has no general knowledge; but if he accurately examines by experience what happens to each individual, as some physicians seem to be the best towards themselves, when they are not able to assist another person in any respect. But perhaps it would still be not less advisable for him, who wishes to become an artist or a projector, to have recourse to the universal, and to make himself acquainted with all the contingencies of that; for we have observed that sciences are connected with that: and perhaps he who wishes to make men better by education, whether many or few, should endeavour to become acquainted with legislation, if it is by laws that we become good. For to give a good disposition to any one and to the particular person entrusted to him does not belong to every one, but if to any, to him who possesses the knowledge: as is the case in medicine and other arts of which there is any study and discernment.

8. Should we not then after this investigate from what quarter or by what means a man might make himself acquainted with legislation, or, as in other cases, must he learn

it from politicians? for it seemed to be a part of political science. Or does it appear to be different in political science from the other sciences and faculties? for in the others the same men seem to teach the faculties, and to act from them; as physicians and painters. But the sophists pretend to teach political matters, but not one of them practises them; those who manage the state do this, who would seem to do it in consequence of possessing the faculty[n], and from experience rather than from reasoning upon it: for they do not appear to write or to speak upon such matters: (and yet it would perhaps be a nobler task, than to make speeches in a court of justice, or before the people:) nor do they make their own sons, nor any others of their friends, politicians. But it would be reasonable for them to do it if they could; for neither could they leave any thing better to their citizens[o], nor could they wish any better thing to belong to themselves, than this faculty, nor consequently to their best friends. However, experience seems to contribute not a little; for otherwise men would not become better politicians by being accustomed to political affairs. Wherefore it seems that those who are desirous of knowledge on political science require also experience. But those sophists who profess it, seem to be very far from teaching it: for they do not at all know either what is its specific difference, nor what is its subject: for then they would not have held it to be the same with rhetoric, nor worse; nor would they have thought that it is easy to legislate, if a man makes a collection of approved laws; for they say that he should select the best; as if this selection was not a work of understanding, or judgment was

---

[n] A man who has studied any science, and practises it strictly according to the rules of the science, without modifying them in any way according to his own ideas, is said to practise that science ἐν δυνάμει: if he changes them in any way, so as to be no longer following the rules of the science, he is then said to act ἐν προαιρέσει. This will explain why δύναμις and ἐπιστήμη are so often made synonimous in this treatise. See the distinction of δύναμις and προαίρεσις in Rhet. l. i. c. 1.

[o] Vide Polyb. l. xii. c. 28. ed. Schweigh.

not really the most important thing P, as it is in music. For the experienced form a right judgment of works in every case, and understand by what means or how they are performed, and what things harmonize with what; but the inexperienced may be contented, if they are not ignorant whether the work is performed well or ill, as in the case of painting. But the laws resemble political compositions. How then can a man become acquainted with legislation from these, or select the best? for men do not appear to become physicians from writings; and yet they endeavour to explain by words not only the remedies, but even in what manner they may be cured, and how they ought to treat them, distinguishing the habits of each. But these things seem to be useful to the experienced; but to those who have no knowledge upon the subject, useless. Perhaps then collections of laws and forms of government would be useful to those who are able to contemplate, and to decide what is done well, or the contrary, or what kind of things suit what: but to those who go through such things without any habit, the power of making a good selection cannot exist in them, except it comes of its own accord; but perhaps they may be more able to understand these matters.

9. Since therefore former writers have left the subject of legislation uninvestigated, it would perhaps be better for ourselves to examine it, and, in short, the whole subject of government, that the philosophy of human affairs may as far as is in our power be completed. First then, if any thing has been well said by former writers in any particular, let us endeavour to understand it: then from the different forms of government being brought together, let us see what kind of things preserve and destroy states and individual governments, and for what reasons some are administered well, and others the contrary: for if these points were considered, we

---

P The sophists say that in order to learn legislation, a man has nothing to do but to make a collection of the best laws; i. e. they assume that he knows what are the best laws, when he is only learning them.

should perhaps be better able to see at one view what form of government is best, and how each is arranged, and what laws and customs it uses.   Let us then begin our treatise.

THE END.

BAXTER, PRINTER, OXFORD.

LaVergne, TN USA
07 November 2010
203866LV00003B/134/P